JORDAN

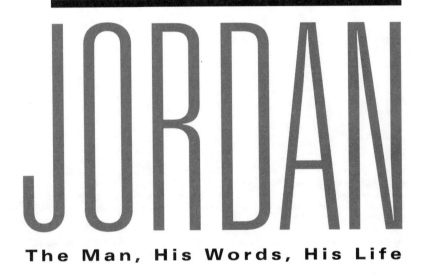

JORDAN

The Man, His Words, His Life

Mitchell Krugel

St. Martin's Press / New York

The extract from Steve Rosenbloom's column in the *Chicago Sun-Times,* June 9, 1993, is reprinted
by permission.

All photographs courtesy of Rob Brown

Design by Jaye Zimet

Library of Congress Cataloging-in-Publication Data

Krugel, Mitchell.
    Jordan : The Man, His Words, His Life / Mitchell Krugel.
        p.   cm.
    "A Thomas Dunne Book."
    ISBN 0-312-11090-1
    1. Jordan, Michael, 1963-   .   2. Basketball players—United
States—Biography.   I. Title.
GV884.J67K77   1994
796.323'092—dc20
    [B]   94-459
                                               CIP

First Edition: June 1994
10   9   8   7   6   5   4   3   2   1

This one's for you, MJ

Contents

Acknowledgments

It's amazing how many people contribute to a book like this. I want to thank them all, and you know who you are.

Specifically my gratitude must go to editor Thomas Dunne and everybody at St. Martin's Press who put in long hours making this work come to pass. I especially want to thank Pete Wolverton, the associate editor who stuck with the project when the last thing the world needed was another Michael Jordan book. Pete stood by me and worked relentlessly to make this book come to life. When you're an author, you dream about working with editors like Pete Wolverton.

None of this, of course, would have been possible without Madeleine Morel, my literary agent. When she gave me my start in publishing in 1986, she knew I had this in me. She never stopped pushing for it. Thank you for working tirelessly to make all the good things happen.

Every writer has to have a confidant, a sounding board, a person who can tell him when ideas will or won't work. Mine was Tim Harmon, the managing editor at *The Times* of northwest Indiana, who served as my personal editor on this project. Many nights were spent eating low-fat meals with Tim, rounding this book into form. You are the Michael Jordan of newspaper editors.

Thanks to all my other colleagues at *The Times:* Bill Nangle, John Humenik, Roman Modrowski, David Campbell, Chris Boghossian, and Bill Greene. I couldn't have done it without each one of you. A special thanks to *Times* sportswriter Johnny O., who worked the Bulls beat with me and generously lent his insight.

Thanks to all the other boys and girls on the Bulls beat. Jay Mariotti, Steve Rosenbloom, and Mike Mulligan of the *Chicago Sun-Times,* Melissa Isaacson of the *Chicago Tribune,* Kent McDill of the Arlington *Daily Herald,* and Mike Greenberg of WSCR Radio in Chicago were all gracious enough to put up with my relentless questioning of Michael Jordan, and they inspired many of the ideas in the pages that follow. A special thanks to Copley News Service columnist Gene Seymour, who was such a good friend on the road following Michael Jordan.

You can't do something like this without support from your family. My beautiful, new wife, Mary, saw to it that our wedding plans did not get in the way of finishing, and I owe everything to you. Ditto for you, Mom. And, Michael, I know how you felt about your father: My Pops was with me every step of the way on this one.

Thanks also to all the NBA players who never hesitated to talk about Michael: Magic, Dominique, Craig Ehlo, Ron Harper, Kendall Gill, Sam Perkins, Orlando Woolridge, Reggie Miller, Rod Higgins, Charles Barkley, John Paxson, Will Perdue, and the rest of the Chicago Bulls and members of the organization. A special thanks to Tim Hallam, David Brenner, and Jeff Nianek. You'll never know how much you did for me. The hours I spent with Doug Collins talking about MJ were among the best I've ever had.

In addition to thanking George Koehler, it is only proper to remember James Jordan. You left us too soon. We all miss you.

Lastly, I must honor Michael Jeffrey Jordan. Never during my fifteen years in this business have I met a man or an athlete as genuine as yourself. You never hesitated to give me your time, even when my questions seemed like they were coming from left field. Thank you for letting me follow you and watch you. You did more for each of us than we could ever do for you. In addition to everything else, these words are an attempt to describe your legacy. Thank you for leaving such a great one.

Mitchell Krugel

Introduction

Never had Michael Jordan shown me this side of his personality. It was April 12, 1993, before a game against the Detroit Pistons at The Palace of Auburn Hills. This was another of the involved conversations Jordan was engaging in with select members of the media. Michael would meet a few of us before road games or stay more than an hour after home games and practices and discuss far more than basketball. Today, he was talking about the arguments he and his wife, Juanita, would have over how they prepared their grits, the summer days he used to spend hanging on the jungle gym as a kid, stretching himself, trying to make himself grow, and how he couldn't travel to Europe anymore. Since becoming both a media friend and adversary the last few years, I had conversed and cajoled with Michael enough times to know the smile that he was sporting now was not one he had let the outside world see too much of lately.

For more than an hour, I kept him off the subject of basketball—or at least basketball and the Chicago Bulls—for these were the times I enjoyed him most. One of the best things you could do for Michael at this point in his career was make him feel like just another guy, like a friend, like somebody who did not have to be an international icon that people were always trying to touch, photograph, or probe. At these times, he would talk forever. He had grown wary of these people—especially those in the media—the last few years, so I was fortunate to be somebody he opened up to frequently.

Game time was upon him when Jordan stood up, stretched out his 6-foot-6-inch body to reveal his only physical imperfection—unsightly toes. He put his hands on my shoulders like a clerical figure about to deliver a blessing and declared, "I just can't wait for the playoffs to start. The championships now are the only reason I'm playing. I still want to win championships. There's still a burning flame in here. Those championships keep me feeling the love for the game. But I feel like these playoffs are going to be my best ever."

When we returned to Chicago two nights later, I jokingly asked Michael if he was ready for the playoffs. He stopped, winked, then ducked behind an army of security guards who escorted him through the throng of fans that awaited him after every Bulls game. The message was clear here. After seven years of knowing him, following him, studying him, it was easy to understand Michael Jordan. He was not a complex man. The Bulls were elbowing with the New York Knicks for the position of superiority in the Eastern Conference going into the postseason. More than ever, Jordan was having to use his individual talents to prop up his teammates. And the two straight years of basketball without a break had extracted some of his statistical excellence.

Still, with the wink and the smile the unspoken message that he was giving me was to keep a close eye on him; the next two months of his life would be more spectacular, more eventful than even he had known before. If Michael had planned the fifty-four days of the 1993 NBA playoffs to be his final days, they could not have been filled with more drama, tumult, and vintage. Each day, each game tested his fortitude and "Air" for the dramatic. Never did his professional life hit such highs. Never did his personal life hit such lows. Never did that smile flash on and off like the "No Vacancy" sign at a small-town hotel.

The final days of his career combined exaltation and misery. Even though he was playing his best basketball ever at a time when the Bulls absolutely needed him to, Michael Jordan could not wait to get the 1993 season over with. Every aspect of his life became open for public scrutiny and/or discussion. Some of that resulted from Michael's own doing. But from what he was telling me during this fifty-four-day melodrama, I knew he could no longer live like this.

Friday, April 30: Ready for the playoffs. Jordan hits 8 of his first 10 shots, scores 18 of his game-high 35 points in the first quarter, and plays just 29 minutes of a 114-90 win over Atlanta in the playoff opener. "Everyone's saying, the message is this, the message is that," Jordan remarks. "If we come out and play the same type of basketball Sunday, start making your predictions."

Tuesday, May 4: "Yeah, I felt the city of Chicago gasp when I went down," Michael recounts. "Yeah, I was limping a little bit. But it wasn't really drama from my standpoint." At the 3:45 mark of the third quarter of this third game of the opening-round series, Jordan twisted his ankle after slipping on a wet spot on the court. He was carried off the floor. He limped back for the start of the final period, then scored 14 of his 39 points to lead the Bulls to a series-ending 98-88 win.

Monday, May 10: An extra-large horde of media have gathered around Michael. He politely answers questions about the Cleveland Cavaliers, the Bulls' second-round opponent. He says that he is eager to get this series going and bored over not playing in a week. He attempts to leave. But he is surrounded by people who want to know about his matchup with Cleveland guard Gerald Wilkins. The Cavs signed Wilkins during the previous offseason to guard Jordan. Michael hears this and says he looks forward to the challenge. He is asked if this guy is really a guy who can guard him, a Jordan stopper. "We'll see," he replies. He is asked if Wilkins doesn't guard him the toughest, then who does. "My shadow," he says and finally ends the questioning.

Tuesday, May 11: After scoring 16 of his 43 points on Wilkins in the fourth quarter of the 91-84 win, Jordan says, "When I'm at my best, it's tough for anybody to guard me."

Thursday, May 13: Panic strikes. Michael scores just 18 in a 104-85 Bulls win. At the end of the third quarter, he takes a chop on his right wrist. He suffers through so much pain that he shoots two fourth-quarter free throws left-handed and then sits out the final ten minutes.

Saturday, May 15: Pre-game practice has to be cut short. More than a thousand Cleveland fans have formed a ring around the first deck of seats in the Richfield Coliseum and appear to be closing in on Michael. His wrist bothers him so much that many pre-game shots are air balls. He passes up all well-wishers and retreats to a corner of the locker room that is off limits to reporters. Michael sits on the floor listening to compact discs. He plays in pain in the first half and scores 22 of his game-high 36 in the second half of the 96-90 Bulls win. Despite Cleveland fans' incessant booing and the media world's incessant questioning about overcoming the pain, Jordan confides that his only flaw was a missed dunk in the second half. "Because of my wrist, I can't throw the ball down as hard as I normally do."

Sunday, May 16: The questioning about the pain in his wrist has become a pain in the ass. Finally, Jordan cracks. "I don't have any choice," he charges, his voice hitting such a low baseline that the echo pounds the eardrums. "I want to achieve something so bad that I'm going to have to pay a little bit to get to that point." He finally escapes to his portable CD player and the voice of Anita Baker when

Gary Bender of TNT asks him for one more interview. He obliges reluctantly but with a smile.

Monday, May 17: "This was one of the moments I dream about," Michael says. This moment came when Jordan hit a game-winning 18-foot jump shot in the Bulls' 103-101 Game 4 victory. The shot knocked Cleveland out of the playoffs. It came about five feet to the right of where he hit a shot to eliminate the Cavs four years earlier. "I'm pretty sure all night long I'm going to lay awake and think about it," he says. This is the crescendo. Life can only go downhill from here.

Tuesday, May 18: Michael finally finds refuge. "I hung out with my kids all day," he reveals. "They didn't know anything about the shot. I can't tell you how great it was to get home to that atmosphere."

Wednesday, May 19: The New York Knicks won their second-round series the night before, setting up an Eastern Conference Final with the Bulls. Consequently, the infamous New York media has come to town to confront Michael with antagonism and lack of manners. The shot is a faded memory. They grill him about his gambling activities, his documented run-ins with Isiah Thomas, and what he calls "a lot of extracurricular stuff." He is asked if the pain in his wrist has affected his golf game. One New York writer challenges Michael to a round of golf. "What's your handicap?" Jordan asks. "I'm blind in one eye," the writer responds. Michael walks away laughing, saying, "They're always trying to get me."

Sunday, May 23: In one of those rare moments before Game 1 of the Eastern Conference Finals, we are sitting around the locker room joking with Michael. He relates a conversation he just had with his kids and plays a little show-and-tell with all the devices that he has received in the mail the last week to help cure his wrist injury. Then, the rest of the media world comes at him, and Jordan is forced to listen to questions as ridiculous as "Is the motivation for meeting Phoenix in the NBA Finals a chance to get out there and play some golf?" Finally, Michael turns the conversation to the new commercial he made for Nike which carries the message "What if I were just another basketball player?" As the media horde relents, he confesses, "I'd really like to be like that now. Everybody's always criticizing me for something."

Monday, May 24: The critics have been all over Jordan after Sunday's 98-90 Bulls loss. Because he missed seven of his nine shots in the fourth quarter and failed to score in the final 6:31 of the game, *New York Newsday* ran a picture of him with the word "Goat" printed underneath it in big, black type.

Tuesday, May 25: Charles Barkley is named the NBA's Most Valuable Player for the 1992–93 season today. After being asked to send up some words of praise for his best friend, Jordan is forced to spend 30 minutes before Game 2 explaining why he did not win the award for the third straight year. "I didn't campaign for it," he explains. "And I think they wanted somebody new." Then, he must defend himself. "I felt my year was consistent with what I've done in the past. As long as that's the case, I'm satisfied." Then, he must concentrate on the game, a 96-91 loss in which his 36 points cannot make up for Scottie Pippen's third-quarter ejection.

Thursday, May 27: A story in Wednesday's edition of the *New York Times* reported that Jordan was at Bally's Casino in Atlantic City Monday night. The story quoted eyewitnesses who said that he was there until 2 A.M. playing blackjack. Late Wednesday night, teammate Darrell Walker called Jordan to inform him of the story. Michael's conversation with fifty-six reporters after Bulls practice turns into a deposition. He confirms his trip to Atlantic City with his father but denies that he was there past 11:04 P.M. He threatens to sue anybody who says he was there beyond that time. He pleads with reporters, "Don't take it out of context. Report what's true fact, which is what I'm telling you." He relates that he needed to escape from New York Monday amidst all the attention of being called the goat. He says this is not a regular pre-game ritual. When a television news reporter asks him if he has a gambling problem and makes references to previously reported betting on golf with convicted felon Slim Bouler, Michael ends the interview session abruptly and angrily, and walks away.

Friday, May 28: Michael snubs reporters, refusing to answer questions. The rest of the Bulls also refuse to talk, saying that they are boycotting the media in reaction to the way Jordan was treated Thursday.

Saturday, May 29: Michael hits just 3 of 18 shots in the Bulls 103-83 victory in Game 3 against the Knicks. He breaks his silence only to grant an interview to NBC's Ahmad Rashad directly after the game.

Sunday, May 30: Word is that Jordan may break his vow of silence at any time. More than sixty reporters wait outside the Bulls practice facility for three hours in case he will. He does not. Instead, Michael's father, James, speaks out for more than an hour. James says that Michael is frustrated with everybody expecting too much from him. "Some demand him to be perfect," James says. "And every time he stubs his toe, someone is there to jump on him. He wants to live his own life, do what he wants. And he can't. And he feels that's not fair. It's scary. How the hell is this possible?"

Monday, May 31: Michael is back to himself. At least on the court. He scores 54 points in a 105-95 Bulls win. He hits 6 of 9 three-point shots and 18 of 30 overall. But he's still not talking. One reporter stands in front of his car in an effort to get a comment while Michael is revving up to leave Chicago Stadium. Another tries to interview his car.

Wednesday, June 2: Forget Jordan's 29 points, 14 assists, 10 rebounds, and last-second block of Charles Smith's shot in the 97-94 Bulls win in Game 5 of the Eastern Conference Finals. An hour after the game a report surfaces that San Diego businessman Richard Esquinas has written a book claiming that he won $1.25 million from Jordan gambling on golf. The book recounts several rounds in which $100,000 was bet on a single putt. Jordan isn't saying whether Esquinas is telling the truth. He isn't saying anything.

Friday, June 4: Jordan issues a written statement through his agent David Falk about Esquinas. He admits knowing and playing golf with him but says reports of the amounts lost were "greatly exaggerated." He thanks those who reported the story fairly. The story reduces the Bulls' 96-88 win over the Knicks that wraps up the series and a trip to the NBA Finals for the third straight year almost to an afterthought, especially with Madonna attending the game.

Thursday, June 10: During halftime of last night's 100-92 win over the Phoenix Suns in Game 1 of the NBA Finals, Michael spoke publicly. During an interview with NBC's Rashad, Michael talked as if he was the witness finally taking the stand in his own defense. He admitted to losing money to Esquinas and insisted he did not have a gambling problem. Now, it was back to the same routine. During the Finals, the NBA asks all players to be available for questions for 30 minutes on days without games. Jordan's sessions went to 40 counting the ten reporters who chased him out of the America West Arena firing inquiries. "This is the worst part of my life, being swarmed," he says. "I mean what is enough right now? It's not like they go back and write the guy is human. It's all a big headache."

Friday, June 11: Michael comes into the Bulls locker room before Game 2 smiling. He does not seem upset by the helicopter that hovered overhead and spied on his golf game the day before. He is not upset by the news that NBA commissioner David Stern held a press conference yesterday to announce the league will be investigating Jordan's gambling activities with Esquinas. It does not seem to affect his play when he scores 42 points and adds 12 rebounds and 9 assists in the Bulls 111-108 win. The Bulls have become the first team to ever win the first two games of the NBA Finals on the road and appear to have all but locked up the third straight title Jordan covets. "Now if I can just get my handicap under an 18," Michael jokes.

Sunday, June 13: Just when he had reason to think about smiling again, the trouble starts again. Michael hits just 9 of his last 22 shots and misses a free throw that would have sealed a victory in Game 3. The Suns come back from a 10-point deficit to win a triple-overtime game 129-121. Afterward, Charles Barkley makes fun of Jordan for taking 43 shots in the game. Kevin Johnson gets credit for defending Jordan and shutting him down in the end. "Just give me a chance to redeem myself for that missed free throw," Jordan says.

Monday, June 14: At the morning interview session, Jordan gives the answers before the question can be asked. "I know you guys will more or less evaluate my missing all those shots. I don't think you should worry about all the individual stuff." There is talk that the triple overtime game could be one of the greatest in NBA history. Jordan says that he knows he can play better and does not consider it so. As he leaves, he admits his body has been aching. So many friends and members of his family are in town, he says, that every one is ringing in his ear. "It's time to get the season over with as quick as possible," he mutters.

Wednesday, June 16: Yesterday, the criticism continued about Michael's failure to deliver a victory in Game 3. The pressure built up so much that he changed the subject to talk about retirement. "This franchise should prepare to make a transition into the next era," he said. Before that, Michael provides one more glimpse of what made the modern era so exhilarating. With his 55-point effort, the second-highest single-game scoring effort in NBA Finals history, Michael carries the Bulls to a 111-105 victory. He carries them within one win of the history-making third straight title. With the game on the line, he drives right at Barkley and flips in a shot as Charles drags him to the floor. At a time when the Bulls absolutely need him to, Michael has his greatest game ever. "Not my greatest," he points out. "The greatest will be the last, when we win the championship."

Thursday, June 17: With the third title all but sealed, Jordan must answer what more there is for him to accomplish. "A fourth title," he quips. He is asked about retirement again and says it will come sooner than later, probably before the Bulls move into their new arena for the 1994–95 season. He pulls a fast one on the media by devising a plan to get out of the interview session 15 minutes early. He hops in his Porsche, runs off a pick set by police escort, and dashes off to the golf course.

Friday, June 18: Michael films a public service announcement for local television, asking the citizens of Chicago not to get destructive if it comes to celebrating the title tonight. The Bulls lose 108-98 even though Jordan scores 41 points on 16-of-29 shooting. He lashes out afterward. "You guys will never know what it takes to play in a game like this. The desire and heart and energy is there to achieve but the body and mind don't act together." That night he takes Charles Barkley to dinner at Michael Jordan's: The Restaurant and responds to Barkley's claim that winning, the Bible says, is the Suns' destiny. Michael tells him, "I don't know what Bible you're reading, but you're wrong." Dinner is served.

Sunday, June 20: The Bulls are falling apart when Jordan comes to the rescue one more time. He scores nine straight fourth-quarter points, including a coast-to-coast run for a layup that cuts the Suns' lead to 98-96. He scores 33 points, and after John Paxson's game-winning three-point shot and Horace Grant's game-saving blocked shot he chases down the game ball. An hour after the game, he has answered the last of the questions, drank champagne, smoked a big cigar, and prayed. He looks down and says, "This is the hardest thing I've ever done. I'm glad it's over. What a relief."

Wednesday, June 23: After receiving his third straight NBA Finals MVP award, Jordan shares parting words with a few friends. When asked what he did on his first day off yesterday, he says, "I played golf. And I didn't play that bad. I didn't lose any money." There is no celebration in the tone of his voice. He says he has no desire to touch a basketball and that he probably won't all summer. He asks that nobody hide in the bushes by his front door looking for a story. We are walking out and he vents. "This is as relieved as I have ever been to end a season. A lot of weight has been lifted off my back. It's been a long, long run and I'm so relieved."

At that time, I knew retirement was inevitable. It was time to put together an overview of Michael Jordan's nine-year career, an inside look. This is not a biographical look at the game's greatest player ever but an overview to examine and explain how life could have so many highlights and so much trouble. And never was that more apparent than during the final days of Michael Jordan's career. When he managed to escape the outside world and find peace only inside his Chevy Blazer, Michael related how life got so good and how it got so bad. An hour after the game was over and all the prying media disappeared, Michael opened up to explain his greatest moments and vent his frustrations.

This book takes you inside Michael Jordan's head, or as close to that point as it was possible for us to get. Each chapter begins with a view of crucial events and issues as seen through Michael's eyes. Many of the detailed perspectives are compilations of conversations we had during the past seven years. Some of the passages are embellished with thoughts that friends, family members, teammates, coaches, opponents, and others close to Michael—and who also understood his thinking—submitted. This is the essence of what motivated and inspired him. To those select few he allowed inside his head, Michael was open and honest for the most part, and consequently you only had to be around him, talk with him a few times, to know exactly what he was thinking or feeling.

The goal of this book is to provide objective accounts of what Michael Jordan dealt with as a basketball player and a person whose life was never his own. The goal is not to provide a forum for Michael to speak, to present only his side of the story on events that may have cast him in a supernatural light or depicted him with a dark side. This is a one-on-one study of Michael Jordan.

PROLOGUE

Looking Back

November 5, 1993, Michael Jordan's: The Restaurant, Chicago, Illinois. It seemed like I've been waiting nine years for the day when life would be this easy, this relaxed. It's been a month since I retired, and now I can finally get up in the morning and walk to the bathroom without limping or walking slow. There are no more aches and pains. A weight has been taken off my mind too. I don't have to worry about doing anything, being anywhere, dealing with any adversity. I can do whatever comes to my mind. That's a big, big difference because for the past nine years my life has been such a demanding routine. The past nine years I didn't even have time to get stuck in the traffic on the Chicago highways. Tonight the traffic was so bad I was a half hour late to a party I was hosting at my restaurant, and I could laugh about it. When I finally arrived I was joking with everybody that I couldn't fly over the traffic, that I was human now. I felt like I really was human.

A few months ago I never thought I would be hosting a party for media—telling jokes, and laughing with them when they made fun of me. When I walked away from the game of basketball a month ago, I didn't hide my bitter feelings toward the media. I think I told them they weren't human and didn't have any sympathy for normal people. Tonight, somebody asked me if I felt like I had replaced Al Capone as a worldwide symbol of the city of Chicago. A few months ago I would have been afraid to answer such a question for fear that somebody might blow it up into a scandal or something. But I spent a few minutes comparing myself to Al. And I found the whole thing funny.

That gives you an idea of how life has changed for me the past month, how much better it has become. Yesterday, I went to visit my old teammates at practice and wound up playing a few games with them. Today, everybody was all riled up, asking me if that meant I was having second thoughts about retirement. It wasn't planned or anything. I was having breakfast with B. J., and he was telling me some of the enthusiasm he was used to the past four years was missing from practice. He asked me to come by and see some of the guys, bring back some of the old times, talk some trash, and all that stuff we used to do at practice. I was standing on the sidelines talking with Phil and Jerry Reinsdorf when some of the guys challenged me to come out and play. Being that I wasn't working and I was dressed for the occasion, I did.

I held my own out there. But the whole time I never felt like I was missing the game. I knew some people would speculate that I was itching to play and I went out to practice to scratch an itch. That's what they said. I knew that wasn't the case. I didn't miss the game. I was able to have some fun with some friends. That was the best thing about going out to practice. Finally, life was becoming a little more normal. I could do whatever I wanted. I was finally getting away from that high, rollercoaster lifestyle where the last nine years I dedicated eight months out of a year trying to get to the mountaintop.

After all that, I just didn't have the desire to step out on the basketball court anymore for more than fun. I had to admit to myself there was nothing left to prove. If I had that feeling, then I knew I would be out there playing for no reason. That wasn't worth it for me. Without something to prove, without something to achieve, there was no way I was going through that scenario again. After every game, after every practice, I couldn't answer all those questions again. Some as ridiculous as, "What would you think if your daughter ever wanted to play in the NBA?"

Going from the hotel to the team bus, there were always hundreds of people standing and watching and screaming, trying to get close. After games, it was the same way. I couldn't leave without four or five security guards. Taking all the time away from my wife and my family and facing opposing players who have geared up for you all season or the Knicks trying to beat you up just wasn't worth it anymore. Walking away from the game meant 110 nights or so when I wouldn't have to deal with that stuff anymore.

I didn't think I could ever have a normal life. But if I could lessen it just a little bit, it would be better than it was. During the past few months, I started to think about the perfect day. That perfect day started to happen a month ago, because I finally had some time for myself, and it began by getting up without any aches and pains or a weight on my mind. Most people probably think that day would be spent on the golf course, but it was also just being a father or being at home vacuuming and washing dishes. I just wanted to do all those things I never had a chance to do.

---

n September 1993, Michael Jordan tried to do something normal, something human, something everybody else would do. He took his sons, Jeffrey and Marcus, to Disney World. They entered the Magic Kingdom through a back door. They had to go through a back door for every ride. When the rides ended, they left through another back door. Jeffrey and Marcus rode with daddy on what he called "Splash Mountain." They went on fifteen other rides. They were there about an hour and fifteen minutes. Anybody who has ever been to Disney World knows that 7 A.M. and midnight are about the only times you can ride "Space Mountain" without waiting more than an hour and fifteen minutes. Unless you're Michael Jordan. In one door and out another every five minutes and Michael still had to deal with the people recognizing him. After an hour and fifteen minutes he may have felt like an exhibit at Epcot Center.

"You know how many tourists there are there. Eventually, we had a really tough time moving without pushing, trampling people, or whatever. After a while it became a hassle, and we had to leave. I had never been able to take my kids to a place like that, and I chose to deal with what I had to deal with. For what little time we were there, I had a great time. The kids seemed to enjoy it. They got scared on all the rides. But that's not a great environment to enjoy your family."

When Michael officially announced that he was retiring from playing basketball in the NBA on Wednesday, October 6, 1993, his comments came off as somewhat antagonistic toward the reporters in front of him. He spoke in the harsh, accusing tone that Perry Mason would use when he was trying to get a witness to confess to the crime. He was defiant of the media, even going so far as to respond to the question of what special contribution he made to the game by saying "the tongue."

He was talking about the tongue that darted out of his mouth on every spectacular move, every score. This response was Michael's way of sticking his tongue out after one more score, the one he had been waiting to make for almost a year—the one against the media.

On the way to the final mountaintop, he had to deal with eight months of persecution over his gambling activities and having his every move examined. He said that was why he had been thinking about retirement the moment the Chicago Bulls defeated the Phoenix Suns in Game 6 of the 1993 NBA Finals and won their third straight NBA championship. Jordan observed that the one good thing now was that his father, who was shot to death less than two months earlier, had seen him play his last basketball game.

After answering more than an hour of questions about his retirement, Jordan grabbed his wife Juanita's hand and walked away from this press conference at the Sheri Berto Center, the Bulls' practice facility in the Chicago suburb of Deerfield. He slipped out another back door and into his black Mercedes Benz 600. Jordan's friends and family maneuvered their cars behind Michael's to make the getaway, forming what easily could have been perceived as a funeral procession. A few feet to the side, Scott Williams, the 6-foot-11-inch Bulls forward who looked like Mr. T without the Mohawk, cried as he watched the convoy pull away.

A dark, grey October sky opened up at that moment and shed some sunlight on Michael Jordan. He smiled. He seemed to know right then that his decision was correct, that the future was bright, and that he would no longer have to deal with so much of what made being Michael Jordan the basketball star and international icon not worth the price anymore.

Perhaps you can only imagine all the things, all the crap, that Michael Jordan went through to become the most skilled, most talented, and most worshiped athlete ever.

November 5, 1991, Chicago Stadium, Chicago, Illinois. I wanted to see if this kid was worth the accolades, if he could answer the challenge. Every time somebody scored 63 points in some playground league they said he's another

Michael Jordan. Every time some kid puts up 50, they said he was the next one—what did they call it?—the Air Apparent. And then they came at me to see if they could build an image or whatever playing against me. There was always somebody who wanted to take my title.

Tonight they're saying this Billy Owens is the next one. And here comes the future, dribbling toward me at midcourt wearing a Golden State uniform. This is when you get into your attack mode: knees flexed, shorts pulled down, hands ready to reach in and wreak a little havoc. You chew your gum almost as fast as your heart beats.

I can test his confidence now. Will he come at me, looking to drive past me and make a name for himself? You can tell right at this instant just how good he will be, if he really has the right stuff. A fearless player will make something happen.

But this kid gets to the halfcourt line and turns his back. Now I know I've got him. As soon as Billy Owens turns his back on me to protect the ball, I'm reaching in to take it away. You hope all the other Baby Jordans out there are watching and learning not to make the same mistake, not to show their fear.

The steal is secondary at this point. The feeling of picking up the loose ball and heading toward the basket isn't nearly as gratifying as shooting him that look that says, "You're not ready for me, kid. Not yet."

Some people have described me as getting a little mean, a little vicious, at times like this. You almost want to stop the game and pat the kid on the butt, partly to tell him not to worry about it, partly to tell him that to get to this level you have to go out and compete every night, even a meaningless night in November. But you know what I have to do. I'm going to steal the ball from him again, just to prove it wasn't a fluke. And when he comes up to midcourt and

turns his back and watches me go to the basket, maybe he will realize being the next Michael Jordan means more than being able to
score 63 points in some schoolyard.

For all the floating dunks and game-winning shots and 50-point nights, no two plays more defined Michael Jordan than the way he tortured Billy Owens that night in early November 1991. What Michael Jordan showed, displayed, flaunted on this night was an ability far greater than any of his athletic gifts. Jordan set up for Owens in that look kids on playgrounds and in gyms forever tried to emulate, especially with the shorts pulled down low. Then, he attacked Owens with compulsive, relentless obsession.

What made Jordan want to play high noon with an overmatched rookie? He will tell us that it is a matter of going out and laying everything on the basketball court. He will tell us the secret is not taking a night off in early November when there are seventy-nine games to go until the playoffs and everybody is expecting him to not go 100 percent. But this does not explain the need to block Shaquille O'Neal's shot the first time that the highly-hyped rookie encountered Michael. Why was Michael Jordan compelled to obliterate Billy Owens? Why did he have to go out on a meaningless night in November and provide one more reason why he was the best in the building?

Why was the man so driven?

December 12, 1992, Bulls Locker Room, Chicago Stadium. A win over New Jersey, 38 points, and the perfect Saturday night should end by having dinner with my wife. But Juanita will have to wait a few more minutes. This writer from France says he has a couple of "off-the-wall" questions he wants to ask me. Just when I thought I had heard every ridiculous question, some guy from France comes up with a few more. These were strange:

"What's your favorite movie?"

"How much money would you give for a drink that would make you invisible?"

"Do you tell bedtime stories to your kids?"

"Are you curious whether there are aliens out there in space?"

"Have you ever been in contact with the Mafia?"

When you were a human interest story the magnitude of Michael, they wanted to know about how you took home economics in high school because you never thought you would get married and you would have to do your own cooking and sewing. They wanted to know about how your brother used to kick your butt playing one-on-one on the court that Pops built in the backyard when you were a kid. They wanted to know about your first job and what you eat for breakfast. They also wanted to know if Michael Jordan has ever been in touch with the Mafia. How many other professional athletes were asked such a question?

Michael continuously faced these situations when he became a phenomenon so deeply injected into the popular culture that off-the-wall questions were a nightly routine. There were media people—an oxymoron if you asked Michael his last year or so in the NBA—who called each Michael Jordan listed in the Chicago telephone book to ask what they thought about having the same name as the superstar. There were people who named their children Michael Jordan. There were some who told Michael Jordan stories to their kids at bedtime.

The prevailing question, then, is, How did Michael Jordan get to be such a walking believe-it-or-not? It's not just the answers that are of human interest. The questions create wonder about what is lore and what is logical. And if Michael Jordan really was asked how much he would pay for a drink to make him invisible, well, how far-fetched was it to wonder if Michael Jordan ever had been in touch with the Mafia?

May 15, 1993, The Richfield Coliseum, Richfield, Ohio. Something had to happen to keep me from focusing on the pain. Deciding to shoot that free throw left-handed the other night because the tendon in my right wrist hurt so much actually made me worry about an injury. And I never worried about injuries. I've always said I know my body better than anybody but this time I didn't know. My right wrist throbbed so much the next few days that practice consisted solely of shooting lefty hook shots. You would think Game 3 of a playoff series against Cleveland today would be enough to keep me from feeling the pain. But we're down 14 points to the Cavs, and fear is keeping me from extending on my jump shot. Fear—and pain like I've never felt before—is making me afraid to shoot. But I have to shoot.

I'm sitting in the locker room at halftime, and we're down three points. I've missed 5 of 9 shots, and I'm afraid to shoot. Now the hype of the competition has ahold of me. If one jump shot can go down, maybe another one will. Now we're winning and the shots are falling. Driving for that layup and drawing the foul to give us a 94-90 lead made me realize I had overcome the pain. Sure it will be sore tomorrow, but you know when you're in the thick of competition you have to find a tolerance for the pain. And when you're on the basketball court, that's the one place you don't worry about the injuries.

f Dr. John Hefferon, the Bulls' team physician, sported some miracle cure, that would explain the way Michael Jordan rebounded from injuries. If trainer Chip Schaeffer had magic athletic tape, then it would not be hard to understand how MJ could sprain an ankle so bad in the third quarter that he had to be carried off the floor, then come back to pull out a victory in the fourth quarter.

His right wrist hurt so much prior to the game at Cleveland that he shook hands with friends left-handed. He spent much of the pregame shoot around practicing left-handed jumpers. Those he shot with the right came up woefully, painfully short.

But after missing 5 of his first 9 shots, Jordan hit 5 of 7 in the third quarter. He finished by hitting 9 of his last 16, some with greater degrees of difficulty than he routinely made when 100 percent healthy. He scored 10 of the team's final 13 points, something Jordan would do on an ordinary night. But on this night when he was talking about pain and fear it was extraordinary.

On a Wednesday night in December, he passed up a game in Boston because of a strain in his left foot and then came back to score 38 points Friday in a win over Portland. He sprained an ankle so bad on a Tuesday in February against Milwaukee that he hobbled out of Chicago Stadium on crutches. Then he scored 36 points in a win at Orlando on Thursday.

Tolerance for pain and getting caught up in the hype of competition were Michael's typical explanations for the ability to bounce back from injury. But this was Michael Jordan, and it was not that simple. His ability to thrive on injury was merely one more component of the man that demanded explanation. It involved extreme mental stubbornness to be sure. But could a trainer with tape create that stubbornness? With Michael it had to be something more, something beyond the medical. Did he know what it was?

May 20, 1990, The Palace, Auburn Hills, Michigan. Joe Dumars has attached himself to my jersey, which you can only admire him for because it means he's always competing, always challenging, and that's the way the game should be played. I can change direction and crossover dribble on most guys, but Joe always gets in my way. When I do shake free, he channels me into a body slam between Rodman and Salley. So now you've got to make the choice: Deal with the hands-on stuff or take the beating. It wouldn't be so bad if Laimbeer weren't waiting with a cheap shot.

This was what I faced every night. This was how they guarded me. There seemed to be one standard Jordan rule: never let go; never let him go to the bucket untouched. Wes Unseld used to tell his Washington Bullets, "Nail him" on every drive. John Starks scratched and clawed and left me scarred for life. Rolando Blackman and Jeff Malone ran me through picks from guys twice my size all night and bumped me off my game. It wouldn't have been so bad getting bounced from one end of the country to the other if Kendall Gill and Reggie Miller would've ever shut up. Those guys talked a better game than they played. They talked the entire game. That was their idea of defense.

They asked me, "Who is the toughest guy to go against one-on-one? Name the one player who defends you the best." It's tempting to say nobody because who knows the last time one guy played me straight up—with just one man—defensively.

For most of six years, Cleveland tried to play me straight up. You would think they'd know better. After I went off for a couple of 50s, a 69, and two game-winning shots, Craig Ehlo said at least he can tell his grandchildren he guarded Michael Jordan.

It's hard to say who was the best. Dumars was the roughest, if not the toughest. I'd be more interested to hear what they said. Like in the 1993 Finals when Kevin Johnson played me in Game 3 and "held" me to 44 points. Listened to that shit for two days, then in Game 4 he played me straight up again and he "held" me to 55. Would have been 60 if I had made my free throws.

It's hard to say who was the best.

The *New York Daily News* devoted two full pages of its sports section Sunday, May 23, 1993, to an explanation of how to guard Michael Jordan. After suggesting such tactics as "Get Physical," "Do not play him 1-on-1," "Make Mike Work," and "The Wave Approach," the article concluded that Kryptonite would be best.

Joe Dumars, who Michael credited with being one of the best at defending him, claimed that he knew the spot where it was toughest to guard Jordan. "Basically when he stepped on the court," Joe D. deadpanned. "That's the spot I feared him the most."

Kevin Johnson learned about drawing the defensive assignment opposite Jordan in Game 3 when the Suns were in mid-flight from Phoenix to Chicago during the 1993 NBA Finals. "I was reading a book at the time," KJ remembered. "I immediately put it away and went to sleep. I figured I was going to need the extra rest and that was the best way to avoid thinking about the nightmare that lay ahead."

Craig Ehlo admitted staying up all night before games against Jordan and plotting his defensive strategies. Guarding Michael became a sport within a sport for some of the NBA's greatest players.

The question here is, Who did what? And what worked? Or maybe more succinctly, What didn't? Most of those who tried to guard Jordan admit that they failed. Why didn't any of their plans work?

*J*une 25, 1993, Sheraton Towers Hotel, Chicago. The season has ended the same way it has the past three years: with a championship, the NBA Finals Most Valuable

Player Award, and another Jeep. Now, everybody wants to know what I'm going to do this summer.

I'm not going to Europe. I used to love to go to Europe. I could get great clothes in Italy, custom-made suits. But going to Europe became like going to New York to play the Knicks. I would walk out of the hotel, and people would be lined up on the street, pushing each other out of the way to get a look at me. I could never leave my hotel room in New York or anywhere.

This was the lifestyle for Michael Jordan, the only player in the NBA—maybe the only athlete ever—who needed police to clear traffic so he could leave after a practice. A practice? After a practice during the 1993 NBA Finals, Jordan, in his Porsche, needed a police escort to get out of the Chicago Stadium VIP parking lot and onto a back street where he could make a fast getaway to the highway. And this was while 500 media men and women were still inside the Stadium talking to Charles Barkley. After a practice, more than 200 people surrounded Jordan.

Michael took his family to an amusement park, and it made the national news. This was the lifestyle that his success created, and he never wasted time complaining about the sacrifices of being on television every five minutes and making millions of dollars. But how did he deal with it? How did he put up with the riot scene every time he set foot in public? And how did he manage to escape unscathed? Did he, for that matter? His strong will, his stubbornness, his relentlessness no doubt helped Michael put up with the lifestyle. But how did he keep the lifestyle from being the source of his undoing? After all, it drove Elvis to depression and drugs, Michael Jackson to legal troubles, and Marilyn Monroe to suicide. Michael Jordan achieved that level of public worship and beyond. More than examining the maladies of his lifestyle, which natural curiosity compels us to, we need to look at how he managed to endure it.

November 11, 1993, Chicago Stadium. The really great players want the ball with the clock running down and a chance to take the last shot. I had confidence in myself and my shot in that situation. And I think all my teammates had confidence in me to make it. Horace was always calling it "Magic Man" and "Superman" stuff, but sometimes I wonder if he was just making fun of me.

You never want to get too excited when you make or miss one of these last-second shots or too disappointed when you miss one. You probably saw me run and jump and shake my fist after hitting the one to beat Cleveland in the playoffs. The one they call "The Shot." The first one. Sure, it was exciting because we moved on to the next round of the playoffs and who knows what would have happened if that shot didn't go down?

But I ran to that spot because all game long there was this one Cleveland fan telling me to get my tee time ready for the next day, that my season was over, and my summer was about to begin. And I had to let him know we were still playing basketball, and it was Cleveland's time to go play golf.

Some shots you just *know* are going in. You *think* they all will go down. We were playing the Pistons early in the 1992–93 season, and the game was tied with about 20 seconds left when we set up for a last shot. Dumars had his forearm in my chest again, but I got a pretty good look at the basket. Thought the shot was going down. It didn't.

We went to overtime, and we were looking at almost the same situation. Dumars hit one over me with 11 seconds left to put them ahead by one.

We had possession with about four seconds left. I got the ball near halfcourt, took two dribbles, and pulled up at the three-point line. I was down the stairs and in the locker room almost before that thing hit the bottom of the net. All I ever asked for was a good look at the basket and enough time to get the shot off. Some shots you just know are going in.

Michael Jordan probably needed less time and less space to get off a shot than anybody who ever played basketball. Explaining how he manufactured such redundant, game-ending drama was nearly impossible for him or anybody else. As Trent Tucker, who played with and against Michael in many of those melodramatic moments, explained: "You just stand and watch with your mouth hanging open. I learned to enjoy those times."

Ah yes, those times—there were so many. There was the time he scored the final 18 points to beat the Knicks in 1986. There was the time that same year when he scored 40 or more points in nine straight games and during the same time blocked a last-second shot by Dominique Wilkins to preserve a victory over Atlanta. These were the times when MJ had "a certain gleam in his eye," said Ron Harper after he watched Jordan gleam all over Cleveland for a career-high 69 points on March 28, 1990.

Timing proved to be an element so important in Jordan's penchant for bravado. He had a knack for picking the right time to produce something extraterrestrial. With the Bulls trailing by 15 points in the fourth quarter at Utah on February 1, 1993, he scored 20 straight points to deliver a victory. In Game 1 of the 1992 NBA Finals, he put up 36 points in the first half in what became renowned as Michael Jordan's three-point shooting extravaganza.

All of which brings us back to how he managed such heroics. After such prolonged brilliance, we have so many questions about Michael Jordan. Why did he look at a meaningless night in November and every other day and night as a never-before-known challenge? Why was he such a relentless practice player? What were the physical and mental skills that made him so great? How could he become even greater in the playoffs? Was he the greatest? How did he compare to Magic and Bird and Barkley and Isiah and Shaq and Wilt and Dominique? How did he compare himself to those players?

How much of who Michael Jordan was as a player and a person had to do with his father and family? What was it like to coach this guy? What was it like to play with this guy? Was he a true team leader? Did he make the players around him better? Did the players around him think that he made them better or that they were just a multi-headed supporting cast? What did they really think of him?

What did it mean to Michael to be an NBA champion? How did he handle the burden of being the offense, knowing that as time wound down, an entire team, organization, city, and league depended on his heroics? How did he deal with his off-the-court troubles? Was he a compulsive gambler or just a compulsive competitor? Why did he retire from the game so suddenly? Did the murder of his father in August 1993 make him decide to walk away from pro basketball? What made him obsessed with trying to play professional baseball less than four months after quitting basketball?

As soon as Joe Dumars watched Jordan get off the eventual game-winning three-point shot on that November night in 1992, he too knew the ball was going in. As soon as the shot left Michael's hands, Dumars looked up as if to provide a reaction replay for ESPN's nightly highlight show. Several minutes after the game, Dumars sat by his locker recounting the play. He insisted he did all the right things in defending Jordan this time. And he was right. He stayed in front of Michael, made him use up time looking for an opening to get off the shot, and forced him to fire while fading away from the basket.

When asked to explain how Michael overcame all that and still made the shot, Dumars smiled and asserted in his soft, high-pitched drawl, "Man, don't ask me to explain Michael Jordan."

PART I

His Work

ONE

Signs of Greatness

March 9, 1993, Chicago Stadium.
Sam Perkins was telling that story again? You mean the one where he talks about the moment he realized Michael Jordan was going to be more than just another good player? It happened back in 1983 and 10 years later he still remembers. It was kind of embarrassing when he told everybody about it during the Finals that year when he was with the Lakers.

But when so many writers are around looking for a story, they pick on one of your college teammates. And Sam certainly had one they never heard before. It's been almost two years since we beat the Lakers for the championship. Sam is with Seattle now and after another loss to us tonight he was telling that story, again.

He actually tells it better than me because he remembers more of the details. He always tells everybody I remember it, and I do. My sophomore year at North Carolina—Sam was a junior—we were playing at Maryland. At some point of the game, Sam hit me with an outlet pass, and there was a clear path to the basket. Instead of going up for a one-hand jam, I kind of turned sideways while rising to the basket. Before you know it, I'm cranking the ball back, rocking it left to right, and slamming it down like with a one-handed push.

Sam said when they asked me about it afterward, my response was something like "It seemed like a pretty good thing to do."

Every breakaway after that gave me a chance to try the same dunk. Sam said that Maryland game was the first time he remembered me doing something different, something other than the normal stuff.

It's funny what some people remember about you from back then. Sam said he remembered the first time we played a pickup game together at Carmichael [Auditorium] when I first arrived in Chapel Hill. He thought I was just another body for the team. "A good shooter," he said, and he was being kind. But he never thought I would be the type of player to take or hit any game-winning shots.

Maybe back then everybody thought of me as just another body.

The summer after he hit the game-winning shot in North Carolina's 62-61 victory over Georgetown in the championship game of the 1982 NCAA basketball tournament, Michael Jordan was still little more than a skinny kid to many people. But about a month before school started the following August, he was playing more pick-up basketball at Carmichael. Not just with Tar Heel teammates this time: the opposition included Walter Davis and Mike O'Koren, North Carolina alums and NBA starters in 1982.

On the first play of the first game, Jordan went right over Davis for a dunk and came down with his mouth wide open and a look on his face that said "Welcome to Tar Hell."

"Michael just dominated," remembered Matt Doherty, another of Michael's college teammates. "His intensity was high, he was taking the ball to the basket, dunking on these guys, not showing these veterans any respect. That just opened your eyes and made you realize he was special."

The same feeling may have overcome a national television audience the opening game of Jordan's sophomore season against a top-10 ranked University of Missouri team in St. Louis. In the first half, Missouri's sharpshooting guard Jon Sundvold was hitting shots over Jordan from all over the court. North Carolina fell behind, and Jordan seemed like just another body on the court.

In the second half, though, he burst out of obscurity. Guarding an opposing player inbounding under the Carolina basket, Jordan jumped three feet straight up and grabbed the ball out of midair with two hands. It was one of those plays that happened so fast that time was frozen solid for a split second. You needed instant replay to see it. Less than a minute later, he darted across the court, intercepted a pass, and sprinted to a slam. And it all happened while he was playing with a broken bone in his right wrist and his hand wrapped in a thick cast.

Even before entering college, Jordan demonstrated star qualities. Certain plays he made and the way he went about trying to improve his abilities provided proof that MJ was going to be a player who could do what no one had done before. There were those who, after their first up-close look at Michael, knew he was going to be one of the all-time greats.

Orlando Woolridge had the first look at Jordan the pro. Ten years later, he smiled almost childishly when recalling the first day Michael showed up for a Bulls practice. Woolridge was a three-year veteran and the established star of the Bulls coming into Michael's rookie season of 1984. Woolridge was the one with the big scoring average (19.3 points per game), the guy who could run and dunk and propel Bulls fans—what few of them there were—out of their seats with a little rim-rattling. Woolridge did not notice any extraordinary ability watching MJ play college ball on television. But he knew that was not the case after the first day of practice, when Jordan tried to win every race, make every shot, challenge every play defensively.

"He was so much quicker than any of us, and he could jump so much higher," Woolridge explained. "He made the game seem really easy. But that wasn't what was special about Michael. I never saw anybody compete like that. He competed every day. He approached every practice like it was a game, like it was the game. Even then, we knew people would be coming out to see Michael and that would create a situation for the rest of us to try and get off."

Kevin Loughery coached the Bulls that season and recognized Jordan's ability when Michael went through ball-handling and passing drills the second day of practice. Loughery said Jordan told him he could not shoot very well. Loughery didn't care. Being around him and realizing how competitive he was helped the coach form a lasting opinion. Even nine seasons after that, Loughery's opinion of what made Jordan special had not changed. "I say this with the utmost respect and reverence," he asserted. "The first thing I realized about Michael is that he would cheat to win. He wanted to beat you that much."

Howard White had to come down and see what Woolridge and Loughery were talking about. Through his work as a national sales representative for Nike, the athletic shoe company that had just invested its future in a product known as "Air Jordan" basketball shoes, White heard all the superlatives that Jordan's play inspired. David Falk, who became Michael's agent in 1984, told White and Nike that Jordan had an electric style that would sell shoes, tickets, and pro basketball. White, who played college basketball at Maryland in the 1970s, knew something about electric style after working with Moses Malone, the NBA MVP in 1983. He figured that he had seen the pinnacle in Moses. Jordan's practice play left White feeling like he had been jolted by an electric shock.

"He played with a tremendous pride and confidence, like nothing I had ever seen before. I'm trying to think of one play that stood out, but he was making one play after another and not letting up. I walked away from that practice knowing there was something very special there. Did I mention he played with a tremendous pride and confidence?"

While Michael's future continued to rise with his leaping ability, legends grew around him. One of the more infamous tales poked fun at the Portland Trail Blazers. Portland had the second pick when Jordan entered the 1984 NBA draft. Houston had the No. 1 pick, and the Rockets opted for a guy named Hakeem Olajuwon. Portland had a shot at Jordan but took 7-foot center Sam Bowie, who went through three injuries and three teams before surfacing as a role player for the New Jersey Nets about the same time the Bulls were winning their third straight NBA title. Dr. Jack Ramsay, the Blazers' coach at the time, supposedly fumed about being known as the one who made that decision. Passing up Jordan reportedly led to his retiring from coaching in Portland. Ten years later, Ramsay still had trouble dealing with being part of the organization that picked Sam Bowie over Michael Jordan. But he had not seen any of the signs of greatness.

"I don't care what anybody says today. Nobody expected this Michael Jordan," said Ramsay, turning up the volume to an accusatory tone as he continued the thought. "Nobody. If the Bulls had the chance, they would have taken Sam Bowie over Michael Jordan. I had two very good guards at the time. Jim Paxson was an All-Star. I also had a guy by the name of Clyde Drexler. I had no center. I think everybody thought Michael Jordan would be good but not all-universe."

Driving through the Weavers Acres neighborhood of Wilmington, North Carolina, it's hard to imagine this is where a young boy named Michael Jordan rode his bicycle in and out of the woods and in and out of mischief. Decked out in middle-class suburbia, the town could have been in Ohio, Indiana, or California. Plain is a good way to describe Wilmington.

But this was the place where Michael started to show signs of greatness. When he was 12 years old, he pitched the Wilmington team within one game of advancing to the Little League World Series. Michael threw a two-hitter in the East Regional championship game but lost 1-0.

This was also the place where on the playground court at Trask Junior High a guy introduced himself to Michael by trash-talking to him with a toothpick in his mouth. That was the day Adolph Shiver and Michael Jordan developed a friendship that rarely let a few days pass without some exchange of trash-talking.

All those stories from his wonder years seemed to be buried in the Weavers Acres archives, including the one that forever defined Jordan. When he was in 10th grade, there was no room for Michael Jordan on the Laney High School Buccaneers varsity basketball team. Bucs coach Clifton Herring decided to take Leroy Smith, one of Michael's childhood friends, over Jordan. As the tale goes, Jordan came home after finding out about being cut, stayed in his room all afternoon, and cried. And that was what supposedly inspired him to become All-State, All-American, All-NBA, and All-Universe. End of story, supposedly.

But that is not where the story ended. When school started the following year, Jordan prepared to make the team. Herring picked him up every day at 6 A.M. and put him through shooting and dribbling drills. Jordan's physical development accelerated as well. He shot up to 6 feet 2 inches the summer before his junior year. He was so dedicated to making the team that he spent much of that summer hanging on monkey bars to try and grow or at least stretch a few extra inches. With nobody in his family taller than 5 feet 7 inches, perhaps this helps to explain how Michael grew a foot beyond any other Jordan.

The most important part of Jordan's unique makeup was quickly developing at the time. It would be easy to credit being cut from the Laney team in 1978 as the reason for Michael's insatiable desire to excel. "I wanted to prove to the guy [Herring] that I was good enough to make the team." Basketball became his proving ground ever since. But the relentless desire is a by-product of two other factors.

As a kid, Larry Jordan beat his little brother's butt so many times playing one-on-one on the backyard court James Jordan built for his kids that Michael learned to hate losing. "As soon as I grew taller than him, I vowed to never lose to him again," Michael remembered. He kept that vow. Equally important was Michael's high school basketball experience. How much do you remember hearing about Jordan as a prep player, the way you heard about such prep All-Americans as Billy Owens, Harold Miner, or Anfernee Hardaway being the next Michael Jordan?

"I never had any of that notoriety in high school and that was probably a blessing because I always had the hunger," Michael observed. "I was never compared with the greatest of all time, and I didn't burn out early as a result."

High school was a proving ground and a time for Michael to find himself as a basketball player. But it wasn't the greatest learning experience. After growing to 6 feet 4 inches his senior year at Laney, he played power forward. That position allowed him to play the post-up game with his back to the basket, which became an inherent part of his offensive arsenal as a pro. Former Bulls coach Doug Collins called Jordan "one of the five greatest post-up players in the game." And in high school, Jordan was a power forward trying to become a guard. During his senior season, Laney won 19 games with Jordan taking rebounds off the defensive board and driving from one basket to the other for a dunk.

"When I finally became known as an outstanding high school player, I was known as a guard because I was 6-foot-6," Jordan recalled. "I didn't have the body of a forward, and I did have the skills of a guard because of all that time I spent in the gym in the morning. But I got to that point strictly off desire and ability. I learned on my own or by watching. I wasn't taught fundamentals until college."

Jordan developed his relentless desire in high school. That provided the foundation for the rest of his game.

Something must have happened at North Carolina that had nothing to do with a shot, a dunk, or a moment to make Michael Jordan better. It didn't have to do exclusively with learning and developing skills, although in Chapel Hill Michael was exposed to methods that helped improve his shooting, ball-handling, passing, footwork, and other basics of the game. Learning basketball was a regimented process at North Carolina. Everything was broken down to a fundamental procedure and taught through repetition. So Jordan no doubt learned about offensive and defensive spacing and positioning and probably gained a cerebral perspective on the game while playing three years for Dean Smith.

But there had to be something more there that helped contribute to his ascension. Jordan always spoke about Carolina with allegiance in his voice, as though it was some sacred temple and it would be blasphemous to divulge too much about what went on there. The national exposure no doubt had an effect on him, for every time the Tar Heels played it was a national event. You had to learn and grow accustomed to always being in the limelight. And this is how he learned to look at every game he ever played since as *the* game.

Michael also learned how to become a dedicated practice player at Carolina because practice play reaped the rewards of playing time in games. But except for isolated moments, such as blocking a jump shot by Ralph Sampson, the 7-foot-4-inch Virginia All-American center during a game in Chapel Hill in 1983, or soaring to that newly created dunk against Maryland, Jordan never had an opportunity to extend as a Tar Heel.

"It was a very regimented atmosphere," he observed. "They taught you how to be a team player, how to lay it on the line for the team. The education of skills was by far the best, but I never really knew what I could do there. I never really knew if I could excel or dominate."

An old joke fingers North Carolina coach Dean Smith as the only guy who could ever stop Michael Jordan. The line started making the rounds after Carolina lost to Indiana in the 1984 NCAA East Regional semifinal. Jordan scored just eight points in that game while playing limited minutes.

The game set up a career for Indiana's Dan Dakich, who guarded Jordan that night and went on to become an assistant coach to Bobby Knight. Dakich also did serious time on the lecture circuit, telling time and again the story about how after finding out he was going to match up with Jordan he immediately went into a nearby bathroom and vomited. Jordan only found it funny that a guy like Dan Dakich actually stopped him because the only thing Dakich did that night was to figure out how to get Jordan into early foul trouble. That allowed Jordan to play just eight minutes of the first half. Michael always called that game the most painful loss of his life, probably because he never got another chance to show Dakich that one night was a fluke.

The Carolina experience did not climax with that game. Jordan had ample opportunity to apply his skills, and he learned how to overcome adversity to an extent. At one point during his freshman year, he considered leaving Chapel Hill and going home until then Tar Heel assistant Roy Williams talked him out of it. Jordan established the same loyalty for Williams that he did for Smith and Carolina. And when Williams went on to coach at Kansas and faced Carolina in the

NCAA tournament Final Four in 1991 and 1993, it was the only time Jordan struggled to root for the Tar Heels. But the Carolina experience left Michael with something considerably more important, though he never was able to put it into words. His father, however, provided insight.

"People underestimate the program that Dean Smith runs," James Jordan explained before a playoff game in Chicago in 1993, which Smith happened to be attending. "He helped Michael realize his athletic ability and hone it. But more important than that, he built character in Michael that took him through his career. I don't think Michael was privileged to any more teaching than anyone else. He had the personality to go with the teaching, and at Carolina he was able to blend the two of them together. That's the only way I can look at it, and I think that's what made Michael the player he became."

Michael Jordan always said that if he woke up one day and thought he could not get any better than he was the day before, he would quit basketball. Such a statement of purpose allowed him to develop into greatness. It's the same attitude that compelled Jordan to build up his body. Six years into his career, Jordan had already established himself as the most talented player in the game. But that was not producing his desired result—a championship.

He felt that the Pistons were always able to beat him by beating on him. That was the only advantage they had. So he set out to get stronger. Through the help of personal trainer Tim Grover, he developed a regimen to bulk up his chest, shoulders, triceps, biceps, and back. His body weight went from 201 to 213 pounds, and his body fat went from 4 percent to 3.2 percent. And he went from losing to Detroit to beating the Pistons. Grover put together a year-round training program that eventually had Jordan working various exercises, lifting five sets of six with as much as 255 pounds. And he continually tried to improve on that because he figured it was another way to develop as a player. That's the approach that led Jordan to greatness.

"Early in my career I was able to drive because teams played closer on me, guarded me closer, guarded me one-on-one. They didn't double- and triple-team me. Then, I earned the respect of the double- and triple-team, and defenses started playing off me, making me take the outside shot. They felt that was the weakest part of my game. I was able to adjust to that, and in adjusting I was able to maintain the consistency I started my career off with in terms of numbers or whatsoever. That showed progression, maturity, and improvement. I think I got better every year that I played the game. Not just physically but with my knowledge of playing the game. And if you ever get to the point where you don't think you need to improve, then why keep playing?"

The game's greatest players play as intensely and play to win as much in practice as they do in games. Jordan practiced every day to prove such a statement. At times during 48 minutes of game, he flashed his brilliance. But day after day, Michael demonstrated his superiority in practice, and it was that way from the moment he became a professional.

He always practiced hard. You have to want to practice to get up at 6 A.M. and do it on a school day—in the offseason. At North Carolina, practice was one of the few times Dean Smith loosened the reins, and Jordan was able to catch a glimpse of what he really could do. But when he arrived at his first Bulls training camp, Michael knew that practice was going to be at once a discovery zone and a place to develop greatness.

"I used to have a hell of a practice," he recalled. "I thought practice was my proving ground to my teammates, where I had to prove to them, 'Hey, I was the third pick in the draft, and I was worth it. I was the highest paid player on the team, and I was worth it.' Once I did it, it was the way I did it that was important."

Like any other practice from the YMCA junior leagues to the pros, there is usually a time to scrimmage. The coach splits the team into two units of five that play against each other. More often than not, the five best players—the starters—scrimmage against the five next best players. At Bulls practices, the starters were known as the white team. The second five wore red.

Loughery had Jordan playing with the white team from his first day. With Jordan and Woolridge, the white team easily rolled up leads of 8-1 or 7-4 in games to 11. The loser of these games always had to run extra wind sprints after practice. It was about that time of the scrimmage that Loughery would switch Jordan to the red team. And the red team would wind up winning more often than not.

"That was his [Loughery's] way of testing my competitiveness," Jordan continued. "But I think it helped me understand my ability, it helped me believe in myself at a time when I wasn't too sure what I could be. It also helped me being in that spotlight in terms of getting all the different things in my career.

"It also gave me a lot of confidence. That was the time when my confidence grew the most. I credit Loughery for that. If he didn't do that, there's no way I would ever have become what I became."

Jordan became a relentless practice player. Even when he was hurt, he could not sit out of practice. Late in the 1993 season, he sprained his ankle so bad in a game against Milwaukee that he left Chicago Stadium on crutches. He was practicing the next day. He did not run through all the drills, but he spent the time developing a regimen to improve his foul shooting. Jordan shot free throws rapid fire until he missed. He hit a string of 23 straight before practice ended.

When Doug Collins coached the Bulls from 1986-89, he had to force Jordan to sit down at practice. "Chain him down," was how Collins described it during scrimmages. Collins would tell Michael to sit down, and a minute later Jordan would check himself back into the scrimmage and take Charles Oakley's place at power forward. He would play center in practice if it meant a chance to work on his post-up play.

"Practice is what made him go," Collins said. "Every day he had this need to show he was the best. It's like 'I'm the best today, and I'm going to show you, and tomorrow I'm going to show you, and the next day I'm going to show you.'

"That's the only way he could do it 110 times a year. If he didn't feel the need to show you every single day, then he would have bad games. It became part of Michael. Some guys take nights off. Some guys take days off. He never did that. It's because he had a great love for the game. But it was also a big part of his greatness. Throw away all the talent. The way he practiced put him on a level above everybody else."

When Collins coached the Bulls he sold Jordan on the idea of becoming a great shooter. After practice every day, the two would work together for 20 minutes on Michael's outside shot. He developed some of his ability through tireless practice. Some of his skills were natural, God-given as Michael used to say.

On the playgrounds of Wilmington, at Laney, at North Carolina, and when he first came to Chicago, Jordan sent up signs of greatness. Before he could get to that level above everybody else, however, he had to put the package together. Whether it happened overnight, after a few years in the NBA, or as David Falk said, "with a strike of a lightning bolt," Michael Jordan had to go through that process of combining all his ability, mental and physical, into what is known in any place where there are two iron hoops, two backboards, and a group of ten willing to play as "your game." Not that commercial crap like "Me and him and the guy over there got the next game." But, "I can play some defense and shoot and drive so well that you can't deal with my game."

TWO

Tools of Greatness

January 16, 1993, Chicago Stadium. There's a new kid in town, so to speak. He's a big, strong kid, too. You feel for what Shaquille O'Neal is going through right now. Everywhere he goes, people come to see him, to see what he can do. If he can score or dunk or break backboards, whatever. That's what it was always like for me when we went on the road. They wanted to see me score 50, and they wanted to see their team win.

Since everybody was watching this game, you think maybe it's another chance to show off your game. People everywhere, even people in this locker room, might say I just want to show this kid who's the best. Especially in my hometown. Deep down, I suppose they're right to an extent. Every great player picks it up a notch under these circumstances. Every great player has a second gear or third or fourth they can go to.

But tonight it's about more than that. This is one of those ultimate moments when you want to try and put everything together. If they're going to have a chance to judge you as the best player in the game, then give them a chance to see why. And it's not necessarily a matter of scoring a lot of points but doing things on both ends of the basketball court. That's kind of the way my entire career was—a progression of developing skills to stay on top. You have to be able to do more than one thing, so this was not a time just to show that to Shaq but to show myself.

You know at first they said about me that I didn't pass enough. So I learned from that. Then, they said I couldn't go to my left. And I practiced that, and they stopped saying that.

Then, they said I couldn't hit the jump shot consistently, that I was primarily a driver and a dunker. I practiced my jump shot.

Eventually, they didn't know where I was going or what I was going to do and that became the most lethal part of my game.

The 64 points Michael Jordan scored against Orlando during Shaquille O'Neal's debut in Chicago Stadium on January 16, 1993, was not just another season high. Jordan did play with that "OK, Shaq, if you think you're hot stuff, I'm gonna show you what this game is like when it's great" gleam in his eye. But because the Bulls blew a six-point lead with 44 seconds left and lost 128-124 in overtime, Michael's final comment after 30 minutes of talking about the game dismissed any feeling of accomplishment. "Those 64 points don't mean a thing when you lose."

Jordan threw away the ball in those final 44 seconds and missed a crucial free throw down the stretch, so he had to accept blame rather than celebrate his earlier heroics. Because Scottie Pippen looked at the box score afterward, he noticed Michael took 49 shots and had one assist. Then, he cracked, "How did Michael manage to get one assist?" Jordan never fully enjoyed the magnitude of his play on this night.

Lost in defeat was an effort that demonstrated Michael Jordan's ever-expanding array of skills. Sure, he wanted to show up Shaq but not by just scoring 64 points. He scored in every way conceivable. He scored any way he wanted. It was one of those nights that his offensive skills were on some kind of wheel of fortune, continually spinning until Michael stopped on the one that would ring up another basket.

Consider that of the 27 shots he hit on this night, only one was a dunk. Two others were driving layups. Nine of the eleven baskets Jordan made in the first quarter came on shots made from beyond 10 feet. He posted up and opened up with a 10-foot turnaround fade. He drove left for a 12-footer, then right to hit an 18-foot fadeaway. After a 19-foot stop-and-pop off an isolation went down, Michael buried a 10-footer.

He finished the game with five steals and six rebounds. He also passed. One assist may have shown up in the box score, but how many of his passes ended up in Pippen's and Horace Grant's 17 missed shots?

Michael always invoked analogies and metaphors after performances like this. If the Bulls had won, he would say he felt like a hurricane gusting more intensely as the game went on. Or like a sports car winding through the gears and hitting that last gear in the final moments to pull away. Except that Michael had many more gears.

There were nights when Jordan shot better, scored more flamboyantly, passed more effectively, or defended more disruptively. To him there were nights more memorable because his team won. But even Michael did not deny this was one night—one of many nights—when his performance featured all of his skills. It was a night to make you want to sit down with Jordan and discuss all the physical, mental, and mystical genius that made him extraordinary.

James Jordan once attempted to explain his son's genius. After stumbling over several words and phrases Pops said, "I think God wanted to make the perfect basketball player, and he picked Michael." When Michael scored 64 points on one Saturday night in January 1993, then made 7 steals in a game the following Saturday night, he was like a gold ring that has the same shining luster all the way around. During that week, Jordan again showed just how well-rounded his game was. The way he shot the ball—easy to overlook because of the way he leaned, floated, or avoided a pair of defenders in one motion—was in a word, perfect.

To understand perfection, pop a tape of Game 1 of the 1992 NBA Finals into the VCR and focus exclusively on Jordan's shooting posture as he hit those six straight three-point shots in the 122-89 victory over the Portland Trail Blazers. With his upper arm parallel to the ground, his elbow extended, and his forearm perpendicular to the court, he formed the perfect U-shaped shooting pocket that coaches say only the most gifted shooters ever achieve. Every shot in that series repeated the motion so exactly that you swear you would be watching instant replay if you knew it was not live. No matter what contortion he was caught in, Michael always squared his shoulders up to the basket. And he always pumped his legs into every jump shot. Perfect.

When the Bulls hit their championship form in 1991, coach Phil Jackson moved Michael Jordan from one attack position to another, like the queen on a chess board. He would start the game as the off-guard, the one who did not handle the ball. Then he would serve as point guard. From that position, he would occupy defenses while other players took shots and scored.

At the end of the first quarter, he would get about three or four minutes of rest, and then come back in while Scottie Pippen rested. Jordan would play Pippen's position at small forward, move without the ball, and look for openings to shoot. Toward the end of a close game, he would become the team's main option in the post, the position about five feet from the basket that is usually reserved for centers. If he did not choose that spot, Jordan would handle the basketball and take on the point guard's role of finding openings to score while trying to create opportunities for other players to shoot.

When Michael talked about the position he played, he rarely used such terminology as off-guard, shooting guard, or small forward. "I'm the utility man," he would say. "I fill all the loopholes, and I do whatever it takes to do that." Translation: I have all the necessary skills to play any position, and I will use them whenever the team needs me to. Michael handled the ball with the perfection of a point guard. He was so repetitive that games seemed like practice drills. He stayed low, kept the ball in front of him, and kept his head up. What he could do from there separated Jordan from other ball handlers. He could dribble from left hand to right quickly and fluidly. He could also do this while changing directions, and he could change directions simply by pushing off one leg to the other, then back again. He could also do it while running full speed from the defensive end of the court to the offensive end.

Some of the best ball handlers in the history of the game could make one change from right hand to left—known as a crossover dribble—to slip a defender. It is an effective move that more often than not leads to a drive to the basket. Michael had the ball-handling ability, combined with speed and strength, to go back and forth several times while moving forward. It was as if he was hopping or jitterbugging with the ball, building up to make a move. Imagine being an opponent trying to defend that.

Remember that Doug Collins called Jordan one of the five best post-up players of his era. The post is the area also called the low block, within five feet of the basket where if you can catch a pass you are a power-turn away from a dunk or layup. Wilt Chamberlain, Charles Barkley, Karl Malone, Hakeem Olajuwon—big, strong, beefy men—were consummate post-up threats.

Jordan flaunted leg strength and arm strength as his tools of success in the post. Jordan had so much forearm strength that he could hold off defenders or keep them behind him with one arm and collect the ball off a lob pass. He had tremendous balance; the hand-checking and bumping that accompanies play in the low block never knocked Michael out of position. Quickness and the mastery of fundamental footwork to take one step and explode past defenders to score also made him hard to defend in the post.

Michael could always spin away from the basket to a counter move the way a boxer jabs to get an opponent to defend one area and expose another. That was when Michael would shoot the high-rise, fade-away jumper that became his trademark shot. Larry Bird had his—the one-handed push from the shoulder off the step-back out of the post—and

Kareem had the skyhook. When Jordan established position in the post, he was more of a threat from that spot than Barkley, Malone, or even Shaq.

Although nobody will take the credit for it, some critics said that Michael could not pass. At least, that's what Michael said.

Collins believes that early in his career Jordan had no confidence in his teammates and that is why he did not pass. It should be noted that during a month of the 1988–89 season Collins asked Jordan to play point guard, and he averaged double-figure assists during that time. Only when Pippen and Grant developed into trustworthy offensive threats sometime in 1990 did Jordan become more freewheeling with his passing.

When Dr. Jack Ramsay provided a review of Jordan's career, one of his initial comments addressed passing. "Michael always had a great sense of what his team offense was and where everybody should be. If somebody was open, he would get them the ball. But he put them in this situation where now you've got to produce. You see, he wasn't the kind of guy who was going to keep giving you the ball if you didn't produce because he felt that hurt the team."

In the opening game of the 1993 NBA playoffs, Jordan scored 36 points against Atlanta and hit eight of his first 10 shots. After his team suffered through a 114-90 loss, Hawks center Jon Koncak could not stop talking about what Michael Jordan did in that game. "I don't know why they ever said he couldn't pass. He beat us with his passing. For his teammates, it was like playing a game of 21—just catching it and shooting it. We started double-teaming him and he hit the open man for layups. I don't know why they ever said he couldn't pass. He can pass to exactness."

Although he did not always use them every game, Jordan had all the basketball skills necessary to excel. He also had other skills, ones not so easily explained, that put him on a higher plane or—as those who played with him or coached him or watched him night after night used to say—on another planet. Examining Jordan's physical attributes was like riding an elevator to the unknown or exploring a cave. Ascending to each new floor there is something more extraordinary than the last; down each tunnel there is darkness, and out of that comes something never before seen.

Dr. David Orth served as the Bulls' team ophthalmologist during

Jordan's career. He also performed the same function for the Chicago White Sox. Dr. Orth used to run a test on all players to measure reaction time. With the player looking into a dark area, he flashed sets of numbers on a tic-tac-toe board in increments of a half-second to a hundredth of a second. The players had to call out the numbers as they were flashed.

Frank Thomas, the 1993 American League Most Valuable Player for the White Sox who hits a baseball thrown at 100 m.p.h., also took the test. So did all his teammates, most of them also pretty good at hitting a baseball, which many experts—and Michael—will tell you is the single hardest thing to do in sports.

"Michael got more numbers than anybody," Dr. Orth said. "What that showed was spectacular vision but more than that a tremendous physical ability to concentrate. He was by far the best of all the athletes I ever tested."

Moving from head to toe, you may be surprised to find out that Michael Jordan was not the best jumper in the game of professional basketball. He didn't think so. Hakeem Olajuwon and Shawn Kemp were quicker jumpers, guys who could go up and down like they were on pogo sticks. Dominique Wilkins was more explosive with his leap than Michael. He went up so fast it looked like he had the help of a mini-trampoline.

When Ed Pinckney of the Boston Celtics was asked whether Jordan was the best leaper in the game, he said, "No. There are others who are better leapers, like Clyde Drexler and Dominique Wilkins. But Michael is the best floater." Hence conception of the terms "Hang Time" and "Air" to describe Jordan once he was airborne. What made his jump unique was what came *after* he left the ground. Jordan was the one player who could leap and gain momentum while in the air. Gravity would naturally bring a player back to the ground. But not Jordan.

"I have no explanation for how I jump," he noted. "I do know Dominique was always a two-footed jumper. He jumped off both feet. Clyde was a one-footed jumper. I'm both, plus I've got a bunny-hop jump."

Check the tape on this one. That bunny-hop jump made Jordan seem like he was preparing for take-off. It is the same motion that Olympic divers use as they run off the springboard into mid-air acrobatics. Michael's bunny-hop gave him extra spring, off which he could twist sideways and slip defenders in midair. So he had to be floating because even Ed Pinckney could not find a better way to explain his extra flight time.

The film shows it well: Jordan finding openings while in the air or maneuvering to spots to get off his shot, score, and get fouled. Fast forward to Game 4 of the 1993 NBA Finals, when in the final minute Jordan jumped into the midst of three Phoenix Suns, floated while they all came back to earth, swung the ball from high above his head down to his head, and flipped in a shot as Charles Barkley fouled him.

His explanation for such a shot and the ability to repeatedly create air acrobatics usually came down to "I was just trying to find a way to get to the basket and maybe draw a foul," or "It didn't really start out like that, but I found an opening and threw the ball up there." The shot against Phoenix fell into the same category. "It was just a continuation, trying to get the ball to the hoop," he explained. "I got a good look, and I was just trying to get the ball to the basket." It was never anything special to Michael, never anything that gave him a feeling of invincibility or superiority.

Magic Johnson had another perspective on the Jordan air raids. "Michael was the greatest of all time at moving the ball in the air. A guy on defense would think, 'I got him now.' But he would just hang there and hold the ball back." As he passes through this explanation, Magic rotates his hand back and forth. "With one left-handed move he could get three guys to jump and then hold it back." Now he's got his arm hyper-extended out to one side.

"Then, at the last second, he could swing it way out to his left and spin it in off the glass." As he says this, Johnson drops his arm, shrugs his shoulder, and smiles. He tried to demonstrate Jordan's ability to move the ball in the air but couldn't finish. "You see, there's nobody else who can do that."

Michael Jordan never relied solely on his physical genius to win basketball games. Intelligence and preparation made his physical tools an undeniable threat. On the night that he scored 64 points against Orlando, he analyzed what openings would occur playing against Nick Anderson and then figured out at which spots Shaq would not be able to challenge him. That is why he was taking open shots all night. Because Shaq was the Magic's only real defensive threat, Jordan never needed to go to the basket to score. In fact, he only went to the basket on three occasions. And when he did set up in the post, he turned and faded from spots O'Neal could not get to while giving double-team help. That's how Jordan would break down an opponent.

"Michael was never the kind of player who would just lace up his sneakers and say, 'OK, I'm a great player, and I'm gonna go out and kick this guy's ass today' " Doug Collins said. "He realized who was playing him and made sure to break the guy down. If he was smaller, he would take him in the post. If he was slower, he would make sure to take him off the dribble. If he was quick, Michael would make sure he gets the ball to a certain area and then jump over the guy.

"He always watched film. He never said anything about it, but he would come to me and say, 'Hey coach, can I have the film when we last played these people?' He was always trying to figure out like if we played Detroit. Dumars is playing him, OK what to do now? Now, they come with Vinnie [Johnson], what do I do know? Now Rodman. Where is the area I can go to on the floor when these guys are playing me? He always knew the harder you prepared, the luckier you seemed to get. Funny, isn't it?"

Preparation always worked in conjunction with motivation and confidence for Michael. Once he determined how he could put his physical skills to work, Jordan needed to find something to put him in the proper frame of mind. Sometimes, he focused on the individual matchup. For example, Indiana's Reggie Miller always worked wonders for Jordan's motivation. If Jordan would shift thorough a series of gears during a game, then he spent the pregame revving up.

Just before a game against the Pacers in Indianapolis February 10, 1993, Jordan sat in the Bulls' locker room watching a tape of Indiana's previous game. "This guy is a fucking joke," Jordan said as Miller came into view. "Look at the way he travels. It's just a joke." Maybe he was like a boxer talking trash to a figment of his motivation.

On the court that night, Jordan and Miller exchanged more trash talk, dirty looks, elbows, cheap shots, and eventually punches, which escalated into a bench-clearing brawl. Miller was ejected. Jordan was booed mercilessly. "I just fed off that," Jordan said afterward. Fed off it for 40 points in a 115-104 Bulls victory.

Cleveland's crowd provided similar motivation. After he hit the shot to beat the Cavs in the opening round of the 1989 playoffs, Jordan was booed in the Richfield Coliseum upon every return. That's the place he scored his career-high 69 points on March 28, 1990. After he hit another "shot" to knock Cleveland out of the 1993 playoffs, Michael said, "When they boo like that, it can get ugly . . . for them. They should know better than to boo me by now."

Johnny "Red" Kerr, who served as the Bulls' television broadcaster Michael's entire career, noticed the way Jordan played to the crowd during a game against New Jersey in 1990. "The Nets were having a down year, and there weren't many fans at the game," Kerr recalled. "But Michael was out there pushing it. After the game he told my wife that no matter where he plays, no matter how big or how small the crowd is, he wants to try and play that one perfect game. He said he wanted the fans to see him at his best. He said he owed it to the fans who paid to see him play."

"Michael would find different stimuli every night, and that put him on the plane no one else could reach," said Collins. "It might be someone in the front row that says something to him when he's warming up. He conjured up something, maybe something another player said. It was like a shot of adrenaline."

From Kerr's point of view, ego and pride always motivated Jordan in ways opponents never could. "He had so much pride that he never wanted to be embarrassed. He wouldn't accept it. And that's where ego came in. Those two things not only made him the greatest player in the world but also gave him supreme confidence."

It's almost easier to glorify Jordan's mental superiority than his physical dominance. Discussion of his powers of awareness tended to come off like a Jerry Seinfeld comedy routine. Take something unique, indigenous to the individual, and joke about it. Michael passed this off as just another part of his game, but somehow he always knew where the cutters were filling the lanes on the fastbreak, where the popcorn vendors were, and what section his father was sitting in. Perhaps that attested to his powers of concentration.

Or maybe this does: On the opening night of the 1992 NBA Finals, Jordan went on that overhyped (as he called it) three-point shooting spree. As soon as he nailed the sixth and final three-pointer, Jordan shrugged his shoulders, spread his palms, raised his eyebrows, and shot a look of disbelief toward Magic Johnson, who was sitting at courtside providing color commentary for the NBC television broadcast. As Michael said later about the look, "I could see him smiling at me, and I wanted to let him know I couldn't explain it either." In the biggest game of the season, Jordan was carving history and noticing how Magic Johnson reacted at the same time. That's like scoring bonus points playing Pac-Man or solving the puzzle on "Wheel of Fortune" and explaining how at the same time. Is it unusual powers of awareness, extraordinary powers of concentration, or just Michael?

The search continues, though it's getting to be like looking through a pile of diamonds for a needle, to find out what vaulted Jordan to greatness. If you had to pinpoint one tool, what would it be? It may be too early to tell, but this extra-gear phenomenon certainly is one worth examining. Yeah, the extra gear. It's that feeling that comes when you're playing in a pick-up basketball game, the score is 14-14, and the next basket wins. Somehow, you make that one spinning move for a layup or throw in that ridiculous bank shot from behind the backboard. Except that Michael did that kind of stuff not only in the fourth quarter but the first; not just the last minute but the first.

"Whenever we needed a win, it was one of those moods I could get myself into," Jordan observed. "To play better basketball I realized that I could get myself in a mood at certain times. It just kicked in, like a fourth gear."

Just a fourth gear?

"Maybe, or a fifth, sixth, seventh, whatever. It was the last, let's put it that way."

Magic Johnson figured he hit the extra gear by luck or by being in the right place at the right time. That is how he said he managed a few game-winning shots in his career. He did not put himself in Michael's class when discussing the overdrive element. He didn't put anybody in that class.

"I saw Larry Bird with an extra gear, just in a different way," Magic remarked. "Michael was more dominant than both of us ever dreamed up. He could do it in 50-, 60-point ways. When I was on, 30 points was good. I thought I did something. But he could score 55 and in all different ways. That's what made him special. If our certain way wasn't going, forget about it. But Michael could go inside, outside, dunk—that's what made him Air Jordan."

Red Kerr actually considered that Jordan may have possessed some supernatural power, commenting, "It's almost like if Michael set the ball down in front of him at the free throw line and went up to it and stared at it long enough, I believe he's got the mystical powers that if he said go into the basket, the ball would pick itself up and soar gently over the top of the hoop."

When it comes to explaining Michael's powers and tools of greatness, maybe Horace Grant's perspective served best. Michael hit a shot from halfcourt just before the halftime buzzer in Game 2 of the 1993 opening round playoff series against Atlanta. Afterward, Grant was asked about how Michael keeps doing that stuff. "He just pulls it out of his hat," Grant responded. "He's the magic man, so to speak."

THREE

Offense Part I:
Being the Offense

Richfield, Ohio, March 28, 1990.
That best-game-ever feeling hit me really only one time. On a lot of nights you feel nobody can stop you. At least not the guy who's going to be playing you. And when you come out hot, run off a bunch of baskets in a row, or put up a lot of points, that's when everybody asks if this was your best game ever. My standard answer was, my best game will be my last game. But I never matched that feeling of scoring 69 points against Cleveland and winning the game in overtime. The two greatest feelings are scoring like nobody can stop you no matter where you shoot from and winning. That was my best game ever by far. You know how I wear a new pair of shoes for each game and sometimes give them away afterward? I kept the shoes from that game.

I can still recall the details. Missed one shot in the first quarter, four by halftime. The Cleveland fans were booing me half the time, but that was just more motivation, more drive to excel. I hit a three with no time on the shot clock in the fourth quarter. You know when that happens, things are going your way. I hadn't felt that since that day in Boston when I scored 63. But I'd been in that situation where I score so many points, yet we lose the game. And I didn't want that to happen again. So I kept pushing myself and talking to myself; saying don't stop, keep going. Everything seemed to fall in line. I just jumped on it and rode it as long as I could.

I always looked back on games when I scored in the 60s and fought that same predicament: Was it just a matter of coming out and getting aggressive and starting to roll or did my supporting cast think I was being a one-man team? But on this night no one could get the offense generated. And since I pretty much felt it, Phil kept coming to me. When you get that feeling, you might miss, but not too many.

"We tried everything and everyone on you tonight," Craig Ehlo told me after the game. He knew I had the feeling because there were no easy points. Ron Harper used to try to play me tough when he was with Cleveland, but he was out with a knee injury for this game. After I made a move where I glided under the basket for a dunk—you know, one of those where it felt like flying—I looked over at Ron sitting on the bench. He was waving his hands, saying he didn't want any part of it.

I had the feeling all right. I had the defense on its heels and for a while I felt like I could pick and chose which way I wanted to go. That feeling really only hit me like that one time.

A fan's chances of seeing Michael Jordan score 40 or more points during his nine years in the NBA was once every 4.4496644 games.

How many of the times when Michael Jordan scored 60 or more points do you remember, do you recount with the same vividness Michael has? Oh yeah, I remember the 63 against Boston. On this one play, he dribbled between his legs, drove past Ainge, by Bird, and went under McHale for a reverse jam. You must have been there for one of Jordan's 50s. Or the 40s. After all, he topped the 40-point mark 165 times. There was not a team in the league he did not light up for more than 40 during those nine years.

Whether it was instant, fresh-brewed, or aged over time, Jordan's offense repeatedly surfaced as an issue, a topic sportswriters used to sit around and debate like members of the Continental Congress. Phil Jackson tried to keep Jordan's offensive outbursts in perspective, if not under control. Jordan forever tried to escape the tag of being just a scorer, even though being the most electrifying scorer was how he made an indelible mark on the NBA. Is he hot or is he a hog? was always the burning, yet unanswerable, question. Just to hear it made Michael burning mad. Questioning his offensive genius was the quickest way to put him on the defensive.

There were nights like the one in Cleveland when the basketball court became his canvas, his block of marble. Call him Michelangelo Jordan on nights like this. After 48 minutes (actually 53 on this night because of overtime), Michael chiseled out a masterpiece blotched with stylings only his talent could muster. That he could score 69 points, or 64, or 61, or more than 50 on 27 occasions commands examination first and foremost. To debate the overall welfare of Michael's ability to paint by numbers is like looking for the abstract in the realism. Let's look at the vintage of the work and then wonder how and why and how and why so often.

November 21, 1986, Chicago Stadium. Research charts this date as the official start of the Jordan can-score-more-and-more obsession. The New York Knicks saw it coming. Michael's outbursts against the Boston Celtics in the past year's playoffs—49- and 63-point games back to back—were the signs of his God-given scoring abilities. On opening night of the 1986 season, Jordan reeled off 40 points in one half against the Knicks in Madison Square Garden. Three weeks later, on November 21, 1986, Jordan scored the Bulls' final 18 points in a 101-99 win over the Knicks. After New York scored the tying hoop in the final seconds, Jordan dribbled the length of the floor with three guys hanging on him and made a 10-foot jump with less than a second to play to win the game. A week later Michael started a streak in which he scored 40 or more points in seven straight games and in 11 of 12 games en route to 37 such efforts for the entire season.

"I had no idea he would be able to do that," Doug Collins recalled about his first year coaching the Bulls. "In training camp, I thought we had a team that wasn't going to win 25 games. I wasn't being negative, I just saw our talent. Michael carried us to 40 wins, but after the first two games I realized this guy was going to do things we had never seen before."

February 26, 1987, Chicago Stadium. Collins said the highlight of this game was when Michael Jordan asked to come out with 2 minutes and 44 seconds left. Certainly a guy who has hit so many game-winning shots has a flare for the dramatic. Upon making his grand exit, Jordan had scored a regular-season, team-record 58 points. He had a record-setting night from the foul line with the third-highest free-throw total in league history (26 of 27), third highest number of free throws made in a half (13), and second-best free-throw percentage in one game (96.2).

The game was filled with Jordanisms: 11 straight points at the end of the first quarter, 15 of the final 17 in the first half, and the record-breaking basket coming via an assault across the lane and an over-the-shoulder reverse layup that drew a foul.

What did Michael remember most about that night? "I was on a roll and everything was falling," he recalled. "It was better than Boston—we won and my shooting percentage was higher."

March 4, 1987, The Silverdome, Pontiac, Michigan. Detroit Pistons fans were actually dancing in the aisles, doing the jerk as they watched Michael work. Pistons fans cheering for Jordan? That was like cheering for the Iraqis in the Persian Gulf War. If all he did was hit that twisting, fade-away jumper from the corner to tie the game at 111 with a few seconds left, it would have been one of those nights to remember. If all he had done was make a steal to preserve the tie and force overtime, it would have been one of those nights. But score one for Michael for making 30,281 Piston fans evoke movements from the hokey-pokey after watching him reel off a series of reverse scoops, drunks, and high-rise, driving jumpers with three defenders hanging on various extremities. Oh yes, he scored 61 points.

"One of those nights where you just had to hope he would miss," said Isiah Thomas, who viewed Michael as the enemy throughout his career. "But he wasn't going to, so you might as well enjoy it. It was a good time."

"No one's ever really unstoppable," Jordan said. "But I felt close to it that night."

April 16, 1987, Chicago Stadium. Michael was chasing scoring history. With the Atlanta Hawks in town for the second-to-last game of the season, he needed 37 points to hit 3,000 for the season. Only Wilt Chamberlain had ever done that before. And Wilt did it in an era when he was the only 7-footer playing against—with the exception of Bill Russell—mostly smaller, weaker players. Michael had 37 by halftime. Oh yes, he finished with 61 points.

It was another one of those memorable nights, but Jordan, in his competitive way, focused on something else from that night. "All I remember is that Dominique hit an unbelievable shot at the buzzer to beat us," he recalled. "That kept us from having a .500 season."

April 3, 1988, The Silverdome, Pontiac, Michigan. What was it like watching Michael go off for one of those 60-point outbursts? Or in this case, 59 points?

"He was in his own little funk, and there was no way I could get him out of it," said Pistons guard Vinnie Johnson, who played against Jordan but never claimed to match up with him. "He hit a few shots I know even he had to be impressed with. On this one drive to the hole, three of our guys jumped at him. We swiped at him, spun him around, fouled him, and it still fell in. He felt like he could do anything out there, which is what he did."

Jordan hit 20 of his first 24 shots in the game. That's a career night for some of the NBA's shooting stars. In retrospect, Michael admitted there was only one way to tell if he was satisfied, even pleased with such an effort. One way, that is, besides winning. On certain nights you remember the details. On others you just remember the feeling. "I don't think too many people could've stopped me," Michael said, describing the feeling he aspired to every day.

January 8, 1993, Chicago Stadium. Talk about your feat of scoring extraordinaire: In the 120-95 defeat of the Milwaukee Bucks, Scottie Pippen and Horace Grant each finished the game with 16 points, Trent Tucker finished with 14 points, and Michael Jordan finished with 20,000. By hitting consecutive three-point shots at 5:36 and 5:10 of the fourth quarter, Jordan, who scored 35 points in the game, hit the 20,000 mark faster than any other player except Wilt. Maybe it should have come on a dunk, but Jordan's scoring should be remembered because in this game he proved he always figured out how to put up points in the quickest, most economical way.

He went back into the game despite a 25-point lead. But this was not one of Michael's most cherished moments. When asked about it after the game, he tried to downplay the accomplishment and turned his back on reporters as he talked about it.

"I went back out there for one reason and that was to score," he confessed. "That's what people carry with them, remember me for. My scoring. That's something I never wanted to be totally remembered for." But, hey, 20,000. For just ten or so guys who played this game, that was a lifetime achievement.

April 22, 1993, Chicago Stadium. With 36 points in a 109-103 win over the Pistons, Michael Jordan wrapped up his seventh straight NBA scoring title. Wilt was the only other player ever to do that.

"Second to Wilt again," Michael pointed out. "Probably something that will have greater impact 15 years down the line. But I don't want to be remembered as just a scorer." Just a scorer? Right, and Michelangelo was just a painter.

So many nights. So many points. If this is Sacramento, it must be time to put up 50 more. If you had to trace one reason for Michael's excessive explosiveness, his flare for the dramatic might suffice. He knew the fans in Golden State and Houston and Utah had only one chance to see him each year. Even in Detroit this one game might be the only time that some fans would get to see Michael Jordan live, and so he was compelled to let that person say, "Yeah, I was there when Michael scored 54 and hit the driving one-hander with five seconds left to win the game."

It was more than a matter of, as Michael said, getting hot and riding the wave. Like everything else he did, Jordan had a methodical, obsessive, almost defiant approach to scoring. Never did scoring at will more accurately apply to anybody.

"The first thing I was thinking about at the start of the game was what did I have to do for us to get to the next level," Jordan noted. "Whatever was necessary, because I felt that was my role. I never knew until I came out for the game.

"You knew about the man guarding you and what kind of situations you can get aggressive in. That's why you can be so confident when the ball is in your hands. But it always depended on the situation of the game. You think, 'I can be aggressive or I can be a decoy. I can be passive.' You have to be a little of each, and you never wanted to make the opponent aware of what you were doing. You go at them early, then you lay off a little, whatever, but I could always read it very easily.

"Your first couple of shots go in, and then you take the initiative. And then all of the sudden you're getting great position to shoot, so you try and ride that. Then you try to find something else.

"So you look for your teammates. But nothing is there; you can't establish another scorer. The next thing you know, you're back at me, and I'm thinking, 'OK, I can try to carry the load for the team, go to the hole, get some fouls, whatever.' Every basket then is a big basket and that would really drive me.

"And in some of those big games, it was late in the fourth quarter, and I was getting within eight feet of the basket. They started to bring the double teams, but you're feeling it, you're hot and I can beat the double teams with no problem. You take advantage of it, and if it ends up with a 50- or 60-point night, as long as we win that's all that mattered.

"Some of those big nights I don't even remember because we lost. If we won and I scored 50, I remembered all the details. But like the night I scored 64 against Orlando, all I remember was blowing a six-point lead in the final minute. So when I say I don't want to be remembered as just a scorer, that's because you want to be remembered as a winner."

So many nights. So many points. So many times it seemed as if the Bulls could give Michael the ball, clear out one side of the floor, let him work one-on-one or two or even three, and call it offense. He scored 50. Bulls win. Everybody went home smiling. But it was never that easy.

FOUR

Offense Part II:
Too Much Offense

May 31, 1993, Chicago Stadium.
Don't ask Michael to carry the load. Phil stressed it a couple of times during time outs in the first half of this playoff game against New York. Sometimes you wonder if that was another way of him saying there's no execution of the offense, especially when I've got one of those good offensive runs going. I know I hadn't shot too well during the first three games of this series, and consequently the Knicks think they've shut down our offense. But we need this game to tie the series, and in the first half the jumper was going. The opportunities were there. You hit the first two shots after half-time, and suddenly it becomes one of those nights when you feel everything's going—layups, dunks, three-point shots.

Then comes the breakdown. Up seven points, I get my fifth foul.

On the bench. We score three points the three minutes I'm out. Forget about winning by 10 or scoring 54 points. That's not what everybody talked about even after we won this game. It seemed like all I heard about was the breakdown of the offense, guys standing around watching and how it made it tough for them to step up when they had to.

It became a real Catch-22 from that standpoint. Early in my career I felt I had to score a lot. Doug used to call it a lack of faith in my teammates. All I wanted to do was win. As my supporting cast improved, I figured I would feed off the way those guys approached the game and decide whether to be passive and try to get everybody involved or be aggressive and attack the basket. But sometimes guys tended to sit back and waited to see if I could carry the load whenever they couldn't seem to knock their shots down. The next thing you know we were totally out of the realm of the system. Then it looked like I'm trying too hard or trying to take all the shots or score all the points.

All I wanted to do was win, but you hear this stuff about "Michael carrying too much of the load" and whether that's good for the team. You hear Phil say things like "when he's hot like that we tend to stand around and watch and it seems to affect us when he scores a lot of points." But you want to do whatever you can to win.

Only a handful of players in NBA history could carry the load like Michael Jordan. None of them ever wore a Bulls uniform. Certainly, there was a time when he had to score 18 straight points against the Knicks to pull out a victory. But when Scottie Pippen elevated to superstar status and Horace Grant, John

Paxson, and B. J. Armstrong matured into reliable scorers, did Michael still feel compelled to score 54 points for the Bulls to beat the Knicks in Game 4 of the 1993 Eastern Conference Finals?

This was a choice example of the controversy that Jordan faced when he performed one of those scoring soliloquies. Maybe this was the Little League parent syndrome invading the Bulls. When the Little League team wins the championship, there's always one father yelling at the coach about why his son didn't get to pitch. On the Bulls, that father was Jackson or Pippen or Grant or Armstrong. Even Bill Cartwright or Will Perdue would go off on Michael after one of his high-wire, solo flights.

And then the questions would come: Can too much Jordan be a detriment? Did his scoring turn his teammates into Invisi-Bulls? Consider what happened in that Knicks game on May 31, 1993, at Chicago Stadium. In the third quarter Michael drilled a 19-foot jumper, followed by a 16-footer and an 18-footer. A layup, two three-point shots, and two free throws later, the Bulls led 82-70. He hit seven of his first eight shots in the third quarter. Grant's dunk was the only other shot any Bull hit, one of eight attempts. During a 17-minute span, Jordan had scored all but one of the team's baskets.

Michael drew his fifth foul, however, with 6:58 left in the game. He went to the bench for three minutes, and the lead fell to four points. The Bulls scored three points while Jordan sat on the bench with a towel over his head, though it was not clear whether he was drying off sweat or he could not bear to watch. When Michael came back, Pippen delivered a three-point play, and Jordan and Armstrong split the final eight points for a 105–95 victory.

Afterward, Pippen made a personal observation: "Michael had a very hot hand. However, when that happened it disrupted us and allowed the other team to get back in the game. It's not that we don't want MJ to get points, but it makes it tough for others to get in the game and step up when they have to."

Being one of the four guys standing around watching Michael led to mixed emotions. Will Perdue called this the ups and downs of playing with Michael. From his perspective, how can you not stand and watch a guy who can drive past three defenders and then jump over a fourth to score . . . when it's a one-point game . . . in the final seconds?

But the last thing anybody wants to be in an NBA game is the guy standing around watching. For Perdue, the toughest part was to watch Michael score 46 against Milwaukee, then look at the newspaper the next morning and read, "Jordan carries Bulls past Bucks." The hardest part to deal with when Michael went off on one of his offensive explosions, Perdue said, was not getting the credit you deserved, the credit you earned.

John Paxson—who had something bad to say about Michael about as often as he missed a free throw, which was almost never—even acknowledged that playing offense alongside Jordan meant being content with increasing the number of spectators in the arena by four. "If Michael would come out and get 24 in the first quarter, you knew it was going to be a night when you didn't get to do much. But, then, you didn't have to do much either." Perhaps the Bulls were upset for not being credited with doing the little things, such as rebounding, setting picks, and staying out of Michael's way when he got into the scoring mode that nobody could stop.

The situation often turned from isolated argument to chronic controversy and eventually became the full-fledged knock on Jordan throughout his career. Here was a player whose teammates had to learn how to play with him, to conform their games to what he was doing. The theory made it seem as if it was a case of building a house so it will fit the window in the upstairs bathroom. Yet Jordan was the big picture window in the living room, the one everybody else was going to look at.

"So it took you a couple of years to realize when he gets in that zone that you can't do anything but stand around," Grant explained. "I was pretty sure Michael wanted to get everyone else involved. But when he was on, he was on."

Paxson attributed Michael's inclination to take over a game to his competitive nature. Aside from Paxson, the rest of Jordan's teammates had trouble expressing admiration for his offensive genius. Some at least made light of the situation. After Jordan scored the 54 points against the Knicks in that memorable Memorial Day game, Bulls forward Scott Williams, who also played his college ball at North Carolina, mused, "It was a good day for the Tar Heels. We combined for 55 points." Pippen would emphasize that the best thing

Michael did was draw defenders and find the open shooters, not take the defenders one-on-three to the basket.

After games, Phil Jackson could be heard lamenting how 10 assists from Michael were as good as 30 points. After he scored the 54, Jackson admitted that "Jordan bailed us out a few times." But after Michael hit the six three-pointers against Portland in Game 1 of the 1992 Finals and carried the load in a 33-point win, Jackson passed off Jordan's contribution with the understatement "Michael had a hot hand tonight."

The argument lingered back and forth, more suitable to a school-yard than Chicago Stadium. "Yes, we won but I didn't get to shoot enough" seemed to be the consistent sentiment among the Invisi-Bulls. And then they would nitpick at Michael. "Look at guys like Dominique Wilkins and Bob McAdoo," those Invisi-Bulls would shoot back. "They scored a lot of points. They led the league in scoring. But what did they ever win?"

If Michael wanted to, he could have shot back with some statistics of his own. In the 32 games in which he scored 50 or more points during his career, the Bulls went 23-9. Seven of those were playoff games, and the Bulls won all but the one in which he scored 63 in Boston. And nobody bitched after that game because everyone in the locker room realized that the Bulls would have lost by 30 without Michael's scoring.

If only the Bulls could have envisioned nights like November 6, 1993, the first home game after Michael retired. They set a franchise record for least points in a quarter with six during the second quarter of a 95-71 loss to Miami, a team that did not even make the playoffs the previous season. The team established another franchise record for least points in a half with 28 in the first half. They shot 28 percent from the field.

The scrutiny over him being too much of the offense tore at Jordan as painfully as John Starks's defense. It eventually forced Michael into a routine of rationalization every time he had a big game. After he scored 64 points in the loss to Orlando, he spent 45 minutes of postgame rendering explanation. After one of the most transcendent shooting exhibitions in the history of basketball, Michael had to apologize for the bad pass he threw in the final minute. He had to explain letting the man he was guarding get off and hit a 35-foot three-point shot to tie the game at the end of the regulation and to defend his scoring output.

"Hey, it was my man who made the shot," he admitted. "I take the blame for it. As for the pass, I was just trying to follow Phil's orders and move the ball ahead of the foul. I thought I was getting fouled. I saw Bill Cartwright wide open but he evidently didn't see me. If I had the chance to do it all over again, I would take the foul."

Then, the question came. "But Michael what happened out there?" From the perimeter of the circle of reporters who cornered Jordan for more than 45 minutes after this game, somebody shot the question about what happened. Jordan turned his head sharply to where he heard the question come from and opened his eyes wide. This was the look of disgust that he would show to Jackson and teammates when he thought they were saying he was carrying too much of the scoring load. To Michael the question of "what happened" might as well have been "Did your scoring do more harm than good because at the end of the game nobody else was there to step up when you clearly needed some help?"

"Did you see the game?" Jordan charged, raising his hand straight to keep from pointing. "Do you know what happened?" Now Michael was pointing his finger, one of his signs of anger. Jordan rarely gets visibly angry in public. The questioning persisted about whether his scoring may have cost the team the game.

"I felt that I had to get everybody involved, and Phil felt that too," Jordan explained. "A lot of the offensive burden was put on me, and Phil wanted to spread it around in the second half so we would have better guns going down the stretch. We tried to find something else, but it just wasn't there and the next thing you know we're back at me. We never really established another scorer."

On a night like this, Magic or Bird or Kareem or anybody else would be talking about the left-handed fall-away hook shot, the driving scoop layup after splitting a double team, or the one over the river, off the billboard, nothing but net. You wonder how Michael Jordan reconciled the need to score against the threat of scoring too much? What do you do if you are Michael Jordan and you can score 50 points and win a game all by yourself but the people around you do not necessarily want to play that way?

"The first thing I always worried about was not separating myself from the unit. It was never a problem as long as everybody was productive. But when they weren't, well, then I had a problem. You see, I knew I could lose the team's aggressiveness if I came out too aggressive on offense. But if I saw no one else was generating offense, then I had to. I had to take the shot because I could feel the tentativeness among the team in certain situations.

"Especially when it got to the fourth quarter. They looked at me as the person to take the big shot or give them that incentive or motivation from a leadership standpoint. I feel I had to do that, it's just that sometimes I wasn't able to succeed. I always felt I was an offensive force to the point where I could take pressure off the guys.

"But that's where it got to be a touchy situation. We would try to go to other areas but there was no response. Then, they had to come back to me and quite frankly that's when I liked to work myself into the offense. Sometimes guys would forget to play because I was going strong, hitting everything, throwing them up from all over. And I never really knew how to read that. Do I slow it up and try and get everybody involved? That's when we would lose games. Or do I try to maintain this streak I've got going? Those were the fragile situations where Jerry Krause would say we have Michael Jordan and sometimes that's a penalty and sometimes that's very healthy. Phil would stress, 'Don't make Michael carry the load,' but deep-down I always knew I could step up my game and put us in position to win. But I always had to worry about how everybody else would read that if I did."

In order to rise above such controversy and hit game-winning shots and win three MVPs, three cars, seven scoring titles, and three championships there had to be so much more to Michael Jordan. The worst part about the situation for Michael was that these scoring soliloquies were what people remembered as his greatest nights. But he wanted everybody to remember him for more than just the offense.

FIVE

Defending Honor

April 2, 1993, Chicago Stadium.
You walk onto the court at the start of the game, see a matchup with Rafael Addison and it's hard not to think this is a guy you can light up for 50. When the first jump shot goes down, everybody in the building, including the New Jersey Nets, thinks you can get 40 or 50. But I'm thinking if I can get all over the floor defensively, maybe I can make a point. Addison's not a guy like Rolando Blackman or Jeff Malone or Joe Dumars where you got to play him straight up and keep him from getting the ball. Get in a passing lane and make a steal, go down and double team on a guy like Derrick Coleman in the post and that's what will make a difference, win the game.

Take it away from Coleman when he first touches it. Force Addison to make a bad pass. The game is two plays and 50 seconds old, I've got two steals, and New Jersey better start worrying about me on both ends of the floor. You have to do this every now and then. The more you disrupt defensively, the more things open up offensively. The first quarter of this game proves my point. Three steals, five New Jersey turnovers, and I hit nine of my first 10 shots. We're up by 14. Nobody will be surprised if I get 40 points this game. Nobody ever expects me to get nine steals.

And when I do, somebody will notice. See, Chuck Daly does. He said, "We couldn't control Jordan's defense. When he gets nine steals, it's too tough to win." Always admired Chuck when he coached Detroit. He knows what he's doing.

After this game, it was the same thing: Everybody asked me about the 40 points, about the great shooting rhythm. When the first shot went down I got in the groove, I told them.

One out of 100 asked me about defense. How many of them ever thought of me as dominating defensively? Sure, some guys gave me credit for being a good one-on-one defender, and it was always a challenge to go out and try and stop the best players in isolation situations. I feel I was known as a feared defender in that respect. But to take over a game, how many people think I could do that with my defense? And because Dumars and Dominique only came along once in a while, I felt it was necessary to do something else to make them think I was as good on defense as I was on offense.

November 20, 1987, was a night at Chicago Stadium most fans will remember just like April 2, 1993. On the latter, Michael Jordan had 40 points in a 118-105 victory over the New Jersey Nets. Against the Atlanta Hawks in November 1987, Jordan scored a team-high 33 points and with 11 seconds left, he hit a 16-foot jump shot on the run from the right side of the lane to give the Bulls a 94-92 lead. Long after he retired, such a shot would become another entry on the Jordan legend ledger. And it would not be a very prominent one at that. But with 11 seconds left, the Bulls still needed one more heroic play to deliver a victory.

Bulls Coach Doug Collins knew Atlanta's Dominique Wilkins would take the Hawks' last shot. Every player on the Bulls bench knew it. The 18,000 fans in Chicago Stadium knew it. "Michael didn't even wait for me to draw up the defense," Collins explained as he described the sequence of events during a time-out with 11 seconds left. The moment seemed fresh in his mind even more than six years after it happened. Collins said Michael's miracles were like that. "He just pointed at himself saying, 'Put me on Wilkins. I'll stop him.' I wanted to create a situation to double-team and get help. Michael said, 'I'll stop him.' "

Wilkins took an inbounds pass near halfcourt. He stood still for a moment, bent over dribbling the ball looking at Jordan. Jordan was bent over. They looked like Big Horn Rams preparing to butt heads, two knights mounted up and ready for a joust. Wilkins moved forward, turned, and backed his way down to the free throw line. Jordan planted himself there as Wilkins turned to put up a jump shot. The ball never made a full rotation toward the basket. Michael blocked the shot, and the ball bounded toward the Atlanta bench as time ran out.

Jordan said he never got the respect for his defensive abilities that he always wanted. Phil Jackson called him the best defender in the game more often than he reveled in Jordan's scoring abilities. Michael figured he might get recognition as the best defender of his era long after he retired from the game.

Two days after Michael announced his retirement from professional basketball, the Chicago Bulls held their annual media day gathering. This was two hours set aside for players and coaches to deal with questions and answers about the upcoming season, the first in nine years without Michael. Assistant coach Johnny Bach, the team's defensive coordinator, talked about what he would miss most about Jordan. For an entire hour, he talked about Jordan's defense. He stressed how the Bulls would have to worry about compensating more in that area than any other. He pointed out that for the Bulls to become a three-time champion they had to invent a method of defense to disrupt opposing teams. Using Jordan, Scottie Pippen, and Horace Grant in a full-court, helter-skelter attack to double-team opposing ball-handlers in the backcourt accomplished that in Bach's mind. Because of Jordan's athleticism, they turned him loose to double-team in halfcourt defensive sets, which caused opponents to pass the ball out of desperation rather than by design.

Jordan may have been more skilled, more naturally talented perhaps, as a defender than as a shooter or scorer. He was named to the NBA's All-Defensive first team in each of his last six years in the league, more than any of his contemporaries. Detroit's Joe Dumars, whom Michael himself often called the best defensive guard in the NBA, made the All-Defensive team four times during those years. Another Piston, Dennis Rodman, was named to the honor five straight times beginning in 1989.

"I think Michael was one of the most feared defenders in the league," Bulls coach Phil Jackson said during the 1993 season while stating a case for Jordan being the league's most valuable player that season. "I say feared because most everybody wasn't aware of where he was on the floor and what he was doing. He could make a block or get a steal and the whole game would change. The first time we played Orlando, he went and blocked a couple of [Shaquille] O'Neal's shots at the beginning of the game. That changed O'Neal's way of thinking the rest of the game." That's just one way he could change a game with just his defense.

Experts on basketball and some who passed themselves off as experts—otherwise known as coaches—usually judged the quality of a player's defensive ability based on fundamentals. How well does he stay in front of his man and cut off his penetration to the basket? Does he make the proper rotations in double-team situations? Does he keep from getting lost on switches and in transition situations? But Jordan could never be evaluated so basically, Bach argued, because his skills allowed him to play a kamikaze style of defense—attack for the kill and risk getting burned. "Like a Doberman," Bach explained. Michael was premeditated in his methods of defense, setting up steals, blocks, and stops like an assassin. He was the kind of defender who made opposing players remember their career-best nights because opposing players just did not get off for career nights on him without paying for it.

Jordan did not lack the fundamental skills of a textbook-correct defender. He stayed low to the floor, and he could cut off any player he wanted to. Darrell Walker, Jordan's teammate during his last season and a player generally regarded as one of the best NBA defenders ever, appraised Jordan's role as a defender by saying, "Anytime Michael wanted to get between his man and the bucket and shut him off, he could." But his long arms, quickness, and ability to change direction enabled Jordan to be more of an attack-type defender. In situations when the man he was guarding was dribbling up court, Michael loved to reach in one way to try and steal the ball, force the man to turn, circle around the other side, reach in for the ball again, and force him to give up the basketball.

"He had unbelievable speed," said Bach, picking up the tempo of his voice, attempting to convey how quick Jordan was defensively. "He had the speed to stop, pivot, and return. Return and coil, very much like a rattlesnake. He could strike and recover so quick. Nobody had that recovering ability. Combine that with his determination and his intuitive sense, and those were his greatest strengths as a defender in my opinion."

Jackson said the best thing about Jordan as a defender was never having to provide help for him. When opponents tried to set picks or screens for the man he was guarding, Jackson never worried because he believed Jordan was too strong to hold with a pick. Jordan's foot speed gave him an ability to circle around to the front of the man he was playing and poke away the ball on an attempted pass. When defending a man in a post-up situation, this technique is known as "circling the post." Jordan was so tough to beat because of his ability to circle the post. He negated an opponent's ability to post up simply because nobody felt confident enough to challenge him there.

"The only guy who could hurt Michael was a stand-up shooter like [Indiana's] Reggie Miller," Jackson said. "He would stand out at the three-point line. Because Michael played such good team defense,

Reggie could stand out there and get some open shots when Michael couldn't recover in time. But we felt it was OK to give some of those up and use Michael as more of a weapon on defense."

Dean Smith came up with the idea of using Jordan as a defensive weapon when Michael was a sophomore at North Carolina. In his multiple, ever-changing defensive alignments, Smith had one man-to-man defense in which he allowed one player to roam away from his man to play in the passing lanes and look for steals. The passing lane is the space between the player with the ball and the spot where another player might move to receive a pass for an open shot or to make a pass that would lead to an open shot. Because of his defensive tools—long arms, quickness, and intuitive sense—Michael could float in and out of passing lanes to disrupt opposing offensive schemes.

When Collins took over as coach of the Bulls in 1986, he initially concentrated on using Jordan as a defensive weapon. "We felt it was important to let him double-team on the big guys—come down and drive the big guys crazy by blocking their shots from behind. I made him our wild card on defense. I told him, 'Michael, you react and we'll cover for you.' I was not going to take away from his greatness and ask him to be handcuffed by playing defense only on the ball. That would have taken away from his strength."

In his first two years playing for Collins, Jordan became the only player ever to top 200 steals and 100 blocked shots in the same season. Most experts, even most coaches, will say that's a pretty good measure of defensive ability. In his second year playing for Collins, Jordan averaged a career-best 3.2 steals per game to lead the NBA. His 2.8 steals-per-game average the year before was better than the 2.77 and 2.72 marks that he posted in 1990 and 1993—both of which led the league.

"He was such an attacker, guys were afraid to put the ball down on the floor against him because they were afraid of losing it," Jackson continued. "I always felt his tendency on defense was overlooked. The great scorers, he could neutralize them or take them out of games. He did that to Clyde Drexler in the 1992 Finals. He did it to Reggie Lewis. Those things were why we won a lot of games."

Jackson used Jordan as more of a designated stopper than a defensive wildcard. He would put him on a forward, such as Atlanta's

Wilkins or Indiana's Detlef Schrempf, when either got into a shooting or scoring groove. Jackson also would switch Jordan to play an opposing point guard. "He would sit back on the bench and say, 'Where can I play Michael now and cause the most damage,' " Bach revealed.

Jackson felt his greatest defensive move with Michael came during the 1992 Eastern Conference Finals against Cleveland. A series whose momentum and advantages went back and forth like windshield wipers was in the pivotal fifth game with the best-of-seven series tied at two-all. Going into the fourth quarter, the Bulls held a 73-71 lead. Jordan came out for the start of the final period with orders to guard Cavaliers point guard Mark Price. Jackson observed that Price's repeated penetration of the Bulls defense was the only way Cleveland was scoring with any consistency. At the start of the fourth quarter the Bulls scored 17 straight points and outscored Cleveland 39-18 in the final frame to steal a 112-89 victory.

Jordan's greatest moment of defensive sustenance may have come after the Bulls beat Cleveland in the sixth game of that series and advanced to the 1992 NBA Finals against Portland. Prior to the start of the series, Jordan was asked how he was going to defend Western Conference counterpart Clyde Drexler, the one player in the NBA considered close to Jordan in terms of athletic ability and flair for scoring. By series end, Drexler suffered through 40 percent shooting from the field, nine percentage points lower than his career average. His 24.8 scoring average for the six games was on pace with his 25.0 average for the 1991–92 season. But Jordan went from a 30.1 points per game average during the regular season to 35.8 against Drexler in the NBA Finals.

"My thinking was that I never wanted to be known as just a scorer," Jordan said as he reviewed his defensive abilities. "I realized it was important for me to score for us to win. But I wanted everybody to realize I played both ends of the floor. It's like when I won the seventh straight scoring title. Everybody made a big deal about tying Wilt for the record. But I was just as proud of winning the steals title that year because it showed I played both ends of the court."

Michael wanted everybody to remember the way he combined offense and defense into a winning combination. But the 69 points he put up against Cleveland in 1990, the 64 he scored against Orlando in 1993, or the 63 he had against Boston in the 1986 playoffs may not be any more significant than the block on Wilkins to save a victory at the beginning of the 1987 season. More than those achievements, there was one attribute most fans will always remember him for. There was something that would make you forget his defense and even overshadowed his offensive outbursts.

SIX

Money: (It's Not the Shoes)

May 15, 1993, Richfield, Ohio. You dream about having a challenge like this. Tie ball game. Eighteen seconds left. You get the ball. You against the defense. Make one shot, they go home for the summer and we move closer to the championship. The fans are booing. They hate me. They're thinking, he can't do this to us again. This one fan under the basket is really getting ugly, but that is only helping me to concentrate because you know God doesn't like ugly.

This is when self-determination takes over. Just come out and do the job. This is a chance for redemption too. In the first half of this game, I'm frustrated, I'm struggling, I'm angry with myself. I needed an opportunity to get the respect back. With all those factors motivating me, there's really no pressure. There's no way I can miss.

Everybody in the building knows I'm going to take this shot. If I don't take it I will wonder for the rest of my life what would have happened if I did. No way I'm going to live with that. But even when I get the ball, I'm very surprised Cleveland doesn't double-team me. I don't know what they're thinking. Don't they know I'm the most confident in this situation?

I'm backing Gerald Wilkins in because there is still plenty of time to find an opening. I feel good in this situation because I'm moving toward the basket and he's back on his heels a little. He knocks the ball away but there's still seven seconds left so I'm not rushing. With 3.5 left, Hot Rod Williams is coming over to double team, and I see him and the clock out of the corner of my eye. I know I have to turn away from the double-team and shoot the fadeaway. Now, I'm a little worried because I haven't hit a fadeaway all night. It's a tough shot, no momentum going toward the basket. Not the way I like to shoot it.

Somehow, I'm able to twist and get my body square to the basket to the point where the shot feels good. Gerald Wilkins says, "No way." Then nothing, silence from the crowd. That's the feeling you play for. You hear that and you know you've won. All my teammates are running onto the court, hugging me.

My first reaction is to find the one fan under the basket and tell him, "I got ya!"

I really didn't know how I was going to make that shot to win the game. I just knew I could respond to challenges some people may not be able to respond to. You think about these things all the time. Maybe that's why they happen. I know I'm going to think about this all night. You dream about a challenge like this.

JORDAN

The progression of events following Michael Jordan's 18-foot jumper from the right of the free-throw line with one-tenth of a second left and the score tied at 101—the one that knocked Cleveland out of the 1993 Eastern Conference semifinals and completed a four-game sweep for the Chicago Bulls—explained why he could manufacture repeated acts of heroism. The last-second shots and fourth-quarter flurries to bring his team victories when the odds seemed virtually insurmountable—he loved these situations, and the revelry and emotion they provided, so much.

When the ball rattled in, Gerald Wilkins smiled the rueful smile of a man who bet it all on a straight flush only to see his counterpart pull four aces. He was the consummate beaten defender. Michael silenced the taunting fan and 20,272 others. He gave a subdued explanation of the moment afterward, focusing more on his three-for-nine shooting in the first half, the pain in his right wrist, and other failures inhibiting his usual standard of performance.

Meandering toward the team bus, he parted a sea of greeters that included such luminaries as former Cleveland guard Ron Harper and Baltimore Orioles shortstop Cal Ripken, Jr. Cleveland coach Lenny Wilkens gave Jordan one of those "beat-me-again" hugs, holding Michael for a few seconds, smiling, and shaking his head. James Jordan lined up family and friends, who wanted to shake hands with, hug, and bow to Michael as he walked out of the arena.

This coronation inspired The Shot: Part II—Son of the Shot—just as it accounted for Part I in 1989 and maybe even Part III in some basketball afterlife for Michael. To win in dramatic fashion, make the media believe the propensity for such heroics is the by-product of some secret alloy buried beneath the woods in Weavers Acres, and then inhale a celebration Elvis himself never knew was like a drug for Michael. He chased the high in all avenues of life but never felt it anywhere as he did on the basketball court.

The scoring titles, the most valuable player awards, the millions of dollars he made never meant as much to Michael Jordan as hitting a game-winning shot. That he could beat somebody, or some team, with a flick of his wrist was the ability Jordan knew separated him from any other player. And he realized this before he ever played a minute of college basketball.

Before his freshman season at North Carolina began, Jordan was enduring fraternity-type pledging in the form of a pickup game with other Tar Heels at Carmichael Auditorium. James Worthy, Al Wood, and Mitch Kupchak were working him over when Michael had the ball, with the score tied and a chance to win the game with one basket.

"Al Wood was guarding me and bumping me the way most guys would when it's next basket wins. I was nervous because people were watching and I wasn't sure I belonged out there. I drove baseline and Al went with me. When I made my move to the hoop, this 7-footer, Geoff Compton, came over to cut me off. I went up and I thought I was trapped. But I just kept going up and dunked over both of them. When I came down, I said to myself, 'Did I really do that?' That was the first time I realized I could do something like that."

We have already established he had the physical skills, the meticulous methods of preparation, and the mental discipline to make such plays. Another element may have enabled Michael continually to provide new or re-defining moments. Those who followed him since he hit the shot to beat Georgetown in the 1982 NCAA Championship game assumed that he was Superman and searched out no further explanation. But it was the feeling of walking off the court with that once-again-I-proved-I'm-the-best, you-never-saw-Magic-or-Bird-or-Wilt-do-this smile and strut that motivated Michael to new highlights.

"I really think that's the trait that differentiates you from all the other players," Jordan explained as he contemplated his flair for the dramatic the day after he hit The Shot: Part II. "You know, I didn't even watch any of the replays. You don't get the same feeling watching it again. So I played with my kids." With his kids, sons Jeffrey and Marcus, Michael could shoot fadeaways over them on the Jordan Jammer basket in the playroom, and have them stand up and cheer like a full house at Chicago Stadium.

"I'm always thinking I can do it whenever we need it," Michael continued. "Whenever we really need it. The higher the competition, the higher the stakes, the higher the rewards, the higher the level you play at. I've always had that. Maybe it's been a matter of perfecting it and applying it through the years. I think that's the mental part of the challenge.

"A lot of these things didn't surprise me after a while. I think this was the time when every person wanted to play his best basketball. Every player wants to excel when it's most needed. I had the appetite, certainly the talent, to apply it when we really needed it. I don't know why. I don't know if I can give you an explanation.

"There was a level of competition out there and that gets you into gear. I can't say it's a switch you turn on. I wish it was. It was more of an attitude thing. I can carry the load. I want to carry the load. Because of all the other shots I made I know what's at stake. I always want the ball in that situation. That's the ultimate situation.

"You can score 40- or 50-something and all you remember is that you win. But you hit that game-winning shot or that great shot or whatever, and that's something that you always dream about. And you keep dreaming about it."

Michael may have earned the moniker "Money" after one magical fourth-quarter flurry on February 3, 1988, in a game at the Stadium against the Lakers. The Bulls trailed the defending NBA champions 83-67 at the start of the fourth quarter when Jordan twice navigated through Byron Scott, around Michael Cooper, and over Magic to dunk. He floated into the lane and hit a pair of jumpers over James Worthy, then buried a hanging shot over Scott. As he finished off a fastbreak by dunking over Kareem Abdul-Jabbar, Jordan scored 22 points in the fourth quarter to bring the Bulls to within 101-97 before losing 110-101. It was then that John Bach first described MJ's crunch-time assaults by saying, "When Michael took over in the fourth quarter, it was like a shark in a feeding frenzy. He sensed the blood in the water and went for it."

Jordan insisted he had no sense of drama for these moments, but after Febaury 17, 1989, you had to wonder. In a game against Milwaukee, he scored 27 points in the fourth quarter to set a Chicago Stadium record. He also hit a 16-foot jumper with one second left to give the Bulls a 117-116 victory. And it all came on his 26th birthday.

James Jordan explained that his son invented situations such as these and The Shot: Parts I and II and all the others to find new venues in which to astound. Michael called these proving grounds.

The week before the Eastern Conference Semifinals series, Jordan filmed a segment for ESPN's "SportsCenter" during which he reviewed some of his great moments in the postseason—his playoff resume. He watched a replay of The Shot (the first one) and said that's why the people of Cleveland came to hate him.

He watched his leaning, reaching bank shot from halfcourt with time running out in the first half of Game 2 of the opening-round series against Atlanta in 1993 and admitted sometimes it is luck, that he is trying to score but the odds are never in his favor. He watched the rapid-fire three-point shooting against Portland in Game 1 of the 1992 NBA Finals and explained it was one of those days when you have everything working and you just want to keep it going.

The final highlight came against the Los Angeles Lakers in Game 2 of the 1991 NBA Finals. "Oh, that one," Michael called it. The one where he took off from the foul line ascending to dunk, then switched the ball to his left hand at the last second to bank in a soft scoop shot. It was the thirteenth straight shot he hit in that game and came right after he threw a halfcourt, no-look, alley-oop lob pass to Scottie Pippen for a dunk. It was the kind of move that compelled Mike Fratello, the analyst for NBC's broadcast of the game, to say, "Michael can't even find a way to miss."

"You ask me to do that now," Jordan said, "and I wouldn't be able to go out there on the basketball court and do it. It's just instinctive."

By the end of the segment Jordan was wearing a diabolical smile. He was preparing for another flash of brilliance. ESPN aired the segment with Jordan the Sunday night between Games 3 and 4 of the Eastern Conference semifinals. Monday he hit The Shot: Part II. Is that sequence of events coincidence or premeditation? A look back at the formula for these crowning moments shows why Michael Jordan hit them so often. Instinct, luck, and motivation from a hostile fan or crowd or opponent who lacked respect combined to create the moments when Michael ingrained a memory on basketball legend.

The Shot: Part I

Motivation: The last game of the 1989 season, the Bulls lost to Cleveland, 90-84, on a day when Larry Nance, Brad Daugherty, and

Mark Price did not play. That was the Bulls sixth straight loss to the Cavs that season, and all experts picked Cleveland to sweep the opening-round playoff series from the Bulls in three straight games. In the third quarter of Game 1, the Bulls were well on their way to a 95-88 victory when Jordan stopped at press row where a group of Chicago sportswriters were sitting and said, "Sweep, my butt."

In Game 4, with the Bulls holding a 2-1 series lead, Jordan missed a free throw that would have assured a series-winning victory. The Bulls lost in overtime and had to go back to Cleveland for a fifth and deciding game. After Game 4, Jordan sat with his father in the Bulls' locker room and made a vow for all to hear. "Daddy, I promise you I will never miss in that situation again." Michael spoke with a hollowness to his voice, the kind children seem to use when they are seeking a parent's approval. For him, however, this was the voice of vindication he used when he felt due for one of his shining moments.

"I remember the Kentucky Derby was run the Saturday between Games Four and Five," recalled Doug Collins of his third season as the Bulls' coach. "The winner of the race was Sunday Silence. I told our guys in the meeting on the plane Saturday, that's what it was going to be like in Cleveland—Sunday Silence. I knew Michael would make the shot. I'd seen it too many times."

Luck: With 12 seconds left, Jordan hit a jumper to put the Bulls up 99-98. But a defensive lapse by Craig Hodges enabled the Cavs' Craig Ehlo to sneak in for a go-ahead layup with four seconds to play. Brad Sellers set to inbound the ball for the Bulls at halfcourt to trigger the final play. Jordan faked a movement toward the halfcourt line that luckily induced Nance to go that way and created an opening for Sellers to get Michael the ball.

Instinct: With 2.5 seconds left, Michael still focused on getting into shooting position rather than catching the ball and launching a shot. He didn't get an unobstructed look at the basket before the shot. He dribbled twice to the foul line and elevated; Ehlo hung right with him. He had to double-clutch—reload, or extend to shoot, then recoil to avoid Ehlo before extending again—before shooting the ball. He knew where the basket was.

"I remember TNT brought in a physics instructor to illustrate why Michael was able to hang in the air longer than I was," Ehlo said. "It was something about muscle mass and body weight—his being greater than mine. Also, if you remember he had to change his shot. He reloaded and shot from a different angle. He had great instincts for things like that."

More motivation: "All game long, there was this one fan telling me to get my tee time ready for the summer, that I was going home," Jordan remembered. "I was also crushed after I missed that free throw. I felt I had something to prove."

Game 3, 1991 NBA Finals

With the series tied at one game each, the Bulls fell behind the Lakers by 15 points in the third quarter of the game at the Forum in Los Angeles. Jordan led a comeback that culminated with his length-of-the-court drive to a 10-foot jumper that sent the game into overtime. The Bulls went on to win that game and the series, 4-1.

Motivation: Michael missed two shots at the end of Game 1 that would have tied the game. But forget that. With the Bulls leading by one in the closing seconds of regulation in Game 3, the Lakers' Vlade Divac scored on a driving bank shot and collided with Scottie Pippen. Pippen was called for a foul, his sixth. To a man, the Bulls questioned the call. Down two points and with Pippen lost for the night, Jordan sensed an opportunity to take matters into his own hands. But forget that. Michael had made just two of his previous 11 shots in the game.

Luck: In a situation like this with 9.8 seconds left to play, most NBA teams would opt to inbound the ball from halfcourt. The Bulls wanted to use the full open court so Jordan could see the situation unfold. As he rushed the length of the court, the Lakers' Byron Scott watched Jordan dribble right past him. Nobody really defended him until Divac picked him up within 10 feet of the basket. As a result, Jordan did not need to waste any time maneuvering into shooting position. "I was surprised I had a one-on-one situation," Jordan said. "That was pretty lucky."

Instinct: Jordan had it in his mind to drive to the basket. But at the last second he saw Divac out of the corner of his eye. The 6-foot-11-inch center was sliding over. Michael had severely sprained his toe earlier in the game, so jumping over Divac, normally an option, was out of the question. He pulled up and nailed the 10-foot jumper. "At a point, I just wanted to get a shot off," Jordan said. "But when I put it up, I knew it was going in.".

February 1, 1993, Salt Lake City

The Bulls trailed the Utah Jazz by 15 points going into the fourth quarter. Jordan scored 20 of his 37 points in the final 12 minutes to deliver a 96-92 victory.

Motivation: Michael had missed 13 of his first 19 shots in the game. A week earlier, he expressed his frustration publicly over how the Bulls were not playing enough up-tempo basketball. He felt they were not running enough and how that put an extra burden on him to fight two and three defenders to score in halfcourt situations. Also a week earlier, he missed a game-winning shot at San Antonio, one of four losses in five games that Michael called "the low point of the season." What's more, a month earlier Jordan commented about Salt Lake City, the site of the 1993 NBA All-Star Game, that "the best thing about Utah is that it's close to Vegas." The Delta Center crowd booed him relentlessly.

Luck: When Michael sank a 47-foot, halfcourt-heave at the halftime buzzer, you had to think luck was on his side.

Instinct: Scottie Pippen and Horace Grant were no-shows on this night. In basketball lingo, a no-show is a guy who is on the court but becomes part of the scenery, not part of the action. Michael's supporting cast lent all the support of an overwashed brassiere on this night. So with the Bulls trailing 84-71, Michael reeled off one of those Jordanesque scoring tears. Two jumpers, followed by a stop-and-pop off one leg and another jumper; Jordan hit seven of his next nine. He fed B. J. Armstrong, who made a three-point shot, and then Michael added three free throws in the final 31 seconds to steal the victory.

"At the end of the third quarter Michael walked by the scorer's table and said to me, 'No way we lose,' " recalled Tom Dore, the play-by-play announcer for the broadcast of the Bulls game on SportsChannel Chicago that night. "After the game, I asked him how he knew they would win. He said, 'Instinct, Tom. I just felt a surge of energy.' "

Postscript: After the victory was all but assured, Jordan glared up into the crowd, raised his arms, and said, "I win."

The Shot: Part II

Motivation: The Cleveland crowd booed Jordan non-stop. His right wrist hurt so much that his first shot of the game was an air ball. Michael was so frustrated by halftime that teammate Stacey King said, "I don't ever remember seeing Michael that down or angry." It's a wonder he didn't score 69 and then hit the game-winning shot.

Luck: Bulls coach Phil Jackson had no other explanation: "You just get Michael the ball in the right spot at the right time. No need to draw up any plays. We're just lucky Michael can do what he does at the end of a ball game." Gerald Wilkins played Jordan as close as possible in the situation. He even knocked the ball away. He hit it again. Basketball lingo for consummate defense is "getting in a guy's jock." Wilkins undressed Jordan with his defense. "I had all ball, and it seemed like he went back a couple more inches to shoot it," Wilkins said. "I made him take such a tough shot. Damn. It had to be luck." Michael figured it was luck. "I'm definitely going to church on Sunday," he exclaimed afterward.

Instinct: Jordan saw Hot Rod Williams coming over to double team and looked at the clock all in one glance. He also gathered the ball after Wilkins knocked it away and turned into perfect shooting posture. Like Ehlo, Wilkins obstructed his view to the rim. He let the shot go just as time ran out, which could be a product of his intense concentration—or instinct.

The shot also featured a hint of redemption. Jordan missed a shot with 30 seconds to play that would have put the Bulls ahead by two points.

The final component to explain Jordan's many acts of heroism: they always came in a situation where he could do something more dramatic or more important than he ever did before. It's like the night he scored 15 of his 38 points in the fourth to lead the Bulls to an 86-83 win over Seattle in 1993. Michael sat out the previous two games with a case of athlete's foot so infected and painful that he spent two days in the hospital. The world's greatest athlete had the world's greatest case of athlete's foot. You would think something more macho, more manly, would keep him out for two days.

At any rate, he missed two games. The Bulls won one, the first time they had done so without Jordan since 1986. The other game was an overtime loss to San Antonio in which the Bulls led by 20 points in the first quarter and Pippen was Jordanesque with 39 points, 13 rebounds, and 10 assists. So Michael had to prove that he was Michael Jordan all over again. He did, despite 41 minutes of play enduring pain so severe that he could not get a shoe on his foot the morning of the game.

The same thing happened in Game 1 of the Eastern Conference Semifinals series with Cleveland in 1993. The week prior to the game, Jordan listened to talk about how Wilkins said he was the only one who could be a "Jordan stopper." Michael went out and scored 43 and promptly proclaimed, "Tough night for the Jordan stopper."

According to Phil Jackson, this ability in Michael was completely innate. Just give Michael a smell of the water, and he goes for it.

"When I got into a situation where it's the fourth quarter, the game is on the line, and we need to win," Michael explained, "I started talking to myself. 'This guy can't guard me.' And I believed it. I never set a goal for myself to go out and dominate offensively. If you can whenever you want to, then what's the purpose of playing the game. The best thing I always had going for me in those situations was that I wasn't afraid of the consequences."

Cliff Levingston, who played with Jordan during the Bulls' first two championship seasons, made a study of Michael in the situations with the game on the line. "He would get this little gleam in his eye, and that's when you knew he would take over," Levingston observed. "You see, we're talking about a guy who if you put a hurdle in front of him, he didn't just want to clear it. He wanted to see how high he could clear it. It stirred up his competitive juices."

When the competitive juices started flowing, Michael could produce miracles. Why was competition such an important part of his life? Did it become too important?

SEVEN

A Zone All His Own

JUNE 3, 1992, Chicago Stadium: Game 1, NBA Finals. You look for challenges in everything you do, every day that you live. The best kind of challenge comes when it turns into a proving ground. You hear them say Michael Jordan will never be Larry Bird until he wins a championship. He'll never be Magic Johnson until he wins two or three. And then you have a reason to push yourself to something that has nothing to do with individual accolades. It's not an individual thing. It's a personal thing.

The past two days they've been comparing me and Clyde Drexler. Some of the stuff you hear you pass off as hype, and some you pay your respects to. Yes, Clyde is a great athlete, and he is a great offensive rebounder. No way I'm going to say anything publicly that might give Clyde an edge. Not with what's at stake. But everybody keeps talking about what a great three-point shooter he is; that he has an advantage on me in that phase of the game.

You might hear me say something like: He's a better three-point shooter than I choose to be. Right there, you know I'm creating the challenge for myself. I'm finding a way to elevate my game.

Now, you start thinking, well, we'll see how much better of a three-point shooter he is. I'll go out and practice my three-point shooting the morning of the game. And if they ask me about it, I'll say I'm just messing around, playing HORSE with a couple of friends. This way you don't lose the edge, you don't lose the perspective of having to prove something.

When the game starts, Clyde gives me the outside shot. I hit a couple of 15-footers, and he comes out a little further to guard me. So now the challenge is to see how far I can extend it. He's giving me the three-point shot, and it's obvious he doesn't respect my outside shooting, or at least I tell myself that. Because that's how you maintain the challenge.

He said I was taking the shots he wanted me to take. I hit the first one, then the second one, and the next thing you know they're falling from everywhere and I'm running to the three-point line. And they're still leaving me alone. So I keep shooting until they respect my three-point shot, but by that time six have gone down and we have a 17-point lead. Sure, I was in a zone that night. But you don't get into that zone by some strange coincidence. You get to that zone by trying to prove that you can be this good a shooter or this good a defender and you take your game up to a level where you say, OK Clyde (or whoever), let's see if you can get there too. And the challenge is to get your game to a level they can't possibly get to.

efore Game 2 of the 1993 Eastern Conference Finals, Michael Jordan sat in the Bulls' locker room at Madison Square Garden talking with a group of reporters about golf, gambling, and challenges. During that 45-minute session he evoked the word "challenges" more than a dozen times. And he used it in reference to golf, gambling, and basketball—three of his favorite pastimes because of their respective challenges.

Challenges became such a buzz word for Michael that reporters covering the Bulls beat during the 1993 playoffs joked about it mercilessly. Let's get a pool going to see how many times Michael will call this or that a challenge. Who's got five? Who's got eight? What's the over-under? Bet the over.

Challenges became like a vitamin for Jordan—One-A-Day. If Michael had redefined Thoreau's necessities of life, for him they would have included food, clothing, shelter, and challenges. Steve Rosenbloom, a sports columnist for the *Chicago Sun-Times,* turned this whole ordeal into such amusement that after the 1993 Eastern Conference Finals, he wrote a column listing 52 challenges Jordan might seek out if basketball ceased to satiate him. Among the more humorous of Rosenbloom's challenges were:

- Determine the difference between North and South Dakota.
- Just try to get it your way right away at Burger King now.
- Find someone who hasn't slept with Mick Jagger.
- Find someone who hasn't slept with Wilt Chamberlain.
- Find out how these two missed each other.
- See if what you want is actually what you get at McDonald's.
- Admit you're a 10-handicap instead of a 2-handicap.
- Stop playing against guys who are 2-handicaps but claim to be 10s.
- Don't three-putt.
- Ask Chicago White Sox general manager Ron Schueler, who selected his 18-year-old daughter Carey in the 43rd round of [the 1993] major-league baseball amateur draft, if he was surprised she was still available at the point in the selection process.

- Teach Sharon Stone to act.
- Teach Sharon Stone to wear underwear.
- Teach Sharon Stone to do both at the same time.
- See if you can make the shot off the expressway, over the river, off the billboard . . . nothing but net.

In 1988, Michael Jordan reached the top of his profession individually by being named the NBA's Most Valuable Player. From that point on, he felt it necessary to look at basketball as a series of challenges to keep pushing himself. Win the NBA Central Division title, get homecourt advantage in the playoffs, win the Eastern Conference, win one championship, win two, win three. We knew how important this was to him—we knew he survived on challenges—when Jordan quit the game. He left because he said he had no more challenges in basketball. He began to look for other challenges, like playing major-league baseball with the Chicago White Sox in the spring of 1994, because he always needed them.

When Michael conjured up a challenge, he could rain three-point shots and score 35 points on 14-for-21 shooting in one half of a basketball game, just as he did against Clyde Drexler and the Portland Trail Blazers in Game 1 of the 1992 NBA Finals. He could actually feel the challenge and show visible evidence of it gripping him. His eyes would become bone-white as if he was trying to make his vision piercing. As sweat ran down his bald head and dropped off his chin it turned to steam. He would chew his gum with metronome precision. He could fix his body in a catatonic attack position, using his will to break down the defender. Off the first movement he would become a wind-up toy, robotic in his execution. Call it a zone, a zone all his own.

What happened when Michael found the challenge could only be discerned through the words of Gerald Wilkins, who became Jordan's old blue blanket of challenges. No challenges around today, well there's still Gerald.

"That's when he hikes his emotions up a little higher. That's when he wants a little bit more than you do," Wilkins explained in a moment of candor prior to the start of the 1993 Eastern Conference semifinal playoff series. "That's when Michael gives you no time to think. You think, he's gone. You don't think, you just do, and you go as hard as you can but you're out there thinking, 'Why me?' "

"When you have the challenge you feel the hunger for the game, the love for the game, the attitude of coming in and working harder in practice," Jordan continued as he described his obsession with challenges. Surprisingly, the Madison Square Garden media barrage grew tired of the rhetoric by this time. So Michael figured he was not giving away any secrets if he kept talking about challenges. And he had at least one captive listener. "This is what enables me to get going right away out on the basketball court and lay it on the line from that very moment. It makes you prepare to know who you are going to play and how to work to get the advantages over who you're going to play. You have a tendency to lose a little bit of the hunger each time you try to do something again. So you have to find something to push yourself to try and regain that hunger."

That was Jordan's mindset, the attitude that got him results. It is not news that challenges were like oxygen to Jordan. But how and why did Michael turn his basketball life into a quest-quest-quest-until-conquer regimen? And why such intensity? Perhaps it is necessary to examine the process that turned Jordan into a gum-chewing, steam-throwing psychopath. There came a point in Michael's career where every John Starks, every free throw, every arena presented some sort of motivation. But did elevation to answer each challenge turn inspiration to obsession? Did it come to a point where Michael could not feel satisfaction in achieving?

James Jordan argued that his son was born this way, that he always searched for something to drive him to continue playing. But if Gerald Wilkins and the rest of the basketball world must find a scapegoat as the one who created Michael Jordan's need to be challenged, look no further for someone to blame than Clifton Herring, the Laney High School basketball coach. Herring cut Michael from the varsity team when he was a sophomore. Michael went home when he found out, locked himself in his bedroom, and cried. For a minute or two. Then he vowed to get even, to make basketball his never-ending proving ground.

Jordan explained his development into the world's greatest basketball player by way of a series of challenges. "I've had so many challenges that it seems like it's always been a challenge. Going to college was one. Getting cut from high school was one. Being known as an offensive player only was one when I first came into the league. Hearing that the scoring leader could never win a title was one. That the scoring leader could never be on a successful team. And they just kept coming. Jordan is very selfish. He's all offense. He can't involve his teammates. He can't make his teammates better. All of them led me to this point where I felt successful. Take one away and you would have had a different outcome in the success of Michael Jordan. I got to that point because of all those things. You kind of depend on it after a while."

When he turned from Michael Jordan to MVP, the challenge act became a nightly routine. Imagine dealing with players in every NBA city circling their calendar on the date the Bulls came to town. From Jordan's point of view, this is when they all tried to make a name for themselves at his expense. In Charlotte, Kendall Gill was waiting. In Orlando, Nick Anderson. In New York a former grocery store bag boy named John Starks wanted a piece of Michael. Wilkins said he and every other player remembered his best night against Michael. Michael said being the focal point night after night would make most players want to take a night off. So in order to keep from taking a night off he put the challenge to himself not to let Kendall Gill or Nick Anderson outplay him.

"It got to a point where I couldn't look at the accolades to drive me anymore," Jordan recalled. "I had won everything I could win in terms of scoring titles, so I was content with that. So the need to drive myself was to continue to improve as a player. And that became the test—are the challenges still there? I guess you could call that the personal challenge. I didn't play well this game, so I wanted to play better the next game. That's why Gerald Wilkins was good for me. I never looked at it as a one-on-one thing. But I knew every little stop he made against me was going to be magnified so I looked at that as a challenge because I needed something to push me."

Two propositions always prompted Jordan to ramble on about defeating the foe with all the fervor of a television evangelist. Winning the NBA championship eluded him long enough that he nearly panicked. The pursuit of the title became a search to find this path or formula to or for success, kind of like his crusade in search of the Holy

Grail. Being the NBA Most Valuable Player forced Michael to find a way to stay continually atop the rest of the players in the NBA. Once he got there, only one thing was more important to Michael than staying there: winning the championship.

Jordan's route to becoming a champion was littered with obstacles and hurdles. Once he cleared the obstacle that he ordained as most important or most ominous, then he was satisfied. The first championship season, the Pistons loomed as the major bump in the road. Get past them and the rest of the way will be a cruise, Jordan thought. It was.

After beating the Pistons in four straight games, the Bulls topped the Lakers in the 1991 NBA Finals, posting an average margin of victory of 13.75 points per game along the way. Everything Jordan did in his previous basketball life led him to that one moment when the Bulls swept the Pistons out of the Eastern Conference Finals. The Finals became a formality.

During the second championship season the title was a foregone conclusion, and the challenge for Michael was to not lose it. That is why he played his best basketball when the Bulls needed it most. He scored 56 points to carry his team past Miami in the third and final game of the opening round. He had 42 in the seventh game of the semifinal series with the Knicks. He had the big fourth quarter (16 points) in Game 6 of the Eastern Conference Finals when the Bulls closed out the Cavaliers. He hit all the threes in Game 1 of the Finals against Portland, had 46 in Game 5 when the series was tied at two games apiece, and scored 10 of the final 12 points after coming up with just two in the opening period in the sixth and final game.

Jordan sustained the third championship run through a series of challenges. In the opening round against Atlanta, it came down to outdueling Dominique (proving Gerald was not the only member of the Wilkins family who could inspire Michael). In the second round, it was Gerald Wilkins and the obstacle of not letting an ailing wrist limit him. In round three against the Knicks, it was Starks.

In the second game of the series, Starks drove baseline on Jordan in the fourth quarter and elevated to a monster slam in Michael's face. For the first time in a long time, Jordan needed to save face and did so with a 54-point nuclear outburst in a Game 4 that the team had to win to keep the title run going.

In the Finals, there was Charles Barkley. And there was Kevin Johnson, who held Michael to 44 points in Game 3, then held Michael to 55 in the Game 4 win that more or less sealed the title. And if the idea of the challenge is continual improvement or surpassing previous heroics, then do not forget that Jordan scored nine of the team's final 12 points in the decisive Game 6.

"Once I made every individual challenge I could achieve it was a matter of a team challenge. What did I have to do to get the team back where it was last year? I really wanted to push myself to keep the team where it was. So when it came time to get that third or fourth win of the series, you wake up every day ready to go out and play the game of basketball. I never realized how hard it was going to be that third year. The more you try to repeat something, the tougher it gets. So it became a matter of finding all the different challenges."

At one point during the 1993 playoffs, Jordan admitted the hardest part of life was finding a challenge every day, every night. At the same time, he admitted the biggest challenge was winning a third straight title. And with that goal not accomplished, he could turn into that Tasmanian devil-like character and whip the opposition with the full force of a tornado.

Conjuring this feeling is not an easily comprehensible process. You really had to have done it to understand it. It's kind of like that dream you had where you wake up and swear it was real. It can't be a dream but then it was. See, that doesn't make sense but you get the point. Or it's like the high from a certain kind of drug, LSD or something that you had to feel to know what it was. There was something carnal or euphoric or physical about the way Michael summoned a challenge.

Magic Johnson vividly remembered one night when he saw Michael go through the process. Magic, Ahmad Rashad, Quinn Buckner, Adolph Shiver, and Jordan were sitting around the card table in Jordan's house playing some rather heated "Bid Whist" when it all began. Two nights earlier, Kevin Johnson of the Phoenix Suns had forced Jordan into missing 15 of his last 24 shots as the Bulls lost in triple overtime to the Suns in Game 3 of the 1993 NBA Finals. When the group reminded Jordan of that the night before Game 4, it was like tightening the bolt on a pipe about to burst. There was no holding back. Jordan blew.

"He's saying, 'OK, OK MJ.' He calls me MJ and I call him MJ," Magic recalled. "Then he starts breathing really heavy and kind of rocking back and forth. 'OK MJ, they think he stopped me. Well, let's see if he can stop me now.' His eyes are getting a little bigger, and he's got that look of determination on his face. I remember getting that when I heard about how Chris Mullin went off for 38 points on me one night. Next time we played him, I laid 44 on him. Michael did that to everybody every night."

Nothing extraordinary or extraterrestrial about Michael getting revenge on Kevin Johnson, is there? No. The obvious challenges were the ones that pushed Michael to his best. But even some of the more subtle roadblocks fired up Jordan. With five games to go in the 1993 season, the Bulls and Knicks were fighting to the finish for the best record in the Eastern Conference and the home-court advantage most experts and players believed would decide their showdown in the playoffs. The Knicks, who had a one-game lead, were playing Indiana that night, a team Jordan knew always gave New York trouble. The Bulls had the Milwaukee Bucks at home. Add in the subplot that Milwaukee rookie Todd Day was getting his first start against Jordan and probably was looking to make a name for himself. The results: Knicks lose, Jordan burns Day for 22 points in the first quarter and 47 overall, and the Bulls tie the Knicks.

But even as Jordan commented after the game that night, he was worried about the team playing its best basketball going into the playoffs, he was in the process of finding another challenge. "Another challenge staring me in the face, you could say," Jordan stated. "We can win when I score a lot of points, so the challenge is for us to win with everybody contributing. And if the other guys can't then the challenge becomes picking up that load."

The process of creating challenges, re-creating them, and meeting them may have pushed him over the edge. What would happen if he ran out of challenges? It is a sad enough statement when the challenge every day becomes finding a new challenge every day. For Michael it was not enough to keep playing better. It was not enough to keep playing longer. Just as he was about to get that third title—what he called the ultimate challenge—he conjured up the idea of playing better, longer. Longer than anyone else. That would be the challenge. There were those who did not buy it.

Magic Johnson was one. His perpetual tooth-glaring smile, the one that seemed to be Krazy-Glued to his face, disappeared when he was asked what challenges he thought were ahead for Michael. "Three was his goal and then maybe four [championships]," Magic answered. "But what could push him for 82 games? He needed something, someone. And there's nobody there. He's crying for a challenge, and I'm thinking, What's it gonna be?"

Magic was prophetic. The night the Bulls won their third championship, Jordan said he realized that he had run out of challenges. When he announced he was retiring from professional basketball on October 6, 1993, he said the main reason was that he could not find anything to create the desire to go out on the court every day and play his usual gum-chewing, steam-brewing brand of basketball. The previous year it had come to a point for MJ where finding the challenge meant throwing his body into a fray, getting knocked to the ground, injured, carried off the floor before coming back to hit the game-winning shot. There were so many times when he did that. Maybe too many.

EIGHT

It's Just a Little Pain

December 4, 1992, Chicago Stadium. Nothing like a dunk to make the pain go away. This was one of those nights we needed to get out of the blocks quickly in the second half. There was no reason to be losing to Portland at halftime when they didn't have Clyde, even though it was my first game in almost a week. The first half went a little slow because of my left foot. That pain was more mental than physical. But when Scottie missed that free throw and nobody blocked me out, the pain went away as soon as I got my hand on that rebound and put the ball in the basket. Not just the soreness, but the mental pain or strain of hearing three days ago that this foot injury—they called it *planta fascia*—could be the end of my career. When I went down in that game against the Knicks last Saturday, I couldn't call a time out fast enough. Something popped and stretched, and I felt the same kind of pain as when I broke my foot back in 1986. Anytime anything happens to that foot, it brings back that memory . . . missing 64 games.

This one was a bad one. As soon as it happened, I told Chip it popped, let's go. Walking to the locker room, I couldn't put any weight on it. We knew immediately something was wrong, even before we got to the locker room and had it checked out. It took me the whole third quarter to make myself more aggressive, so you know it's a mental thing. In the fourth quarter, I told Scottie Pippen I couldn't move much, and I would try to post up. That was the physical pain. That always led to some mental uncertainty and I was afraid to fall back on it.

The key for me always was the mental part, and when I hurt my foot I was trying to see if I could go back out and play without doing any further damage. The only thing more painful than the injury is not playing, so if there's any way I can come back I'm going to. But you know it's bad when you're more worried about feeling out the pain than losing to the Knicks by 35 points.

The next three days were like walking around on a stress fracture. Every time I pushed off, I could feel the pain. I didn't want to make the road trip to Boston because once I got near Boston Garden I would be tempted to play. This being the same foot that I broke, I didn't even want to be around the game that night. Didn't want to be around anybody. I was as irritable as my wife was with that third baby due in a couple of weeks.

During the day of the Portland game, there was still a lot of pain. But the team lost without me at Boston two nights ago and that hurt even more. If we have a better chance of winning with me playing hurt, then I will play. And there's nothing worse than missing a game, whether it's Portland or New York or whoever. Doc made a good point before the game. He said when you have pain and you have other things that will take your mind away from it, you don't feel the pain as much.

After I hit my first couple of shots, the hype of the competition had me focusing on the game, not the pain. Then I missed four in a row at the end of the first half, and you start to think that you haven't played in six days and wonder, Is everything OK? It's a mental thing, and that's what you have to overcome.

Then came the dunk. Scottie missed a free throw, Portland didn't think to put a guy in front of me where I was standing behind Scottie and now I had so much going on I didn't think about the pain. I just ran right down the lane like it was an airport runway and jammed the missed free throw back in the basket. Evidently, I must have something that really helps me concentrate when I'm in pain because there's no other way to explain how I can feel so bad it hurts to walk one night and dunk with ease two nights later.

When Michael Jordan came back from a foot injury that caused one national newspaper to beam a headline "INJURY MAY END JORDAN'S CAREER" and scored 38 points in a win over Portland, it was not extraordinary. It was no more dramatic, no more legendary than, say, the time Willis Reed limped onto the court moments before the start of the seventh game of the 1970 NBA Finals and inspired the New York Knicks to a championship win over the L.A. Lakers. It was no more poetic than Larry Bird bouncing face first off the Boston Garden parquet in the third quarter of a playoff game against Indiana in 1992, then coming back to score 13 points and lead the Celtics to victory in the decisive game of the best-of-five series.

Athletes make celebrated returns from painful injuries all the time. But with Jordan, this was never a once-in-a-lifetime incident. It was just 17 games after he missed 64 due to a broken foot in 1986 that Michael came out and scored 63 points in a playoff game at Boston Garden. Few athletes ever rebounded from injury and pain with the magnitude and impact Michael Jordan did.

Perhaps the stubbornness he inherited from his mother compelled Michael to look at injury or pain as nothing more than John Starks scratching at his forearm or the Pistons' defense ganging up on him. Imagine Michael looking at his swollen ankle, the kind that blows up to the size of a 12-inch softball when you roll it over after landing on somebody's instep, and thinking, "What if I can get 40 playing on this?" His eyes would light up and "proving ground" would flash before them. Indeed, Michael's ability to overcome injury, and the drama with which he did so, created another reason to marvel and wonder about his makeup.

By the end of his career, Michael made performances like his back-to-back games against Seattle and Milwaukee in January of 1985 seem human. Midway through the third quarter of a 93-76 win over Seattle, Michael suffered a sprained ankle yet finished with 22 points and 8 assists. By his own admission, the injury forced a bad limp. But as he walked out of the Stadium, he asserted, "Do you think this is going to keep me away from the game tomorrow night?" He endured doses of treatment the next morning and before the game, then scored 45 points and added 10 assists, 8 rebounds, and 4 blocked shots in the 117-104 win over Atlanta.

Frequency and timing, not to mention desire, had a lot to do with this ability to bounce back from a knockdown like a pop-up toy. There were those experts around Jordan who insisted he had supreme, even superhuman, powers of recovery. After injuring the big toe on his left foot in Game 3 of the 1991 Finals, Michael cut a hole in his shoe to free the swollen toe from further irritation for Game 4, scored 36 points and left everybody—Bulls trainer Chip Schaefer and team doctor John Hefferon included—convinced he had a unique way to overcome the pain.

For Jerry Krause, the Bulls' vice president of basketball operations during the Jordan era, his most vivid memory of Michael had nothing to do with any game-winning shot or championship. It was December 5, 1986, when Jordan put up 43 points in a 114-112 loss at Phoenix. Michael was nursing a foot infection at the time that filled up with blood and pus during the game. As doctors examined Jordan, it was not hard to tell this was the kind of inflammation that when cut open would squirt streams of pus and catch you in the eye if you were a few feet away. A look at this infection would cause that somersault in your stomach that pulls the oxygen from your head and makes you dizzy. Jordan asked the doctors to cut open the infection, "and he bled like a stuck pig," Krause recalled. "So much blood flew around the room, it was the ugliest thing I had ever seen."

Doctors prescribed three days of rest for Jordan, who promptly insisted on playing in the game the next night in San Antonio. "He begged Doug (Collins) and I to take him," Krause continued. "We said, 'No, you go home and rest.' I think if you look it up, he got 48 or 50 the next night. And it didn't even look like he was hurt. I'll never forget that."

Jordan actually scored 43 against the Spurs. But the point stands out like a stuck pig. He had extraordinary recuperative powers and understanding of how to modify his game to be successful while playing within the limits of an injury. The challenge to come back induced a desire to exceed the limits of the injury. Michael probably sensed the drama accompanying such incidents and used that to further the challenge, the proving ground, the motivation. Those were the qualities that enabled him to scoff at pain. And a magnificent, almost inexplicable series of events at the end of the 1993 season and in the playoffs provided astonishing, if not implausible, evidence of how Jordan used those assets to overcome serious injuries and singlehandedly deliver victories in must-win situations.

On May 4, 1993, the Chicago Bulls faced anything but a must-win situation. They led the best-of-five, opening-round series of the 1993 NBA Playoffs against the Atlanta Hawks two games to none going into Game 3 at the Omni in Atlanta. But every game now packed an element of desperation for Michael Jordan because every win moved him closer to the one goal he was now playing for—a third straight championship. He inspired himself on this first obstacle to three-peating by calling his team and himself the underdog. That was his feeling after a less-than-sparkling regular season left them behind the Knicks and having to face a playoff showdown in which New York had the upper hand, or at least the homecourt advantage. For Jordan having to face somebody being better than him, some team being better than his was like a threat to his manhood. So he came out against Atlanta with machismo as the Bulls won the first two games. Game 3 was falling into place, and Michael's 24th and 25th points off a fallaway, 19-foot jump shot that ended with his trademark backpedaling put the Bulls ahead 68-61.

But Jordan never made it back to the defensive end in the transition. As he turned to run back, he slipped on a wet spot and went down near the halfcourt line. He curled up and squirmed in pain holding his right leg. His agony quickly spread through living rooms all over Chicago. You could feel that sharp pain shoot up the ankle and into the thigh like the shade on the bedroom window suddenly rolling up. The somersault in the stomach drained all the oxygen from the brain. Gasping gave way to breath-holding when Jordan went down because, he said, "I heard something pop, and I thought it was a tendon."

Jordan rose, draped one arm around Stacey King, the other around Scott Williams, and hopped off to the locker room without putting any weight on his right foot. With 3:45 to play in the third quarter, Williams left his teammate propped up on a table in the Bulls' locker room, walking back to the court with a stone-faced look that suggested, "Oh my God."

"I was in agony at the time," is how Jordan described his feeling as he rolled around the Omni floor like a bug who had just been hit with a dose of RAID. Once he made it to the locker room, Jordan learned the tape around his ankle, and not a tendon, had popped. Within minutes desire overcame pain. Jordan was up and walking, bouncing up on his toes, feeling his way around the locker room. At that point he remembered feeling, "It only bothered me when I landed or jumped off of it."

Jordan watched his teammates maintain their seven-point lead through the end of the third quarter. He hobbled back to the court at the start of the fourth quarter, and 15,141 Hawks fans rose and cheered him. With a hero's welcome from enemy fans, Jordan could not possibly shirk the part. That was not his nature. After making his first shot, a pull-up 15-foot jumper on the run, Michael landed only on his left foot and bounced to maintain his balance like a bowler trying to keep from crossing the foul line while using body English to get the ball to trip the wobbling 10-pin. He dunked and hit three-point shots, including one with 1:20 left that compelled him to turn to a group of people sitting courtside and mouth the words, "It's all over." Fourteen points in the fourth quarter. Fourteen points on one leg. Fourteen points after being carried off the court. How?

"I've been there before," he explained later. "I'm in good tune with my body. When the doctor said no tendon had popped, I knew I was coming back. My main initiative is to go back and play, so the first thing I'm doing in the locker room is finding out the extent of the injury and what limits that puts on me. Then, I'm thinking about what I can do if I get back on the floor. I know I'm going to limit my cutting and just shoot off it. Figure out the motions you can make and use those.

"Then I saw what the team was doing. I'm not thinking about whether they can win without me, but how much better a chance we will have if I can get in there and contribute. And then the cheers made me feel better. If this were Cleveland and the fans would have been booing and all that hatred had been out there, there would have been some drama. But I sensed the opportunity to complete the sweep, and you think of all the effects that will have. We get more rest, the other teams see we have moved on to the next round, and they know that Michael Jordan isn't really hurt that bad. It hurt when it happened, but all this other stuff made the pain go away."

The pain would not go away this time. His right wrist hurt so much before the start of Game 3 of the 1993 Eastern Conference semifinal series against Cleveland, he spent 20 minutes on the Richfield Coliseum court practicing left-handed hook shots. He hurt the wrist at the end of the third quarter of Game 2 against Cleveland. It hurt so bad that when he came out for the fourth quarter and was fouled, he shot both free throws left-handed. It hurt so bad that Jordan did not even care that his streak of 59 consecutive 20-points-plus playoff games ended with an effort of 18.

X rays showed nothing more than a sprain, but between Game 2 on Thursday and Game 3 on Saturday Jordan could not even shake hands. His first shot of Game 3 did not come until more than half the first quarter had run out; it was an air ball. His second shot was a layup. In the first half, Michael made just 4 of 9 shots, and none of them came from more than 10 feet.

But the third quarter started with a bang—a Jordan 20-footer. Bang, an 18-footer. He made 5 of his first 7 and 8 of 15 in the second half. He scored 22 of 32 points in the second half, and even hit Gerald Wilkins with a few taunts of "You can't guard me now." From air ball to Air Jordan in less than 30 minutes. Maybe the hostile Cleveland crowd helped Jordan overcome his limp wrist. But to understand how Michael could go from lost to legend in the flick of a wrist, well, we must get inside his head, go through the ordeal with him and feel the pain.

"With every follow-through I could feel the tendon stretching," he said after the game. "It hurt whenever I flicked from the tip of my middle finger to my wrist, an irritation that wouldn't go away. I shot a couple of air balls, but I knew I was in trouble when I found myself thinking about it more than I wanted to instead of playing instinctively. I knew there was going to be a point when I had to exert myself, but I was wondering when that time was. I didn't know what I could give in the first half. Maybe I could be a decoy early or penetrate and dish off. I said to Scottie, I was very limited. I was going to be more passive. Maybe I could just rebound. But I also knew if I had the shots I must take them to set up my drives.

"They were giving me the shot, and I wanted to see if I could make it. I had to prove something to myself. I put up a three and really felt the pain on that one. Hurt more when I missed it. I was shooting more from the elbow instead of my wrist. At halftime, I was frustrated. I was thinking about it too much, and I had no sense of touch.

"I talked with Doc [Hefferon] at halftime to see what I could do to get over the mental block. I figured if I could get over the mental part, everything else would be OK. I couldn't shoot without pain. I didn't feel like I should extend my wrist on the shot. He said to go ahead and shoot it anyway. Extend it.

"Once he said that, I knew I didn't have any choice. You want to achieve something so bad that somehow you got to make some sacrifices to get to that point. I thought if we wanted to win, I would have to pay. But that was OK because I know when you pay on the opposite side you reap some dividends. I was just nervous that I was thinking about it too much. But in the second half, I said forget about it. The throbbing just stopped. The first shot that went down, took my mind off of it. We were still within striking distance, and the next thing I know I'm flicking my wrist almost pain free."

After 48 hours of icing the wrist and squeezing putty to strengthen it, Jordan's miraculous recovery was complete. He went from handicapped to handcuffed to single-handedly winning Game 4 of the series with that miraculous last-second shot. He could do things injured most other players could not do healthy. But he never could explain the powers of healing or recuperation.

In mere medical terms, there was no explanation for how Jordan came back so quickly. Bulls trainer Chip Schaefer more often than not came out of a clinical analysis of a Jordan injury shaking his head. The process was always the same. Jordan would make a speedy recovery, and Schaefer would try to explain how. As he stood outside his training room and offered explanation, he left a feeling of mystery, as though behind those doors were men in hooded coats, dancing around a boiling pot and reciting incantations in century-old dialect.

The situation was never more precarious than on February 23, 1993. With 8:36 left in the fourth quarter of a home game against Milwaukee, Jordan tried to cut off Bucks guard Jon Barry on a drive to the basket. As he went for the block, Jordan landed on top of Milwaukee forward Anthony Avent's foot and rolled over on his right ankle. He was carried from the court, came back to score five of his 34 points in the final 2:28, and carry the Bulls to a 99-95 victory. Forty-five minutes after the game, Michael limped out of Chicago Stadium on the support of crutches. Two nights later he scored 36 points in a

108-106 win at Orlando. He had spent an entire day in bed icing down his ankle, but then carried a team that played without three starters including Pippen.

Recoveries like that come out of bad made-for-television miniseries and bedtime stories. Experience began to factor in, for Michael played hurt so often that he simply learned how to play in pain and play well. With a goal, such as winning a basketball game, in front of him, Michael said he could ignore or tune out the pain. But in the end medical science could not explain how Jordan could hobble out of Chicago Stadium on crutches one night and score 36 two nights later. For some reason, it seemed, Jordan could work with Schaefer immediately after the trauma point, check to see if there was any permanent damage, such as a broken bone, then lace the Nikes up tighter and return to the game. Like so many other things about Jordan, his ability to play through pain, and play well, transcended explanation.

"From my experiences with pain tolerance, Michael was a fairly typical person," Schaefer explained. After Jordan rolled his ankle in the Milwaukee game, the Bulls trainer forced himself to figure out how Michael could make such a recovery. The results of his findings were anything but typical.

"To his credit, he always chose to play hurt, and I think his mind played a great role in healing. It was all about maintaining a positive attitude. I never found anything unequivocal with him that tissue healing was only a mental thing, and it didn't result without incorporating some kind of therapy. But if you talk about whether he had some physiological ability to overcome injuries or heal, you're not giving credit where credit is due. I think it was more a matter of professionalism, discipline, and dedication. We had back-to-back games against Portland and Sacramento one year [1991]. He hurt his back against Portland and was very stiff and sore. But he knew Sacramento was a city we visited once a year, and this was the only time these people would get to see him. That made him want to play, and that's where his mind would just take over.

"He just loved to compete so much that the games were what he lived for. So he found a way, any way, to rise to the occasion come tipoff. I think there's a mind-body connection there. Exactly scientifically what it does, I don't know. Sometimes, it was borderline miracle."

The determination to not let injury beat him the way Ron Harper would take him off the dribble drive may have caused Jordan to burn out on playing pro ball after nine years. Letting Harper or anybody else score on him hit 10 on the embarrassment scale for Michael. It is not that he could not handle sitting out with an injury. He could not deal with what happened to the Bulls when he did. After sitting out 64 games with a broken foot in 1985–86, he missed seven games the rest of his career. The Bulls won one of those. The obsession consumed him during a March 9, 1993, home game against Seattle.

Jordan spent three days in the hospital the previous week getting treatment for a bacterial infection between two toes on his left foot. It was a very bad case of athlete's foot, but Dr. Hefferon believed that if the infection had not been controlled it could have spread and threatened his life. Imagine that recovery. JORDAN COMES BACK FROM THE DEAD TO LEAD BULLS PAST SEATTLE. Michael even saw bacteria as a challenge. That's the way it was with him.

Jordan came back against the Supersonics to score 38 points and add nine assists and six steals in an 86-83 victory. He came back playing as if he was pain free, hitting his first five shots and scoring 15 points in the first quarter. When the layoff would take a toll on an ordinary player, Jordan dug into the side of the mountain and continued scaling. He scored 15 of the team's last 19 points, playing the entire fourth quarter. He said afterward, "The pain feels like it should subside substantially by the weekend." Two days later was the first time in a week that he woke up pain free.

When Jordan announced he was leaving pro basketball, Jerry Reinsdorf, the Bulls' owner, believed the game had become too much of a physical strain for Michael. "I remember watching Jim Brown run with the football, get hit by a bunch of guys, and knocked to the ground. He would pick himself up and drag himself back to the huddle," Reinsdorf reasoned. "It got to be that way for Michael. How many times could he go to the hole, be hit by three guys, and pick himself up to do it all over again? It came to a point where there was no more return on investment. It wasn't worth it anymore."

Why Jordan found it worth it for nine years explains the makeup of this man. Whether it was pain or Gerald Wilkins, Michael could never turn his back on a competitive situation.

NINE

Comp Time

March 20, 1993, Capitol Center, Landover, Maryland. Embarrassment. Never had a guy embarrassed me like that by outscoring me so decisively. I've had games where guys put up 28 points or something like that, but I usually had 56. So giving up 37 points to LaBradford Smith last night made me feel like I didn't compete hard enough and that's the worst feeling. No one's ever done that without me putting the same numbers back at them.

Some of my friends say getting beat—losing—made me a little nasty, a little vengeful. That's the competitor in me. That's what made me tell B. J. this rematch with the Bullets was going to be a big game for me. It was a personal thing. Knowing the same guy would be there in a back-to-back game situation, I'm thinking this time I will get him back on his heels early, and he won't respond well to that. Getting nasty, I don't know. Getting competitive, always.

Whenever you get an initiative like some guy scoring 37 points on you, you know what you want to do the next time around. So when we got on the floor the next night and I hit my first eight shots over LaBradford Smith, I told Scottie I wanted to get all 37 points back by halftime. He told me to go for 60. So then I started telling my teammates to help me in whatever way possible. I'm hot, get me the ball and get out of my way. I always worry about taking it out of the team concept because I didn't want the other guys to stand around and watch. But I was so hot and I wanted to get this guy so bad that they didn't have a choice but to stand around and watch.

Then LaBradford is saying, cool off, cool off. I said, you didn't cool off on me last night, why should I cool off on you? That's not trash talk. That's competitive spirit. I put myself in the right frame of mind to compete—in this case a combination of being pissed off and embarrassed. When you get into a competitive situation like this, LaBradford Smith has to walk away embarrassed. When he missed six of his first eight shots, that was it. But that's not it, not when you feel like this is not only a matter of getting even with a guy but proving what kind of competitor you are. That's why it was so important to get the 37 points back in the first half. If I hadn't missed that free throw at the end, I would have had it. That made me mad. But for me, being competitive in anything took a little bit of getting mad, also getting focused, getting even and ultimately getting a win.

When LaBradford Smith went zoning for 37 points on Michael in the first game of a back-to-back series with the Bulls, Jordan walked out of Chicago Stadium embarrassed. If only he could have walked out triumphant with the feeling that he came back to score 11 straight fourth quarter points and lead the Bulls to a 104-99 victory on this March 19, 1993, night. But if he could have, he would not have been Michael Jordan. Instead, he cut his post-game media conversation short. He went home. He didn't sleep. He took no mercy playing his son's video games.

While his teammates joked about LaBradford Smith's impending place on Jordan's hit list before the Saturday night rematch with the Bullets in Washington, Michael sat alone, quietly working himself into a competitive frenzy. Perhaps he pictured himself on the back-yard court in Wilmington trying get even playing one-on-one with Larry. Or he was trying to get in touch with his mean streak, the vicious alter ego that enabled Michael to do whatever his mind willed on the basketball court. This was how he prepared to put his signature on a game as if it were his own Sistine Chapel. This was how he prepared to create a masterpiece only he was capable of producing.

"We were just waiting for the fireworks to start," reserve center Stacey King remembered. "We knew what was coming, and we were waiting to watch Michael do his thing. Kind of felt sorry for LaBradford."

After the Washington Bullets lost to the Bulls 126-101, LaBradford Smith sat in front of his locker, upright, shirtless, smiling. Hardly the look of a beaten man, beaten for 47 points, beaten for 36 in one half or one point less than he had in an entire game on a career night the night before. "That's the way it goes sometimes," said Smith as he laughed off Michael Jordan's 47-point outburst. "He came out and he was on. Hey, it's hard enough when he isn't on."

LaBradford Smith was no fool, however. He was smiling afterward because he got to stand around and watch Michael do his thing too. In fact, he got an up-close view, kind of like the guy who stood there and handed Michelangelo his brushes.

Jordan managed frequent brushes with the extraordinary because of his competitive nature. This enabled him to make being great or being the best on the court on any and every given night his standard operating procedure. This intensity, which allowed Jordan to miss 17 of his first 21 shots, then finish the game the night before playing the hero with 11 straight points, may have been his tragic flaw, the one that drove him away from the game prematurely. To call this trait an intensity is like calling Cindy Crawford cute or what's on the ceiling of the Sistine Chapel a mural. To understand Michael, you must understand his competitive drive. It's what he used to dominate the NBA and without it, well, he never would have been Michael Jordan.

Whereas challenges inspired MJ to be something better today than he was yesterday, he felt only in competitive situations could he flaunt his true brilliance. Jordan wanted to walk off the court after every game and every practice leaving no doubt who was the best player that day and every day. He was like that off the court. "When we were in college, it would be time to go to sleep," recalled Cleveland's Brad Daugherty of his UNC days with MJ. "Michael would be lying in bed, and I would say something to him like, 'Bet I can beat you in a game of pool.' He would be up all night playing you, beating you to prove you were wrong." Challenges merely presented an opportunity for Michael to push himself. Competition presented an opportunity for Michael to win. There was nothing he loved more than winning. There was nothing he hated more than losing.

James Jordan pinpointed his son's competitive fire as the single most important quality that made him stand out. Pops called it a gift from God, a perspective many others shared because there was simply no better or logical way to explain why LaBradford Smith's career night could piss off Michael. It really was a gift from his mother, Deloris, a stubbornness she needed to keep from giving in to her children. Michael inherited that and manifested it playing one-on-one on the backyard court with older brother Larry.

Jordan often evoked these regular matchups by way of explaining his ascension. If Michael was Air Jordan, then Larry could have been Stratosphere Jordan the way he could jump over his younger brother. Michael said this is where he learned to be relentless. Never give up until you get even unless it's time for dinner, and Michael never one-upped Larry until he outgrew him shortly before he entered high school. So there were many times when Michael was really taking Larry to the basket in an NBA game because, ultimately, LaBradford Smith never presented enough of an obstacle.

Jerry Krause loved to talk about the competitive makeup of athletes. When you are short and stumpy and built a little like the *Star Wars* villain Jabba the Hut, you do not get to the lofty status of general manager of a three-time NBA champion without a competitive feistiness. Krause, who knew what it was because he used it every single day of his professional life, said he never saw competitive hunger in an athlete as he did in Jordan. He knew there was only so much of it Jordan could have developed playing the game. "I think Michael's parents did a hell of a job raising him," Krause said. "The way he would chase a goal or try to do everything in practice perfectly—that came from his family background."

Certain influences allowed Jordan to develop his competitive stubbornness. Obviously, getting cut from his high school team ultimately had a positive effect. At the end of that season when he did not make the team, Michael had to carry a player's uniform and make like a team equipment manager to be allowed in the gym to see Laney play a postseason playoff game. That experience undoubtedly stuck with Jordan forever. It was one of those rare occasions that made him feel like a loser, and afterward he vowed publicly to "never let that happen again."

It was North Carolina that tapped Michael's tireless competitiveness. The system Dean Smith created at North Carolina was based on using players as parts instead of the superstar-and-support method the NBA ultimately employed to become an entertainment extravaganza. Jordan learned to battle for everything, playing time, shots, opportunities to touch the ball. North Carolina also played a high-profile schedule, arguably the most competitive in the country each season. "We used to go into a lot of those games as the underdog," Jordan said. "That was the driving force to compete and because we had to do it over and over again it became a routine. That's where I learned to love, to relish those competitive situations."

"Why did he need to do that to LaBradford Smith?" asked Matt Doherty, one of Jordan's teammates at North Carolina who witnessed the coming-of-age of Michael's competitive abilities. "Coach Smith used to create this environment for us at practice. He'd put us in a lot of little games with winners and losers. Like a defensive drill where the team was broken up into groups of four and alternated trying to make defensive stops. Whichever group made the most stops won. The losers would always have to run. Michael usually won. Coach Smith always talked about coming from behind, and Michael had the ability to do that.

"Before practices, he used to look around the locker room, point to somebody and say, 'I'm going to get you today.' Then, he would dunk on them. I would conveniently leave the room at those times."

In 1985 and 1986, a joke made the rounds in the NBA that the Bulls had put together a team consisting of Michael Jordan and 11 back-up centers. Granville Waiters, Jawaan Oldham, Mike Brown, Steve Johnson, Earl Cureton, Dave Corzine, Mike Smrek, Sidney Green, Brad Sellers—they were all 7-footers who journeyed from team to team in and out of the NBA. These were Jordan's teammates, his supporting cast, through his first three years as a pro. Add in an Ennis Whatley and two guys who had drug problems, and it's no wonder John Paxson is the only player to remain a teammate of Jordan's during his entire career. His first year, the Bulls were a joke. Jordan made light of it early. After coming from a North Carolina team that lost once his last year, Jordan looked at the roster and stated during his inaugural press conference in Chicago, "Well, I don't think we will go undefeated."

Perhaps the only thing Jordan hated more than losing was being laughed at. And so during his rookie season he vowed to do whatever he could to win, which meant coming out every night at his competitive best. A team that went 27-55 the year before finished 38-44 Jordan's rookie year. The talent pool stayed thin until the Bulls added Scottie Pippen and Horace Grant. But those early years fueled the competitive fire that began to smolder at North Carolina. Now, add in the games he missed his second season with a broken foot and all the pent-up frustrations from watching the team lose, and you have internal combustion with enough charge to wipe out a mid-size country. "I remember watching them play, go down by 10 at half and throwing cans at the television set," Michael recited as his most memorable moment from that season. "So many times, I couldn't watch all the way through to the end of the game."

Doug Collins saw this frustration in Jordan when he became coach of the Bulls. Jordan would team with the starting five in practice scrimmages, watch his side miss shots or throw the ball away, and feel his head expand, his temples pounding with anger. Sweat increasingly flowed as Jordan moved toward a boiling point. He would take over and score every point. Collins would switch him to the other team, and the gym actually would heat up several degrees with Jordan's steam. If the others could not compete, Michael figured he'd take them one-on-five.

"One thing I had to be very careful of was how to direct his competitive energy," Collins said. "It could be a positive. It could be a negative. It was very difficult for him to accept mediocrity in others when he was so damn good. He used to destroy guys on our team with his greatness at practice—get in their faces, yell at them— almost demanding them to bring their level of play up to his. Until Pippen and Grant came along and could bridge that gap somewhat, Michael was very frustrated by it. There was that operating theory that Michael Jordan and four guys are going to take you to the promised land. He was so much of a competitor that he actually tried to do that."

If Jordan's competitive fever could have been measured with a thermometer, the mercury burst through glass sometime in 1988. Michael actually led the Bulls to a taste of the promised land on April 3, when he scored 59 points to carry the Bulls to victory in Detroit. That was the night Pistons coach Chuck Daly officially termed Jordan's output "Astro Points." It was also the night Daly unofficially began to devise the "Jordan Rules." When the Bulls met Detroit in the second round of the playoffs in May, the Pistons' as-yet-unnamed triple-teaming defense held Jordan to eight shots during Game 4 of the series. The Bulls lost the series in five games, and Jordan spent many a sleepless summer night trying to figure a way to break the Jordan Rules.

Jordan had reached competition on the highest level. He was made the object of devious defenses because he was the league's scoring champ, Defensive Player of the Year, and Most Valuable Player that season.

Now it became a quest to stay at that level, and so competing all the time became even more important. It was already part of his nature, and Michael figured remaining on top of his profession became a matter of creating a way to constantly juice his competitive persistence. It was as if he was scaling a mountain and somebody—the Pistons he would say—kept pushing him back down the rope whenever he neared the top. The only way to be the best defensive player, the best offensive player, and the most valuable player every night was to get more competitive. Maybe that would rub off on Grant, Pippen, and Paxson, and they could help Jordan achieve the ultimate goal of being a champion.

"If I didn't do that every night, I figured I would lose a little bit of the edge," Jordan explained. "If you don't sit back and evaluate and realize you had something special—that edge—then you've lost it. I was always fighting to find an angle to push myself. That led to turning everything into a challenge. And I loved that competition, playing for that top spot or playing to keep that top spot. I thought it was never in your best interest to be given things. So I was thinking every night you had to go out and work to get it. That gave me a purpose to step on the basketball court the next day—to maintain that level."

When describing the "level" that Jordan was talking about during a private conversation in the spring of 1993, Magic Johnson held his hand high above his 6-foot-9 frame. A bit of envy seemed to touch Magic at this moment, and he stretched his words as if to try to reach a descriptive level that he never quite made it to as a basketball star. When Magic did come close to that level, he did so by jumping on Kareem's shoulders. Michael had to get there by himself, and only two years removed from the NBA, Magic realized what Jordan had inside that made him so competitive and why it was so important to him.

"The man had pride, and he had a level where he had to maintain that," Magic observed. "He created a monster, and he had to stay up there. Otherwise how's he going to react to everybody saying that Kevin Johnson held him down and come back the next time and score 55 points? He had to stay up there, and creating this competitive attitude was the only way he could do that. That's how he was always able to come through when it was the biggest time, and it was in the spotlight. Can't do it any other way. And that's how come nobody else could."

Michael knew that the great players lived from victory to victory or from great performance to great performance. The greatest let the losses burn their competitive organs. This is why Dominique Wilkins will be remembered for slam dunks and 40-point games and Michael Jordan will be remembered for three straight championships. When Michael compared himself to Dominique, the major difference, he explained, was that he had more competitive fire. Competing became Michael's reason to carry on.

"People always asked me what I remembered about that 63-point game against Boston," Michael related. "Was it this shot or that shot? I remember that we lost. If I had done it in a situation where we won, I would remember it far better. Losing had a tendency to make me forget things like that. I remembered the losses. We would lose and every time you looked at television you would see it. I remembered the losses, and I always thought for a long time afterward how I could have changed the outcome of the game. That was part of my competitive attitude."

Imagine Michael becoming this competitive monster, as Magic called him, as if it was some out-of-body, Incredible Hulk-type transformation. That's what it seemed like. Sitting on his living room couch or in front of his locker or on the bench at the Palace of Auburn Hills, that blank stare on his face. You know this stare, the one in which your eyes are locked open and the rest of your voluntary muscles are in the same mode while inside your mind is racing at 1,000 paces per millisecond.

Understanding Jordan's competitive makeup meant getting inside his head when Dominique was in town and they were matching jumpers and dunks.

These were *High Noon* moments for Michael. One came about 8:30 P.M. on February 27, 1993, at Chicago Stadium. With the Bulls leading Atlanta 55-50 at the half, Wilkins had outscored and outshot Jordan in the first half. Michael opened the second half with a 17-foot jumper; Dominique hit from 20. Jordan hit from 20. Wilkins came back with a three-point shot, so Michael hit a three-point shot, then converted a steal into a layup, foul, and three-point play. Wilkins dunked. Michael smiled and pulled up for another three-point shot to give the Bulls a 70-57 lead. "He looked at me and said, 'I can do this all night,' " Jordan recounted afterward. "I said, 'That's OK, I can too.' "

Atlanta coach Bob Weiss knew his team had no chance in such a situation and admitted, "When it turned into a competition, it broke our backs. I wish they wouldn't have gotten caught up in that. You can't beat Michael in a situation like that."

Phil Jackson knew there was no holding back Michael. "In the third quarter when Dominique hit the three, Michael looked over at the bench and said, 'That's enough. Let's get back at this.' He had a certain element there in every game he played. I just hoped he would always realize when it was time to put that aside and do the important things to win a ball game."

To Rod Higgins, a journeyman NBA player and the first friend Jordan made in the NBA when both played for the Bulls during Michael's rookie season, Michael's competitiveness showed with nasty tenacity. A cockiness, intestinal fortitude, obsession with excelling were what Higgins said appeared in Michael when he turned on his competitive side.

That was early in Jordan's pro career. In later years, when the obsession became maintaining his stature, the competitiveness overwhelmed all parts of his life. "Don't beat him," warned George Koehler, Michael's chauffeur, friend, and assistant, when discussing his competitive side. "Because he will come find you. He will redeem the loss." Sure he got a little testy, a little on edge. That was his way.

"Michael had a mean streak. He could be vicious," said Collins as he leaned forward to emphasize the point. "You got him upset, and he would cut your heart out to win. It's like the thing with Billy Owens, stealing the ball from him. What Michael's saying is I don't care what these people are writing, you're not ready for me. He let his actions speak for themselves. Why did he have to block Shaquille's first shot? He was sending a message. I'm still here. I'm still the man. That was how he competed.

"All the great geniuses of the world were like that. We're talking about the Einsteins, the Edisons, the Roosevelts. These people came across something and worked to perfect it. You played one-on-one with Michael, and he was not going to let you score. A lot of guys will play, it will get to game point, and they will win. Michael wanted to shut you out, like you didn't belong there. That was how he competed.

"I don't think there was anything Michael did for fun. You couldn't play cards with him for an hour. You played for 10 hours. Michael would go out and play a pro like Chip Beck in golf and in the recesses of his mind, he believed if he had a great day he could beat this guy."

In practices, Michael challenged every call in scrimmages. One of Krause's greatest challenges was finding a player who could stand up to Jordan in practice. Darrell Walker scratched and clawed his way through half a season in 1993. Rodney McCray lost all his confidence trying to do so. Bobby Hansen, who played with the Bulls during the 1991–92 championship season, was the only player who ever made it an entire season practicing against Jordan. Eventually, Jackson had to resort to playing Pippen against Michael to make practice games work.

"The thing about Michael's competitive spirit was that you couldn't tell him there's something he couldn't do," said Johnny Bach, a Bulls assistant coach who spent seven years with Jordan. "No one was ever able to tell him no. Crowd reaction, the booing in Boston and Cleveland, would stimulate him to a higher performance. If I were in the other camp, I would suggest to my crowd nice quiet applause or heavy adulation. You didn't want to add fuel. He was such a competitor that Michael Jordan and fuel made for some combustible situation."

Finding somebody who does not have an incident to relate or has not been touched by Michael Jordan's competitive extremes would be like defending against Jordan in the open court. On a breakaway. From behind. For Tar Heel teammate Matt Doherty this came on a road trip in 1984 when the two squared off in a game of pool. Besides basketball, golf, and cards, Michael always thought of himself as somewhat of a pool shark. On this night, however, Doherty hustled a victory against Michael. "He slammed his pool cue on the table, looked around all flustered and said, 'This table is not regulation.'"

For Buzz Peterson, Jordan's roommate at North Carolina, the moment came when he and Jordan battled in a game of Monopoly. When Peterson took an overwhelming lead and upped the rent on Boardwalk and Park Place, Michael picked up the board and let it fly.

He was so distraught over losing that he couldn't face Buzz. Michael spent that night sleeping at his sister Roslyn's apartment on campus.

On the basketball court, the stories are even more fantastic. Johnny Kerr remembered a sequence of events during a game in Utah in 1986 when Jordan posted up on 6-foot guard John Stockton, jumped, and dunked over him. "As Michael was running back down the floor, some guy yelled at him, 'Pick on somebody your own size,' " Kerr related. "Now that's hard to hear in an NBA game with 20,000 fans there. The next play Utah came down, Michael stole the ball, drove in on Mel Turpin, a 7-footer, flew over the top and stuffed the ball. As he ran back downcourt, Michael yelled to this guy, 'Is he big enough for you?' "

Doug Collins always noticed Jordan's competitive best when he played against guys who were touted as great defenders, would-be Jordan stoppers, for the first time—such as Dan Majerle, who played for Phoenix, and Stacey Augmon, who was with Atlanta. For the record, Jordan put up 53 points on Majerle the first time around (March 22, 1989) and 37 on Augmon in their inaugural match-up (December 21, 1991).

But the real competitor in Jordan came out during his confrontation with Xavier McDaniel late in the first quarter of Game 7 of the 1992 Eastern Conference semifinal series. After McDaniel pushed Scottie Pippen and threw down words of provocation that would never make the Disney Channel, Michael went nose-to-nose with him, exchanged four-letter words with him, and drew a technical foul. Then he went on to score 18 of his 42 points by the end of that quarter.

Certain stimuli seemed to detonate Jordan's competitiveness like pulling the pin on a grenade. During a lackluster game against a wounded Golden State team in January 1993, Tim Hardaway, the Warriors point guard and one of the league's young guns, attempted to guard Jordan like an old wool blanket, the kind that leaves scratch marks. For a while Hardaway affixed himself to Jordan's back. Jordan was not happy about this. Like a bolt of lightning, Jordan flashed across the lane on defense to block a Hardaway layup attempt, grabbed the loose ball, threw an outlet pass to Scott Williams, then dunked the ball when Williams missed a fast-break layup. "Tim Hardaway had to learn there are some things you can't get away with in this league," Jordan explained of his motive to make such a play. "He had to learn some respect."

The chance to teach other players and teams respect or show them they were not ready for him, as Collins explained, sparked Jordan's competitive side. The Charlotte Hornets beat the Bulls for the first time ever at Chicago Stadium on January 22, 1993, and Hornets guard Kendall Gill, among others, let Jordan know about it as he walked off the court that night. Charlotte came back to the Stadium in March, and Jordan scorched Gill for 52 points in a 15-point victory.

Miami gave the Bulls the same treatment after pulling out a 97-95 victory in March that year. Jordan put up 34 and sat out the fourth quarter of a 119-92 victory when the Heat came to the Stadium in April.

"Those are games where you don't want to come back and say I wished I had done this or I wished I had done that," Jordan remarked. "You don't want to have any reservations about it when you step away. I remembered what they said when they beat us. I'm waiting to see a banner that says 'First win ever over Bulls.' But if they think they are on the same level, well, I had to show them I just didn't agree with that. You don't bother talking while the competition is still there. You get rid of that. I felt like I could expand my role in those times. Then you get the last word. That's what you compete for."

A hint of anger marked Jordan's tone when he talked in depth about competition. Normally, Michael spoke in a very deep voice in very proper English. When he was angry, however, his voice picked up pace and became laced with dialect. Competition was the one aspect of his character that he never tolerated opponents, media, or fans to question. It was the one aspect of his makeup that threatened to consume him.

Michael pushed himself to a limit in every venue. Simple things, such as driving, he would approach like an old arcade game that awarded more points for keeping the accelerator floored and swerving in and out of lanes. Jordan's teammates described times when he would pass them on the shoulder of the highway in excess of 125 m.p.h. Some wondered whether his life would end in a ball of flames on the highway, which prompted the question of whether Michael's zest for competition packed a dark side.

This was more than cheating on lines calls while playing tennis with Rod Higgins, Howard White, and Ahmad Rashad. Though he did do that because of his inability to accept losing, according to Higgins. This was more than telling people he played golf to a five handicap instead of a 10, which his competitive rounds on record showed he was. This addiction to competing led Jordan into gambling on golf and playing cards with Eddie Dow, a bail bondsman who wound up murdered. It also led him to an Atlantic City casino between Games 1 and 2 of the 1993 Eastern Conference Finals and, reportedly, to losing $500,000 playing golf with San Diego businessman Richard Esquinas. These blemishes on Jordan's character did not indicate an addiction to gambling.

"What it was, was an addiction to competition," explained James Jordan. When Michael was persecuted for his escape from New York to Atlantic City, which led to his prolonged boycott of the media, Pops took the time to explain why gambling afflicted his son. He believed it came down to competition. "It was a chance for him to compete against chance and bet on his own strategy," James continued. "If he played for match sticks or straws he would have had the same level of competitiveness. It could be for franks (hot dogs, not the Swiss kind), and he'd play just as hard. When he played golf, whether it was for pennies, quarters, or dollars, that was his way of getting on top of his game. It was a competition problem. He was born with that. If he didn't have a competition problem, nobody ever would have written about him in the first place. And he never would have got to the level he did. That's the one thing he had more than anything. The person he always tried to outdo more than anyone else was himself."

That desire compelled Michael Jordan never to allow himself a chance to relax on the basketball court. He probably did a fair amount of that off the court, which is why he would end up playing cards for 10 hours at a time. In fact, that desire probably led to a life that needed never-ending opportunities to compete and win. The day after he scored 55 points against the Phoenix Suns in Game 4 of the 1993 NBA Finals and the day before Game 5, a beautiful summer Thursday in Chicago, Jordan sped out of practice in his Porsche and with a police escort right to the golf course. After at least 18 holes and a little dinner, he played cards with Magic, Ahmad, and Quinn Buckner late into the night. When competing consumed him that much, Michael realized that it was time to step back and walk away from the life of basketball after nine years.

TEN

One-on-One:
How They Played MJ

Sunday, May 23, 1993, The Plaza Hotel, New York City. In Detroit they had the Jordan Rules. This morning I'm reading the *New York Daily News* about the Knicks' three-part plan on "How to stop Superman." I was the focus of so many different defenses. But all the different varieties of the way teams used to play me made me think no one player could guard me.

Every player in the NBA supposedly had some special strategy to guard me. It seemed like I was the one guy everyone got psyched up to play against. But one player? I never felt there was one who could stop me when I was playing my best. When Jeff Malone was at Washington, he was pretty tough—I will always remember my worst night came against him. Dumars played the best man-to-man defense, but he had a lot of help against me. And John Starks did a good job scratching and clawing me. But for most of my career Rolando Blackman was the guy I looked forward to playing against the most, and he was the guy who probably had the most success against me in terms of stopping me. I always wondered what this one-on-one matchup was like from his perspective.

---

n a 1992 interview Rolando Blackman explained what it was like to guard Michael Jordan: "A lot of players admitted to being intimidated by Michael Jordan, but I never had any success against him until I passed the point of being nervous or intimidated. I never felt like Rolando Blackman had something to prove playing against Michael Jordan. You couldn't look at it that way because he would get the best of you in that situation.

"When I was at Dallas, I made it point to not watch a lot of extra film of him or anything like that. That would have been intimidating. I didn't seek a lot of extra advice, and I never went into a game setting number goals as far as how many points under his average I wanted to hold him. Basically, I realized the main thing in stopping Michael was that you had to have help from your teammates. He's right about no one being able to stop him one-on-one, so forget about approaching it as a personal challenge. You needed help just to hold him a few points under his average.

"The first thing I tried to do was make him work hard to catch the ball. Then, it became a matter of staying in front of him and not letting him get into the middle of the lane. If he got to the middle of the lane, he was devastating, because he could jump over everyone, even most of the centers in the league. I wanted to give him the jumper rather than the drive and dunk. He was more dangerous slashing to the basket because he could get the big guys in foul trouble.

"Michael used to say it was tough playing me because we used to run him through so many picks. So you could never ignore your offense, worrying about what he would do to you when you were on defense. Keep him busy, wear him out or at least try and maybe that would slow him down. As the years went on, you had to worry about making him the entire focus of your defensive strategy because his supporting cast really improved from the time he first came into the league.

"Then came crunch time. It was no treat to watch the guy when you were the man guarding him at crunch time because he was the man."

Blackman knew why it was so hard to guard Jordan. The man could take off from the foul line, hold the ball in his right hand, extend it, then switch the ball to his left hand while still rising, and flip an underhanded shot off the backboard and into the basket. The man could dart toward the basket on an angle, face the basket head on and turn his back on it at the last minute, and flip a shot over his head and in—with a defender hanging on both arms. These were some of the moves Michael Jordan made that forced former Milwaukee Buck Alvin Robertson, acclaimed as one of the NBA's most tenacious defenders, to say the best defense for the man was to make sure you yelled "help" loud enough.

Ask players, ex-players, coaches, and ex-coaches to explain how to guard Michael Jordan and each one answers, "You can't." Craig Ehlo, the man opposite Michael during some of his most offensive moments, said that he used to stay up all night before games against the Bulls and think of a way to stop Jordan. Gerald Wilkins didn't bother breaking down Jordan's abilities to look for a weakness. Wilkins didn't look at it as a matter of taking away the jumper or the drive or overcoming MJ's foot speed and quickness. To Wilkins, the only way to defend Michael was to match his determination. During his years in Charlotte, Kendall Gill found that approach futile and followed an even more simplified game plan. "Don't try anything fabulous; don't try and embarrass him. You don't want him mad at you. There's no way to stop him."

There were as many different varieties of defenses designed to stop Michael Jordan as there were players and teams that he matched up against. He made himself more difficult to guard by expanding his game for each new meeting. Playing Jordan was like matching wits with Kreskin, the famed mind reader. You waited for him to come on "The Tonight Show" again and again because you had him all figured out. Except this time he came up with a new way to baffle you. It's a wonder that in 14 confrontations, Blackman managed to hold Jordan to a 27-point average, five below his career average.

There was almost no way to describe the feeling of playing against Jordan. "It sounds like a good question," said Detroit's Joe Dumars, who found sitting down and discussing defending Jordan more frustrating than playing him. But prior to his last matchup with Michael in April 1993, right before Michael went off for 36 points to wrap up the last of his seven straight NBA scoring titles, Joe D. finally put the feeling into words. "You're in a position where you're at the height of your adrenaline, and it's just stress, it's exhilaration, it's all of that."

To thoroughly feel Dumars' perspective, it would be necessary to play against Jordan. In lieu of that, it is most productive to view such a matchup through the eyes of some of the league's best players and coaches. This is the way to understand the pre-game plans tailored for him; to relate the feeling-out process of the first quarter when Michael determined which moves to use and how to attack his foe mentally and physically. This would be the only way to feel the second-quarter dilemma of deciding what to give up and what to defend or the third-quarter perspective of dealing with Michael playing on fresh legs, knowing exactly how he could beat the defense. This would provide insight to the peril of guarding Jordan in the fourth quarter when he would take control of the game. What was it like to go through the motions and emotions of those who faced the challenge of playing a game against Michael Jordan?

Pre-Game: The Approach

For so many players going one-on-one with Michael Jordan was a no-brainer. You cannot stop him so why try? Dan Majerle, the 6-foot-6 Phoenix guard regarded as one of the players with the physical attributes to defend Jordan during his last three years in the NBA, took this fatalistic approach. His strategy: Just don't let him go crazy; let him get his 30 and hope you win the game. Jordan averaged 35 against Majerle for his career and more than 40 in the 1993 NBA Finals. This approach can be called the "Plead No Contest" strategy. The idea was to make Michael work to beat you by himself, get a hand in his face, make him work for his shots, and do not waste time double-teaming him and leaving teammates open. Jordan was good enough to find them for open shots. If he gets 50, hold all the other Bulls under 10 and force him to win a game by himself.

During his eight years in Milwaukee, Robertson took on the sole responsibility of confronting Jordan. He devised a plan from watching game film. Robertson tried to come in with an approach that would alleviate thinking and save all time and energy for reacting. He started by trying to stay close to Jordan when he had the ball. The idea was to not back off and be forced to deal with Jordan's maneuvering. Robertson's strategy was like mapping out Michael's movements into a play-by-numbers game or a connect-the-dots exercise in which the numbers and dots went up to infinity. This approach meant predicting what Michael would do with the ball. But there was one problem with that. "With Michael nothing was predictable," Blackman noted.

Even Dumars gave into futility with his strategy. "Just stay in front of him and make him take the toughest shot you can," Dumars prescribed. "You couldn't strip (the ball) from him. You couldn't steal it. You weren't going to block his shot. You could look at some guys and pick out a spot where they would be dangerous from. In the post or driving from the wing and keep him from getting to that spot. But Michael had so many spots that the spot I feared him most was the one where he first stepped on the court."

Starks was the last defender to have real success against Jordan. During a stretch of five regular-season and playoff games at Madison Square Garden in 1992 and 1993, Starks and the New York Knicks coerced Michael into missing 90 of 142 shots. He did it by keeping a hand on Jordan at all times and using it as leverage to force him to the baseline or sideline or into another defender. Starks found making such a tactic work meant using all his strength to lean on Michael like a human brace, keeping the door from bursting open after being hit with a hurricane force wind. "I watched Michael. I studied Michael, everything he did," Starks explained. "I figured out what to try and tried it all. Didn't shut him down, though. That was impossible. I never went out with a game plan. You couldn't say you'll take this away from him, you'll take that away from him. You couldn't stop Michael Jordan. That was a given."

The problem with giving Jordan 30 was that so many times he

scored 40 or more points. The problem with trying a single defender on him was that there just were not that many to go around. Even Dumars, a four-time selection to the NBA's all-defensive team, said that he could not match Jordan one-on-one.

Chuck Daly had seen enough of the results from matching Jordan with one defender by the end of the 1988 season. You can watch a guy burn you for 59 points only so many times before realizing you do not fight a nuclear war with a slingshot. Daly figured defending Jordan, and more importantly beating him, should become a group concept. That's what led to the approach known as the Jordan Rules.

"Because he had as good a shooting touch as you had ever seen, athletic ability that allowed him to get free for a shot anytime he wanted, and intelligence, I didn't think it was feasible to play him with one man," Daly later observed. "I never thought that man existed, and we had two of the best defenders in Dennis Rodman and Joe Dumars. You could put one of those guys on him and hope a lot, but we wanted to get two guys on him all the time. We wanted to get close to him with guys who would fight him and keep him under control. Use a forearm in his back was one of our Jordan Rules. Never back off was another. Always be physical. The last part was to change up our looks. Double him in the post sometimes, double him on the wing other times. Come fast or use a slow trap. That way you could limit his movement by forcing him to react to you instead of you reacting to him."

What the Pistons proposed was forcing Michael to move to the spots they wanted, not the ones he wanted. Take away his physical advantage and exploit the mental stubbornness that made him say, "No way anybody is going to stop me." The more the Pistons ganged up on him, the more Jordan tried to take them one-on-three or -four. The Pistons used double-teaming to force him into the lane, where Bill Laimbeer or John Salley could bang him or give him a body shot as he finished a drive to the basket.

"Michael was so competitive that he played right into it," said Doug Collins, who coached the Bulls when the Jordan Rules worked most effectively. "Michael would play and play and play and try to take the ball to them until he beat them." That was the Pistons' game plan.

The idea of turning defending Jordan into Wrestlemania was always a usable concept for a team with the right personnel. The Knicks discovered that they could bully Jordan during the 1992 playoffs when they forced him to play from the perimeter. This version of the Jordan Rules made significant adjustments. Starks used his forearms, his hands, and clawed at Jordan while staying close. Instead of doubling with one line of defense, the Knicks used waves of defenders so he could never penetrate straight toward the basket and find passing lanes to open shooters. The Knicks tried to wear him out by constantly forcing him to change direction. If he managed to break the first two or three lines of defense, Patrick Ewing and Charles Oakley waited with Laimbeer-like contact. This strategy forced Michael to use up precious time on the 24-second clock and put up bail-out shots with Starks, Oakley, or Anthony Mason banging his knees and thighs in an attempt to break his shooting form.

Michael induced players into digging in, giving in, or staying up all night contemplating which would be the best way to face him one-on-one. He prompted coaches to create new tactics using everything within the rules and some things not within the rules. Washington coach Wes Unseld put together a formula to stop Jordan using offense. He would run an offense that set a series of never-ending picks for Jeff Malone. In trying to chase Malone, Jordan hopefully would suffer enough bumps and bruises to be slowed by fatigue. But if he did not tire, Unseld ordered his players to set picks and screens to nail Jordan on every pass. These methods were formulated to counter what Jordan had done. But they still had to deal with what he could do the moment he stepped on the court.

First Quarter: What You Face

This was the time each defender had to deal with the entire range of Michael Jordan's offensive array. This was the time for which Doug Collins prepared Jordan by making him shoot jump shots for 25 minutes after each practice during the three years he coached the Bulls. "Shoot, shoot, shoot, shoot, I told him," Collins emphasized. "If you can shoot, there would be no way anybody could ever defend you."

Defenders had to deal with the jump shot and the move in the post when Michael would catch the ball, turn around, and put up a fadeaway jumper too quick for anybody to defend. Robertson used to give Michael that one because he figured he had a better chance defending him on the 15- to-18-foot jump shots. "And to open up that shot, he would give you this little fake like he was going to the basket," Robertson continued. "Since you were always worried about him going to the basket, that gave him just enough time to get his legs underneath him to shoot the jump shot.

"If you were lucky enough to take that away, he could go to the crossover dribble to create room to shoot. It didn't matter how quick you were. When I was younger I was quick enough to stay with him on the first step. But he changed directions so quickly that you were always chasing from a step behind."

The first quarter of NBA games tends to feature more open court, fast-break play. Shooters are not always warmed up at that point, which leads to missed shots, long rebounds, and the chance to run. In addition to all of the above, defenders had to deal with Michael in the open court. On the break, he had the option of pulling up and shooting or driving for the dunk, and your momentum is going backward and you must defend. Kind of like running full-speed on a balance beam. Lean just a touch to one side and you fall. He's open. With a jab step Jordan could make a defender lean too far in one direction and create an opening.

If that was all there was to deal with, maybe more than one in 27 defenders could have matched Michael one-on-one. But then you had to deal with his will, his attempt to mentally dominate you. Ron Harper, who played for the Cavaliers and later played for the Los Angeles Clippers, projected the illusion of being able to match Michael's physical skills. But he could never compete with the mouthful of trash talk Jordan hit him with. "Can you guard me?" he would say to Harper. " 'Can you stop this? I'm going this way, are you with me?' " Harper recited. "It made you want to compete with him, which is what he wanted. When he got you into that, he had you." At the beginning of games, Jordan figured that working his opponent mentally would cause physical lapses.

"I just wanted to get inside their head," Michael explained. "I would be playing against a rookie, and I might say, 'You watched me on TV, now you're going to see me for real. On TV, you can change the channel; you can't now.' It wasn't like trash talking, you know, attacking them. But if I could put some kind of doubt in their mind then I had an advantage. In my last few years, no one really tried to talk trash to me anymore. Except for the young guys who didn't know me. Veterans like Ehlo and Wilkins rarely said anything to me. So I had to say that stuff to myself."

The first quarter was when Jordan was most lethal. His biggest scoring nights came when he could put up 20 or more points in the first quarter. When he scored 64 points against Orlando on January 16, 1993, he had 22 in the first quarter on 11-for-15 shooting from the field. In the Game 7 victory over the Knicks in the second round of the 1992 playoffs, Jordan scored 16 of the first 25 points and had 18 of his 42 by the end of the period. It was that day when Gerald Wilkins, then playing for the Knicks, learned what it was like to play Michael Jordan in the first quarter.

"If he started rolling in the first quarter, it was going to be a nightmare," Wilkins explained. "You could throw five guys at him, and nothing would happen. For Michael it was predicated on how well he was going early. The shots are going, he's made up his mind what he's going to do before he takes the shot. His emotions are a little higher then, and he wants it a little bit more. If I was successful against him in the first quarter, I felt I would be pretty successful against him the rest of the game."

In the first quarter, Jordan showed his defenders all his moves. In the second quarter, they had to figure out what to try and take away.

Second Quarter: Give and Take

How do you stop this guy? The Phoenix Suns collectively asked themselves this question during Game 4 of the 1993 NBA Finals. Give him the jump shot, maybe. So Jordan opened the game by hitting a 17-footer, then added a 20-footer from the top of the key. After another 17-footer from the wing, a 10-foot pull-up, and a 21-footer to beat the 24-second clock, Jordan had 11 first-quarter points, and the Suns trailed by four.

OK, take away the jump shot and make him drive where you can get more defensive help on him. The second quarter begins with a Jordan layup and a foul. Then another layup. Then a dunk. Then another layup. By the time he put down a final dunk with 49.9 seconds left in the quarter, he had scored 22 points in the second period.

Give Michael the jump shot, and he would kill you. Take away the jump shot, give him the drive, and he would hurt you more. Take away both, and you leave John Paxson and B. J. Armstrong open for pitch passes and three-point shots. What to give up and what to take away from Jordan, that was the question. Were there acceptable losses?

"You come out thinking, Should we concentrate on him and worry about concentrating on him too much," said Phoenix coach Paul Westphal. "You had to decide just how much you would concentrate on him and when. But he would always find another way to kill you. You could never be too preoccupied with him. You just had to determine how much you had to concentrate on him. It could be very distressing.

"You can go and say you're not going to let him catch the ball, try to force him to help, make him take tough shots, and hope that he misses. Remember, this was the greatest player of all time. I think he was the greatest point guard offensively and defensively, the greatest shooting guard, the greatest small forward. And he was probably up there in the top five at power forward and center. He was such an unbelievable offensive player, I don't think Michael could have guarded Michael."

The second quarter is when defending Jordan came down to coaching. He usually caught his first rest of the game at the start of the period and had time to formulate adjustments. Also, when he came back, Pippen usually went to the bench, which further limited the Bulls' options. Michael had two choices at the time of the game: He would score from outside, or he would score on the drive. There was never a better time to double-team him. In the fourth quarter, double-teaming came out of desperation on help situations when he beat his man. You could not afford to double Jordan as much in the fourth quarter because he was surrounded by his best personnel at those times and also because he lived for the challenge of those moments.

Charlotte coach Alan Bristow developed a unique attack for this part of the game. "When he was nailing the 15-to-18-foot shot, he was real hard to double. We tried to play him hard when he didn't have the ball. Make him move as much as possible. Take something out of his legs." Bristow's presentation of this attack came after a loss to the Bulls on March 12, 1993. The theory worked to the point where Jordan was so tired, he managed 22 of his 52 points in the third quarter. More times than not, a half spent figuring out how to play Jordan yielded nothing successful.

Third Quarter: The Heat Is On

The third quarter is when many of Jordan's toughest defenders recall seeing him make his best moves. "These were the ones you dreamed about or that you had nightmares about," Ron Harper remembered. "You would see the highlights on ESPN all season. If I wasn't there watching him beat me, I probably would have paid to see him. I remember one move he made on me when I was with the Cavs. Start of the third period he went baseline on two guys. He went up to jump and just kept jumping, kept gliding. When the two guys—I think it was me and Larry Nance—came down, he had passed the rim. It looked like he thought to himself, 'I forgot I had the ball.' So he reached back and slammed it nice."

Harper knew the third quarter was the one time he did not try to match Jordan athletically. That's when Michael asserted his physical strength. He had his defender expecting him to shoot the fadeaway in the post, so he would bump his way in, draw the double-team, and spin to the basket for a layup. That was Michael's third-quarter move. "Had one on me last year (1992) where I got all ball, and he still made a half hook," Ehlo chipped in. "It's still on all the highlight films."

Jordan could make his best moves in the third quarter because he was strongest both mentally and physically at that time. He knew the spots that he could get to and score, and he came off a 15-minute rest. Jordan could never sit down in the locker room during the halftime break. It was as if he was waiting to explode.

"One thing that always worried us was Michael's ability to pick up his game in the middle of the game to a level nobody else had ever been able to pick themselves up to," said Utah coach Jerry Sloan. "He could play to a certain level and be very effective. And then he could go to another level. That's what made him so rare."

Sloan's praise came two weeks after Jordan scored 20 points in the fourth quarter to rescue the Bulls from a 20-point deficit in Salt Lake

City in February 1993. The danger about playing Jordan in the third quarter was that if he was hot, he would only become more dangerous in the fourth quarter.

Fourth Quarter: The Fear of God

It's playing Michael Jordan in the final minutes of a game that forever kept Ehlo awake. There was nothing unexpected about what happened in the fourth quarter. The ball came to Jordan. The Bulls had this set in their renowned triangle offense in which every other player would react to the move that Jordan made. He would set up on the wing and face his defender or try to back him into the post. Either way, he still elicited the same emotions, the same uneasiness from the defense.

"I could be playing with him all game, scoring on him, and maybe getting a stop or two to boost my ego," said the late Reggie Lewis after he and the Boston Celtics lost a mid-January battle to Michael. "You feel like you have a lot of confidence being able to stop him one-on-one. Then, you get to that final position of seeing him with the basketball knowing you have to stop him one-on-one. It was pretty scary the first time and every time after that."

Ehlo remembered the look in Jordan's eyes and the feeling of helplessness. He was in good company. Starks' technique of pushing on Jordan, using his body to keep him from getting to the spot that he felt most comfortable to shoot from, has some success. "And he was the only one who came into that point of the game with the same cockiness I had," Michael said when explaining his 10-for-27 effort in Game 1 of the 1993 Eastern Conference Finals.

Because of the way Jordan usually wasted opponents in the fourth quarter, Kevin Johnson's effort at the end of Game 3 of the 1993 NBA Finals drew serious review. Johnson was pressed to explain how he had forced Jordan into missing 13 of his last 22 shots. This request cast KJ in a situation where he was a professor working on a new experiment: We have a theory about this, but we have yet to prove it.

"You know, nobody ever wanted to guard Michael over and over again," Johnson observed. "To be matched up against him one-on-one was an impossible task for someone to come out victorious. Reality set in during the fourth quarter, and I just reacted. I had watched some game film and figured out where he liked to go. But he was just too fast to know exactly what he was going to do. He just missed a few shots. I didn't do anything."

Jordan could strike so quickly in the fourth quarter because that was when he combined his athleticism and determination into reaction. No more taking what the defense was giving. Find the one move that was working and go right at it so the defender did not have a chance to react. Jordan rarely used pump fakes or hesitation dribbles in the fourth quarter. He would set up in the post, feel the defender, turn, and explode. Indiana's Reggie Miller called Jordan's knack for quick hits in the fourth quarter the "two-minute drill."

The Pacers were hanging in with the Bulls on a January night in 1993 when Miller hit a 14-foot jump shot to tie the score at 86 with 7:53 to play. Thirty-three seconds later Jordan returned to the game. With the Bulls leading 93-90 at the 5:24 mark, he posted up on Miller, turned, and dunked. He posted up again and drew a foul. After the two free throws, he posted up again and hit an eight-foot fadeaway. At the 3:33 mark the Bulls led 99-92 and went on to win 109-100. Miller never scored another point.

"It was hard to win close games when he was around," Miller said afterward. "There's just no way to play him down the stretch, not with one person. And even with two, it's not what you do, it's really him. You can try to limit him, make him do things he's normally not accustomed to doing. Maybe make him pump fake a couple times before he shoots. But if he's having a night, you can't do anything to stop him."

To stop Jordan, defenders had to push on him, bang him, and hope for help—which was only a hit-and-miss proposition. He was the guy everybody else got psyched up to play. He was the guy who only Rolando Blackman had success defending; if success was never holding Jordan to less than 23 points, then Blackman excelled. Blackman also knew the other side of it when Jordan hit 40 or more on him three times. Jeff Malone held Jordan to 16 points on March 11, 1985, by turning him into a human pinball bouncing from one pick to another and wearing him down. But that only happened once.

The lengths opponents went to guarding Michael Jordan became as important a part of his story as his ability to deliver game-winning shots or compete on a plane nobody else could reach. He was, for a time, the game's greatest offensive player as well as its best defensive player. Even semi-serious injuries could not slow him down in the heat of a game.

Although there were so many who marveled at these abilities, a select few had to deal with the trials of such tribulation. Those were the players known as his teammates, the supporting cast. Michael Jordan could exalt them to victory and make them angry for being left out in the cold while he performed his one-man heroics. It was tough to play against Michael Jordan, no doubt. It may have been tougher to play with him.

ELEVEN

Teammates Part I:
The Supporting Cast

May 31, 1993, Chicago Stadium.
The car was running. Juanita and Ahmad and Quinn Buckner were all waiting, and this was going to be the perfect Memorial Day. Scoring 54 points, beating the Knicks to tie the series at 2–2 and proving to everybody there was no shooting slump—that the defense couldn't stop me—righted a lot of wrongs from the past few days. I was about to drive away when Scottie said something that made me put on the brakes.

Since the media created a big controversy about my trip to Atlantic City last week, I stopped talking publicly. That left Scottie to speak up for the team. It's good practice for him because one of these days I'll be gone and he will have to be the guy who spends 45 minutes after every game explaining what's right and wrong. He was talking about my game, and he said something like it's not that we don't want MJ to get points, but it makes it tough for others to get in the game and step up when they have to.

Comments like those make you wonder how your teammates really feel about you. I was always conscious, even worried, about creating jealousy or animosity. But you can't let that stand in the way of winning or succeeding. You hear some of the different comments after a game like this and think, do they really feel that way or are they just saying that? Scott Williams said it was a great day for the Tar Heels; we combined for 55 points. He's a Tar Heel, so you don't worry about how he feels. Pax said I was spectacular, and even Bill called me unreal. Bill hasn't always had the best things to say about me, but I thought we had a kind of mutual respect.

There was always a lot of teasing that went on behind closed doors. I used to kid these guys about how much money they made, and they would make fun of my hair or all the shots I take. My relationship with my teammates always made me feel uneasy. At North Carolina it was easy to be one of the guys, but in Chicago I came in as a high-profile, high-paid rookie and always worried about being thought of as just another teammate.

You probably heard the story of how during preseason my rookie year when we were on the road, I went to see what some of the other guys were doing in the hotel, knocked on somebody's door, and they were in there partying, getting high. That wasn't me, so I walked away. Told them to have a good time. Aside from a couple of guys like Rod or Cliff or Darrell Walker, I never was able to get real close with any of them.

Apparently, they understood how hard life in the spotlight could be. When the Atlantic City thing came up, all my teammates defended me and supported me publicly. But then Scottie said what he did after the game, and Stacey King said something about when I went to the bench with my fifth foul in the game how the fans shouldn't have worried and should have had confidence in the guys on the floor. Maybe they never really accepted having to conform their games to mine. Maybe they didn't believe that I always wanted to get everybody involved on the floor. How did they really feel?

P laying with and being a teammate of Michael Jordan's required adjustments, sacrifices and understanding. If the corporate and political climate of team sports did not create a hierarchical structure among the players, then the NBA's star system certainly did. And what degree of separatism did not result from that, Jordan created with his otherworldly talent and obsessive compulsive competitiveness. Being a teammate of Michael Jordan's meant you had to get out of his way a lot of times. Off the court, you had to endure the constant talk about him and the wait on the team bus until he was ready to leave the arena.

Some Bulls accepted it. John Paxson always remembered Jordan as the guy he made a living off of for so many years. Some Bulls hated it. B. J. Armstrong called Michael just another co-worker. Yeah, right, and the guys in the Continental Congress called Thomas Jefferson just another co-worker. There were good parts to being Michael Jordan's teammate. He led them to championships, public adoration, and financial gain that they may not have otherwise had. There were bad parts to being Michael Jordan's teammate. You had to give up your game to conform to his. You had to give up some of your shots because he was going to take the most. You had to deal with his wrath in practice if you did not play as hard or compete as hard as he did.

Jordan's teammates accepted him, co-existed with him, benefited from him, and justified why it was OK more than they did outright enjoy playing with him. Or at least, that's the way they made it seem. Then Michael picked up and left them after nine years. He said he was like the father sending his kids off to college, which may have done more to explain Jordan's relationship with his teammates than anything else. But as Michael was pulling away from the Berto Center, the Bulls' training facility, after his farewell press conference, Williams followed him out the back door, stood, and waved as he watched Michael drive away. A tear came to his eye, and he spoke in the tone you hear at eulogies. "I just lost one of my best friends," Williams said, his voice cracking.

Sixty-four guys played with Michael Jordan during his NBA career. Three of them were named "Jones." John Paxson was with him the longest, eight years. MJ was a member of seven different starting line-ups that opened the Bulls' season. Some teammates were as renowned as George Gervin, an NBA scoring leader with San Antonio from 1978 to 1980, who played with the Bulls in 1985 and 1986. Some were as obscure as Fred Cofield and Perry Young, who were only with the team long enough for Jordan to dunk over them in practice. Certainly, all of them had mixed emotions about being on the same team with the greatest to ever play the game. Some said it was a godsend. Some said it was God-awful.

Before a game during MJ's final season, John Paxson spread out on the red carpeted floor of the Chicago Bulls dressing room, put an ice pack on each of his perennially ailing knees, and discussed the virtues of playing alongside Michael Jordan. Pax presented himself as a down-to-earth guy even when he was not sitting on the floor, and as often as he spoke about how good Michael had been to him, well, you had to believe for some it was a positive experience. No other player benefited more from Michael than Paxson. The most memorable example of how came in the fourth quarter of Game 5 of the 1991 NBA Finals when Paxson set himself in open spots, waited for Michael to find him, and scored 20 points in the Bulls 108-101 victory.

Paxson's contract expired after that season, so Jordan went public with his plea to Bulls management to re-sign his backcourt mate and even hooked him up with David Falk, who negotiated a million-dollar deal for Paxson. It is indeed fair to say Paxson got rich off playing with Jordan.

No other player may have felt the genuine affection for Jordan that Paxson did. The two never hung out together as Jordan did with other teammates, such as Rod Higgins, Cliff Levingston, or even Pippen. Paxson respected what Jordan went through in life and always wanted to give him breathing room. But the way Paxson revered Jordan revealed that some of his teammates understood the value of playing with Michael.

"I have a place in basketball history because I played alongside the greatest player ever to play the game," Paxson submitted as his blanket statement for describing how he viewed Jordan. "It's almost impossible to describe. I ran out of adjectives a long time ago. Sure, he added years to my career, and I fed off him a lot. So how can I say otherwise about him? But Michael always told me I meant a lot to him. He always told us there would be a time during the game when he would need all of us. If you didn't harbor any jealousy, then playing with Michael wasn't anything but fun. It wasn't easy for some guys, but that's not the way I choose to look at him. He was the greatest. I can say I played in the same backcourt with him, and I know years from now I will be able to call him, have dinner, and talk about anything with him."

Playing with Michael, however, mostly wrought a struggle within his teammates. You wanted to be like Pax—hit the game-winning jump shot off a pass from Michael escaping a double-team—and praise Michael. But it was hard to do because when the great plays happened, no matter who made them, the credit went to Jordan.

Nobody experienced this dichotomy more than Pippen. He was the one Bulls player, perhaps one of the few in the NBA, who had athletic gifts similar to Michael's. Some of his were even better. By 1993, his sixth year in the NBA, Pippen reached certified all-star, if not superstar, status. He led the Bulls in assists and rebounds and was second in scoring and steals that year. But he often heard how much his success resulted from playing with Jordan and that tempered his sentiment.

Pippen, for example, explained during the Bulls' 1993 playoff run, one in which he accounted for several victories in Jordanesque fashion, that there were no disadvantages to playing with Michael. But he never extolled the advantages of having someone to haul in his alley-oop passes and dunk them or to team up with to form the NBA's most feared defensive tandem. Pippen could play Jordan in practice and match him competitively, but Jordan never credited him with being more than a member of his supporting cast. And that did not always wear well with Scottie.

"In the public eye, everybody wants to be the All-American hero," said Pippen while considering the plight of being Jordan's teammate before a playoff game in Cleveland in 1993. "There was always this feeling that success came about because we had Michael. We never were able to achieve a measure of success by receiving success. There was never that feeling, we did well, now everybody gets justice. I was able to step out of Michael's shadow and receive some things, endorsements. But did we ever get the justice just by us having success?"

The more successful the Bulls became, the harder it became for Jordan's teammates. Everywhere they looked, they heard themselves being referred to as his supporting cast. And they heard that from Jordan. Because he could take over a game and demand the ball on every possession down the stretch, he also commanded the credit. After games like these, Horace Grant would be asked about how Jordan came through again. "He was in charge," Grant would say. "He called the plays."

A typical Jordan rescue mission came when he scored 20 fourth-quarter points to bring the Bulls back from a 17-point deficit to defeat Utah in February 1993. Several nights afterward, the comeback still was a popular topic of conversation when B. J. Armstrong was asked about it. Armstrong had scored the team's other 12 points during that 32-point fourth quarter and even hit a three-point shot to give the Bulls a five-point lead in the final minute. But Armstrong was asked about what it was like playing alongside Michael that night.

"I never really thought about what it was like playing opposite Michael Jordan in the backcourt," Armstrong answered in the kind of tone many players used when they felt they were being asked stupid questions. "I didn't look at Michael as so incredible. I looked at him as my teammate, a guy I worked with. I gave him his space and let him do what he had to do. Then I incorporated what I had to do. That's how I looked at it. He's just a guy I played with. I'm trying to get something accomplished. It never entered my mind who he was. You don't just meet someone and they make you a different player. Michael is Michael, B. J. is B. J., and you're just people." Only after Jordan retired did Armstrong form a public friendship with Michael. When the 1993–94 season began, Armstrong would have breakfast with Michael, ask him for advice and defer to his guidance. But that was after he had space and freedom to play his own game without having to tailor to MJ.

Not that it was Michael's doing, but the rest of the Bulls often felt as though they did not matter. The situation never changed even when they figured it should. In Game 3 of the 1993 Eastern Conference Finals, Jordan made one shot in each of the first three quarters and did not take any in the fourth. He made just 3 of 18 field goal attempts, an effort that would normally doom the Bulls. But they won this game 103-83. Afterward, the questions came about Jordan's shooting and then the demands to praise his 11 assists in the game. Finally, Pippen heard enough.

"We're a championship team," he charged. "We're not a championship team with just one great individual. That's not what made us win the last couple of years. Michael knows he has guys like me and Pax and B. J. who can step up."

Did he? Jordan was not talking at the time. And sometimes he did not say the things to make his teammates believe that the Bulls were more than a team of Michael and company. He would stand around at times and praise the play of certain individuals when asked to. But he would also criticize the Bulls reserves for not stepping up and ultimately land on that draining phrase, "supporting cast."

More than two hours before a game one night at the Stadium, Jordan went through some shooting practice. With just a few people watching, he began to imitate the shooting styles of some of his teammates. Observers would yell out "Cartwright," and he would go through the elongated, elbows extended motion that made Bill Cartwright's shot look like a catapult. When he heard "Grant" he went in for a layup. When he heard "Walker," he put up a shot with no rotation, no spin on it. His teammates would look at such exhibitions and wonder if Jordan was not condescending to them. He would challenge them to shooting contests after practice, wager on it, and demand to be paid. This was no way to create a bond with your teammates.

The bond was not there. His scoring outbursts spawned jealousy more than camaraderie. After each one, it seemed one teammate would downplay the magnificence of Jordan's effort. They didn't think his ability to score 50 points was merely a matter of Michael having more ability or athleticism than they did.

"I don't think the guy's a prophet," Armstrong said, after Jordan scored 47 points against Washington on March 20, 1993. "Can he foretell the future? What he has is freedom and opportunity. The rest of us have to wait for the game and figure out where we fit in. But he has the freedom to pick and choose. I don't know what's so amazing about it. We've all done it in our careers. Him being Michael is more amplified. But to be honest with you, I don't even look at him as anything special."

Because every member of the championship Bulls came to the organization after Michael, they had to conform to his style of play. Much of that approach was generated during Jordan's first three years, when he did not have a lot of talent around him and dominated the ball so much because he felt that was the only way to win. As other players improved, he began to have faith in them and give them an opportunity to shoot the ball, score, and excel.

But during his entire career, you excelled only if Michael let you. Trent Tucker was an established scorer, a 10-year veteran, and one of the league's best shooters when he came to the Bulls in 1993. He never expressed anything but admiration for Jordan's abilities. But he also recognized the cold, hard fact of playing with Jordan. "It was an adjustment to learn to play with him because you had to produce when he gave you the ball," Tucker said. "If you didn't you had to deal with the reality that he might not give it to you again."

Teammates had to play up to Jordan's level. He demanded that. But nobody else could. Bulls assistant coach Johnny Bach observed that Jordan only demanded that his teammates be competitive. That is what Michael loved. But Bach also decribed Jordan as an attacker, a destroyer, especially in practice. That is what Bach felt separated Jordan from the other superstars in the game. Nobody else had that, and that is what Jordan's teammates suffered from.

"Guys used to come in, and it was weird," said Will Perdue, who played with Jordan for five years. "You didn't realize what you were getting into. From what I learned, all he wanted you to do was play hard. If you came out, played hard, gave it 100 percent, and he knew that, he appreciated you. But if you came out and didn't try, he would get mad at you. He did that to me. But every player did that. But when he did that, everybody took notice. Like oh, Michael is disappointed the team is not playing well or this or that. I could have said it and nobody would have cared. But he said it, and it was emphasized."

When Michael Jordan wanted to get the guys on the team together outside the arena of basketball, most of them usually jumped. Once, after a Friday night home game during the winter of 1993, he led a big car rally to a local restaurant. Or on the road, he would invite the team up to his suite to watch the Knicks play the Hornets in the playoffs. Most of the consorting Michael did with his teammates, however, came in the locker room before games, on the team bus going to and from games, and on the team plane flying to games.

None of his teammates ever blamed Jordan for being a separatist, even if he did choose to sit at the end of the bench whenever he was not playing. They may not have accepted life with Michael, but they understood the lifestyle. When Pippen was asked if he should be considered an equal to Jordan on the court or elsewhere, he replied, "No, I still want to be able to go out in public."

The rest of the Bulls could not befriend Jordan because that meant staying in a hotel room all day playing cards. And he had his own friends travel to away games for that. So while the prevailing emotion may have been jealousy, that was on the court. Off the court, his teammates felt sympathy.

When Jordan was subjected to a media roasting after his trip to Atlantic City the day between Games 1 and 2 of the Eastern Conference Finals, his teammates had never been more of a supporting cast. Tucker asked the media to give Jordan a chance to lead a normal life. "The guy cannot even walk through a shopping mall," Armstrong said. "Give him a chance to do something to break up the routine." Additional comments made Jordan realize that his teammates may not always have liked being a supporting cast but that they understood and supported him.

There would always be questions about whether Jordan's presence created a double standard between him and his teammates; about whether he was really a leader; about whether he made them better players as Magic and Bird had done for their teammates; and about why they struggled to win without him. But that's what it was like, playing alongside Michael Jordan.

TWELVE

Teammates Part II:
Internal Affairs

*F*ebruary 12, 1993, Highland Park, *Illinois.* Missing a game was never easy, but not just for the obvious reasons. Certain games you look forward to more than others and tonight's against the Knicks was going to be the toughest challenge of this season so far. Even injury couldn't have kept me out of this one, not that it ever could.

Only the NBA.

Looking back, I should have been ejected in that game at Indiana the other night for punching Reggie Miller. But the refs missed the call, so the NBA suspended me to prove there is no double standard, that I don't get treated differently than anybody else in the league. They proved the whole double standard thing by suspending me a day's pay and fining me $10,000. Reggie lost $6,000 on

148

the deal. I lost $58,000. That's a double standard as far as I'm concerned. Some of my teammates would also say I get preferential treatment, but that's not the only issue here.

The problem is, I can't do anything about the situation sitting here watching the game in my living room. Not the Knicks, but all those same questions that come up whenever I miss a game. My teammates will have to deal with how they can never win without me. It's always hardest on Scottie, because everybody expects him to step up and be me. What nobody realized is that I had him to take some of the pressure off me. So if he plays my role, who will play his? And that question of whether the other 11 guys can step up and win without Michael makes it seem like they're not as important to the team as I am.

That's what everybody looks at when I miss a game. Can they win without me? They should have beat the Knicks tonight. If it hadn't been for a bad goaltending call on Scott Williams in the second half, they probably would have. I was up and screaming on that one. Losing by six points to the team challenging us for first place isn't bad, but the public perception is that they can't win without Michael.

Why doesn't anybody ask why or what it is I contribute that makes a difference? I bet nobody would ever say they miss my leadership or my ability to make my teammates better.

The more he excelled individually, the more Michael Jordan struggled to be the ideal teammate. He always said the other players had to want to step up with or without him in the lineup. But he was blamed so many times when they did not.

Michael could be sitting at home watching them play or sitting in a hospital bed watching them blow a 20-point lead and lose to San Antonio in overtime and still have to be the one to answer for why the Bulls could not win when he did not play. Michael demanded that his teammates answer for themselves, yet he had to be there to answer when they did not.

Maybe it was more interesting for his teammates to find fault with Jordan than it was to continually accentuate his magnificence. But for all his game-winning shots, scoring titles, and MVP awards, Michael Jordan's leadership abilities remained in question as long as he played the game. For all the games and championships the Bulls won with him, he never was accorded definitive status as one of those players who made his teammates better.

Instead, being a teammate of Michael Jordan's meant succumbing to a double standard that accorded him things the rest of the Bulls could not get. And it meant facing constant scrutiny of why you were never as successful without him as you were with him.

The questions about whether Michael was treated differently, whether he made his teammates better, whether they could ever win without him were constant distractions for a team that won three straight championships. These issues hung over the Bulls and Jordan like a dark cloud, threatening the reign. These were the circumstances that separated Jordan from his teammates more than any of his individual accomplishments or abilities. These were the arguments constantly rehashed when Jordan came under ridicule as something less than a team player.

Jordan never did anything to diminish the feeling among his teammates that a double standard existed. If anything, he took advantage in small ways, but ways that irritated his teammates like a basketball shoe that did not fit right and rubbed against the skin. And the more he did it, the more the rest of the Bulls perceived Jordan as selfish or superior.

Jordan's shooting form was as fundamentally perfect as any player's in the history of the NBA.

"I always wore a new pair of Nikes for every game."

Michael always enjoyed sneaking up from behind and trying to steal the ball from players, especially former college teammates like Sam Perkins of Seattle.

Even when he was not speaking to the media during the 1993 playoffs, Michael always had time for an interview with close friend Ahmad Rashad, an NBC commentator.

Michael wasn't always patient with teammates like Stacey King. Sometimes, that inspired jealousy and animosity on their part.

Never were the cheers louder at Chicago Stadium than when the lights went out and Michael was introduced before the start of every Bulls home game.

"I was never known to argue with officials, but I stood up for myself when I thought I didn't get a call."

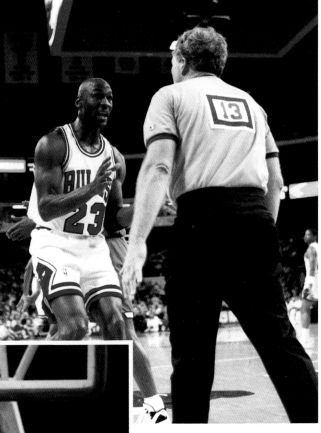

"Jeff Malone, #23 (*right*), guarded me better than just about anybody else I played against."

"There were guys like Seattle's Gary Payton who I would play against for the first time and tell them, 'You've seen me on TV. Now, you're going to see me for real.'"

The New York Knicks tried every tactic they could think of to slow down Michael during the 1992 and 1993 playoffs.

Michael looks out at a crowd of more than 1 million Bulls fans during the 1993 championship celebrations at Chicago's Grant Park.

"The great thing about golf was that it presented a new challenge with every hole."

"I was more nervous playing golf with Arnold Palmer than I was during any game."

As soon as he pulled his car into the Chicago Stadium parking lot before a home game, Jordan was met by a flock of security guards who escorted him to the Bulls lockerroom. He needed the same treatment to make it back to his car.

A media horde followed Michael wherever he went during his final years in the NBA. But more than 500 reporters from around the world attended the retirement press conference on October 7, 1993.

After talking it over with Juanita (*right*), Bulls owner Jerry Reinsdorf (*left*), and teammates (*rear*), Michael said at his 1993 retirement press conference that pro basketball didn't hold any more challenges for him.

Air Jordan

The incidents were not ones that his teammates complained about specifically. If they made an issue over Jordan being allowed to park his car under the stadium while the rest of them had to park outside, they would be thought of as petty. They would have been thought of similarly if they had complained that Jordan was always able to round up as many tickets as he needed to a game whether it was at home or on the road. During the 1992 NBA Finals, Jordan said that he was using up to 50 extra tickets per home game. If Bulls chairman Jerry Reinsdorf had asked ticket manager Joe O'Neil for 10 extra tickets, O'Neil admitted, he would have told him, "That would be hard to get." Jordan got his tickets. When the Bulls played at New York in the 1993 Eastern Conference Finals, Jordan was short on tickets because he had so many members of his family there. With no tickets available, the NBA and the Knicks granted him VIP and media credentials to get them all in the building.

Even if the Bulls could not live with most of the attention accorded to Jordan, they learned to laugh at the disparity it caused. Scottie Pippen and Horace Grant never hid their jealousy over a headline like the one that appeared in the newspaper December 1, 1990. Pippen had 19 points and 15 assists while Grant added 14 points and 9 rebounds in a 124-95 drubbing of Indiana. Jordan scored 20 of his 37 points in the first quarter. The headline read "Jordan's Act 1 Does It for Bulls." "Talk to Michael," Grant muttered after practice the next day. "He gets all the credit anyway." John Paxson realized he had to accept the difference in status. During the spring of 1991, Paxson related how the league perpetuated the double standard. "We get a speech at the start of the season from the head of referees [Darrell Garretson]. He tells us if Michael Jordan and John Paxson are double-teaming a player and there's a foul on Michael Jordan, it'll go to John Paxson. We're in the entertainment business."

But Jordan figured that the double standard worked both ways. After he and Reggie Miller squared off in a fight on February 10, 1993, that was a bad parody of Sunday morning wrestling matches, Jordan complained that he was a victim of the double standard. Miller, who clearly took more shots than he delivered in the brawl, was ejected from the game while Jordan stayed, played, and scored 40 in a Bulls victory. The NBA reviewed film of the fight, which became a standard practice long before Jordan and Miller battled, and ruled that the game officials made a mistake in not ejecting Jordan. He was suspended without pay for the next game, two nights later at home against the Knicks, and fined an additional $10,000. With a $48,000 per-game salary, Michael dropped $58,000 on the fight.

After the game in Indianapolis, Miller moaned about his ejection and charged that Jordan's being allowed to stay in the game came down to money. "If Michael Jordan is ejected, everybody loses money," Miller said. "The ballboys lose money, the vendors lose money, television loses money, the scalpers lose money, the league loses money. Let's face it, Michael Jordan runs the league."

In order to prove there was no double standard, the NBA would have to suspend and fine Jordan. At least that is the way he figured. "All the double-standard talk led them to be pretty harsh," he explained. "I knew the league was going to be hard on me. After the fight they said I was suspended for landing a punch, but if I had thrown a punch that missed I wouldn't have been suspended. That was very strange. I think it all goes back to the double-standard talk."

Jordan also felt the hierarchical structure of the team made him a victim of a double standard. After an overtime loss to Orlando in January 1993, he was the only member of the team talking about the loss. Other players made mistakes that led to the defeat, or so he said, but 45 minutes after the game he was the only one in the Bulls locker room talking to the media. Jordan said afterward that one of these days he was going to walk out and let his teammates speak for themselves.

The way Michael saw it, his success and his abilities placed superior expectations on him. He had to speak up for the team. He had to take blame for the failures. And he had to be sure to pass the credit around when the Bulls won. Otherwise he worried he would be accused of being selfish or superior. His teammates did not exactly see it that way.

When Jordan failed to accompany the team to the White House to meet President George Bush after the Bulls won their first championship in 1991, he was not greeted with understanding. That was two days before training camp for the 1991–92 season opened, and Jordan also showed up an hour and 45 minutes late for the first official session known as Media Day, a time reserved exclusively for reporters and photographers to conduct interviews and take pictures. When no reprimands came down from the Bulls' front office, that inflamed the double standard feeling among his teammates.

"If any of the other guys had missed (Media Day), we would have caught flak from the organization," Horace Grant charged. "There was a double standard between Michael and everybody else since I became part of the team. Other guys felt the same way. I had an appearance scheduled the day we went to the White House, but someone in the Bulls' organization canceled it for me. They could have done that for him. He was a spectacular player, probably the best in the league. But I thought that double standard always threatened to destroy the team."

Over the course of time, the rest of the Bulls learned to accept the double standard. Grant continued to battle it. During training camp for the 92–93 season, Phil Jackson allowed Jordan and Scottie Pippen to miss some of the early practices while recuperating from their summer playing in the Olympics. Jordan spent the time filming commercials and meeting some of the endorsement obligations that the Olympics did not allow him time to fulfill. During this period, Grant felt that he had to work twice as hard during the daily double practice sessions. One day he stormed out of practice mumbling about why Jordan and Pippen should get time off when he thought he was important to the team too.

"Nobody ever wanted to admit it, but Michael and the other stars received preferential treatment," Bulls center Will Perdue observed. "After a while, we had to learn it was a way of life. There were privileges given to him and not given to others. But what were we going to do about it? You deal with it like it's nothing out of the ordinary."

"I always tried to operate fairly and claimed there was no double standard," said Doug Collins of the time he coached the Bulls. "But guys always knew that when it came to Michael, we had to take certain steps to alleviate some problems. We had a different level of standards. When we checked into a hotel, we got him to his room first to avoid the mob scene. But you know it worked both ways. Michael could never come out before a game and shoot because he would get mobbed. He could not even hang out during open locker room periods before games because he would get mobbed."

Double standards, 50-point games, the constant reminder that Michael carries the Bulls to victory—all of these overshadowed

Jordan's ability to lead his teammates and make them better players in the same vein that Magic Johnson made James Worthy a star or Larry Bird enabled Kevin McHale to become the NBA's most devious low-post scorer. Overshadow? Vendela overshadowed Joe Montana when she was on the cover of *Sports Illustrated's* swimsuit issue. Jordan's propensity to win games on his own made his leadership seem non-existent or unnecessary.

Because of a white linen screen—what some people used to refer to as the Bull Sheet—that Phil Jackson placed in front of the media-room window, very few people ever had the chance to see what transpired at practice. This is where Jordan did his leading by example. He would go at Pippen in a scrimmage and do everything possible to beat Scottie. He never wanted to lose at practice, and Perdue said remembering those incidents helped him get his competitive spirit going at game time.

For the most part, Jordan's attempts to lead were subtle and spontaneous. During a game at San Antonio in February 1993, the Bulls faced a double-digit deficit at the start of the fourth quarter. Jordan huddled Grant, Pippen, Armstrong, and Scott Williams around him and told his teammates to get it in gear and play open-court, running basketball. The Bulls had a chance to tie the game in the final 20 seconds, but Jordan missed the shot.

Jordan, however, was never known as a vocal leader. "I saw him walk over to Scott Williams and really go out of his way to help him," observed Johnny Bach, the one who paid more attention to the things Jordan did in this realm. "He was never a Salvation Army worker, the guy who was going to solve everyone's problems or fix everything in the world. He picked the times that were important.

"I remember times when he would lead by indirection. With a single word or a look, in his case. There were times when I saw him look across the dressing room at someone who he thought was taking a night off. That look coming from a guy who never took a night off would get you going."

Jordan had a side to his personality that could really touch his teammates. When the Bulls lost Game 5 of the 1993 Finals at home, a game in which everybody but Jordan came up with a substandard effort, he absorbed the pressure and alleviated the misery. He defended Grant, who had but two points on the night. As a result of the loss, the Bulls had to go back to Phoenix to try to close out the series. Jordan boarded the team plane the next day wearing a straw hat, sunglasses, blazing away on a big cigar. "Everybody looked at him like he was crazy," said Johnny "Red" Kerr, who was on the flight. "He said, 'How you doing, world champs? Just getting started on the victory celebration we should have had the other night.' That really got everybody going. The whole flight there was a feeling like no way we were going to lose."

"I was never one of those vocal, rah-rah type of guys," Jordan mused earlier that season. "I may have given some vocal leadership here and there. But that rah-rah stuff was immature to a certain extent. I was not the person to do that. I tried to inspire the guys to have some sense of motivation. It was tough to find a certain driving force for these guys to focus in on. I had one from a personal standpoint—to win that third straight championship and go one better than Magic and Bird. But my role as leader was to help them find different types of challenges, keep them hungry, not complacent with what we achieved."

This was how Michael Jordan made his teammates better. He took on entire teams of defenders and delivered victories. The problem was there were nights when he could be Magic-like or Bird-like.

Every one of those nights seems to carry an explanation of how Jordan was reluctant or even unwilling to pass the ball and the glory on to a teammate. Perhaps the most famous of those nights was June 12, 1991, the fifth and final game of the NBA Finals. That was the night Jordan set up John Paxson for his fourth-quarter shooting flurry, which lifted the Bulls to the 108-101 win over the Lakers. Six months later, the story that made the rounds depicted Jordan as the heavy and Jackson asking angrily during fourth-quarter time outs, "MJ, who's open?" Jackson berated Jordan several times before Michael finally gave in and admitted, "Pax" was open. The same scenario seemed to plague Michael after he shot 3-for-18 in the playoff win over New York in 1993. Afterward, Jackson said he had to remind Jordan 10 assists were as good as 30 points. But when Michael went out the next game and scored 54 points, it presented another one of those cases in which his determination to be the star overshadowed his leadership ability.

"Michael was a player whose presence made his teammates better,"

Magic Johnson explained during the long discourse comparing Bird and Jordan to himself. "I had to move the ball around to do that, but I also had more weapons than Michael ever did. So did Larry. But when you got Michael Jordan on your team, you develop your game because everybody was always paying attention to him. That's how Scottie became such a good player. And John Paxson. I doubt he ever would have stayed in the league as long without Michael Jordan. There's more to that than the eye can see. They had to understand that when Michael was dominating, their best move was to get out of the way. That probably caused his teammates some problems. But did they realize that if you took Michael Jordan away from that team, you had just a lot of average players."

Take away Michael Jordan from the Chicago Bulls and what do you have? The question really incited animosity among his teammates. John Paxson called it a silly argument, pointing out that if you did take away Michael there would be another scorer in his place. "I'm not knocking Michael's greatness," Pax continued, "but we've only played without him a handful of games." Funny thing is, Paxson expressed such feelings when he was making a case for Jordan being the most valuable player in the NBA when he did not win the award in 1993.

After Jordan missed 64 games with a broken foot during the 1985-86 season, the Bulls played seven times without him the rest of his career. They won once, that coming in 1993 with a 125-97 whipping of the Dallas Mavericks, a team that would have struggled to get an NCAA tournament bid that year. Michael missed that game with a foot infection and also missed the following game against San Antonio. The Bulls missed 21 of their last 30 shots. Trent Tucker had a shot to win the game with four seconds left in the fourth quarter but missed. The question that the team had to face afterward was, What would have happened if Michael had been there to take that shot? Pippen, who scored 39 points and added 13 rebounds and 10 assists for his 11th career triple-double in the game, was so enraged about having to answer such a question that he posted a sign above his locker that read in big, black letters "NO COMMENT." He grabbed his clothes and dressed in the training room where nobody could get to him.

Four days later, Pippen was still riled. He asked why nobody wanted to know how they won without Michael. "You guys probably think it was just Dallas. It was nothing. And when we lose without Michael, that's the way you see it in the paper. It should just be 'The Bulls lost.' You never get that stuff, 'The Bulls lose with Michael.' It's not fair. It's not right."

The Bulls first regular-season game with Jordan gone forever came on November 5, 1993, against the Charlotte Hornets, a team many picked to supplant Chicago as the Eastern Conference champion. B. J. Armstrong scored 28 points that night; Pippen had 20. Horace Grant added 22, including a last-second tip in of a missed shot that gave the Bulls a 124–123 overtime win. Grant showed more emotion that night than he did after blocking Kevin Johnson's last-second, potential game-winning shot in Game 6 of the 1993 Finals the previous June. "It was one of the sweetest victories ever because we didn't have No. 23 out there," Grant said the next day. "We didn't have a go-to guy. We were all go-to guys. We finally had a chance to show ourselves."

Grant's reaction seemed to echo the team sentiment. Michael Jordan was bigger than the team, and that was something they fought as long as he was around. The Bulls as a unit did not blame Jordan for all of it. They recognized that he was more talented and that certain distinctions came with that. But could he have said some things to diffuse some of the negativism aimed at them? What did Michael Jordan have to say about his teammates, anyway?

THIRTEEN

Jordan's Rule

April 12, 1993, The Palace of Auburn Hills. These were the kind of games that used to make me wonder what the hell my teammates were thinking. It made me question whether they were ever going to be winners, whether they wanted to be winners. We were up 19 on Detroit early in the third quarter. Horace was playing out of his mind. He was boxing Rodman off the boards and scoring at the other end. Trent was spotting up for three's, and even Stacey hit a 10-footer when I found him open on the baseline. We were up 15 at halftime.

But the Pistons came back with like 20 straight points. Phil called a time-out, we came to the bench, and I wouldn't talk to anybody. Just kind of stared at them all with that not-this-shit-again look.

This is why I had such a hard time with my teammates. It

seemed like they never wanted to win quite as bad as I did or work as hard. They probably did, but I never always felt that way.

I used to tell Doug Collins when he was thinking of adding a player to the team to check and see how competitive he was. It was hard to deal with a guy who wasn't competitive. I was always testing that aspect of my teammates' character on and off the court. You pick on them to see if they will stand up. If they don't take it, you know you can trust them to come through when the pressure is on in the game. Maybe because of that feeling I had, they perceived me as being better than they were.

When you want to win so bad, the one thing you rely on your teammates for is not to fold in crunch time. If they did, they were liable to hear from me about it. During the first couple years, I got into this pattern where the only one I could rely on to come through with the game on the line was me.

And here it was happening again . . . against the Pistons. Scottie and Horace were getting called for offensive fouls, Cartwright dropped the ball and nobody could keep Rodman from getting any rebound he wanted. They scored the last eight points of the third quarter, and we're down by one, and I'm thinking, If I don't do something fast, who will? Then Stacey King, a guy I figured could never do anything to help us win a ball game, scored six straight points.

I remember those plays because I was sitting on the bench at the time. I didn't always pay much attention to what the team was doing when I was out because I was just trying to get my rest and get ready to go back in. That's why I would always sit at the end of the bench. When my teammates came back against Portland in the last game of the Finals that year, it made me realize they were capable of coming through with the game on the line.

JORDAN
159

Stacey put us ahead by five with his seventh straight point, and I'm ready to come back. I know my teammates are going to be looking for me to score, but Stacey has a good thing going and I don't want to break up his rhythm. For some reason, everything seems to stop. Suddenly we're down two when Dumars gives me an opening for a layup. Stacey hits two more free throws, B. J. hits a jump shot, but Dumars comes back with a three. The game is going down to the wire, and I figured it would be in my hands. But with 4.2 seconds left, we're leading by one and Stacey gets fouled. They call time out, then Stacey nails both foul shots. After that I just had to go up to him and pat him on the head and tell him how proud I was. We were both so fired up coming off the court we couldn't even sit down.

Moments like that with my teammates were rare. When I left the game, I realized I really loved each one of those guys. But aside from pointing my finger at Scottie to say nice pass after he threw me a lob for a dunk, we didn't share a lot of celebration or whatever. I wonder if they knew how I felt about them. With all the publicity about how I was selfish or felt superior, I wonder if anybody really knew.

After the Bulls 98-95 victory over Detroit at the Palace in which Stacey King supported Michael Jordan's team-high 23 points with 17 of his own, reporters hovered over Michael as he provided his account of the game. The visitors' locker room in Detroit is split into two sections separated by a shower room. On one side, Jordan, Pippen, and Grant dressed. The rest of the team used the other side. Weaving around to find King was a chance to let the 6-foot-10-inch forward know Jordan was on the other side explaining King's heroic efforts.

"Really?" King said more inquisitively than sarcastically. "What did he say?" Well, Stacey, he said you were the reason the Bulls won tonight and that's how guys should respond in those situations and how proud he was of you for hitting those two free throws. By the way, what did Michael say to you after you hit those two foul shots? "Same thing," King answered.

Those reporters standing around King did not know whether to laugh or be stunned. Michael Jordan never really praised his teammates, especially not publicly. He complimented them, described what he felt each of them could do to help the team, and credited them when they complied with those roles.

But many times he came forth with comments like the one that lingered after the Bulls win at Indianapolis two nights before the win over Detroit. B. J. Armstrong was a shooting star in that victory. He hit his first five shots of the game and scored eight straight points in the first quarter. Jordan, in the meantime, struggled with his shooting and more or less watched as Armstrong kept the Bulls within three points through one period. Armstrong led the second-quarter assault that put the Bulls ahead by three with Jordan on the bench, then hit a three-point shot to start the third quarter. Armstrong added seven points to Jordan's 10 in the fourth quarter, when the Bulls held on for a 92-87 triumph. But Armstrong scored four of the team's last five points, and the rest of the Bulls circled him as they walked off the court at Market Square Arena.

Earlier in the season, Jordan had criticized Armstrong's play as the team's new starting point guard. He felt John Paxson, who had been the starter the past five years, complemented his game more. Now, after Armstrong scored 27 points, one short of his career high, to lead the team, Jordan was asked about his play.

"B. J. was very helpful to the team tonight," he said. Very helpful. Help like that usually only comes after dialing 911.

That was Michael's way with his teammates. After not having faith in them for so many years, he struggled to build relationships with them. Some, he could actually hang out with. Cliff Levingston became a good friend because he would play pool and cards and be someone who could help Michael fulfill his insatiable need to compete. Many times Jordan would make comments like the one he made about Armstrong after the Indiana game and be perceived as critical of his teammates. Many times he was. And many times Michael Jordan could sit by his locker, talking about his teammates in a solemn tone that suggested a quiet respect and even admiration for the guys he played with.

John Paxson explained why relationships between teammates could be tough to build in the NBA. "You have time on the road together, but that is often time you want to take to get some rest and relax. When you're home you want to get away from it all and spend time with your family."

When Michael Jordan was on the road with the Bulls, he lived a most restrictive life. He could not leave his hotel room without drawing a crowd, so except for going to practice or to the golf course on off-days in warm cities, he never left his room. As a result it was hard for Jordan to find time to spend with his teammates away from the game. He tried to build his bonds on the court, but because of his exceptionally high demand for success this was not the easiest place to get to know Michael either.

Still, Jordan broke his on-the-court seclusion enough times to let observers know that these guys meant something to him or that he felt something for them. And Michael's expressions stunned like the surprise twist in the movie *The Crying Game*.

One of these unexpected moments occurred during a home game against New Jersey in December 1992. Jordan never went out of his way to pay homage to Bill Cartwright. The Bulls co-captains often walked to center court to meet with the officials before games without saying a word to each other. Before games, Cartwright was one of the few Bulls who lounged in the locker room with reporters. Most of the players stayed in the training room, which was off limits to the press. Now, Cartwright was not a player who had a lot to say to reporters before or after games. So most people covering the Bulls figured Cartwright hung out in the locker room because he did not want to be in the same room with Jordan.

But during the third quarter of a night when New Jersey was hanging tough, Jordan had the ball at the top of the key when Cartwright moved into an opening at the foul line. This was a standard play in the Bulls triple-post offense, designed to free players up to shoot when they made sharp cuts without the ball. But Jordan rarely gave up the ball to Cartwright in this alignment. Except for this time.

He passed to Cartwright and faked movement one way to fool New Jersey's Drazen Petrovic, who was guarding him. Then Jordan darted back toward the basket when Cartwright dropped a no-look bounce pass that hit Jordan in stride to the hoop. He picked the ball off one bounce, laid it in, and drew a foul on the Nets' Sam Bowie who tried to help out on defense. The eventual three-point play made the score 87-80 and more or less was the turning point in the Bulls 95-89 triumph.

After he scored the basket, on his way to the foul line, Jordan made eye contact with Cartwright, extended his arm with a closed fist that Cartwright in turn bumped with his fist. The two shared a moment of warmth perhaps only soldiers who had been through battle could relate to. You wonder what Jordan was feeling at this moment.

"Bill was a unique pro, very quiet in a sense, and I respected how much everybody else respected him," Jordan noted. "He went out, he did his job, he led by his actions. Which was something I liked to do. He was our quiet leader. A lot of his statements came through emotions, with actions. Very few pros in the league could do that. It was like he was from a different era but could compete in this era. He was also a very cerebral type of player, and I admired all those qualities."

Otherwise, Jordan formed big-brother relationships with some of his teammates. Because of his increasingly receding hairline, some of the Bulls players teasingly called Michael "Pops." And in a way he wanted to be a father figure, a guy who could make everything seem all right and not by merely delivering the game-winning shot. Horace Grant used to find himself sharing these kinds of moments with Michael. When Phil Jackson would berate Grant during time-out situations because things were not going well, as he often did, Jordan would come up to Grant and say, "I'll take care of it, Horace." Then he would shoot Jackson one of his in-the-heat-of-battle, pissed-off looks. Another time, the Bulls were in the process of closing out a rout of Cleveland at the Stadium when Cavaliers forward Jerome Lane tried to lure Grant into some pushing and shoving under the basket. Lane tried to bully Grant by bumping him with his chest sticking out, as if to say, "You want some of this?" Grant stood up when Michael said, "No, Horace." Grant continued to mince words with Lane when the two were lined up across from each other on the free-throw lane waiting for the Cavs' Craig Ehlo to shoot a foul shot. Jordan put his hand up and said, "I got this one, Horace." After the missed free throw went out of bounds off the Bulls, Lane caught the inbounds pass. Jordan hounded him on one side, then as Lane turned away Jordan circled him, stole the ball and threw an outlet pass to Grant, who had the last word in the form of a dunk.

Michael always said that he had this teammates-come-and-go philosophy. In the upwardly mobile NBA, teams stick with five or six core players—eight or nine if you have a championship club. During the Bulls title years, three players changed each season. Michael said the new blood kept him going because he wanted each new player to feel what it was like to win and be a champion. After the Bulls clinched their third straight title in Phoenix, the made-for-television postgame celebration was underway with all 12 players in uniform and coaches up on a makeshift stage in the locker room tipping champagne all over NBC sportscaster Bob Costas. Jordan realized something was missing.

"He saw that Corey Williams wasn't up there," Jerry Krause explained. "Corey Williams was a rookie, a guy who was on the injured list and didn't play in the playoffs. But Michael knew he contributed and he wanted him up there for the celebration. So he called him up there. That's the kind of teammate Michael Jordan was."

When Jordan picked on one of his teammates, it was his way of expressing the ties that bind. After Michael overcame his excruciatingly painful wrist episode in Game 3 of the 1993 Eastern Conference Semifinals at Cleveland, he explained how the injury affected his jump shot. "Only for the first half," he began. "But I figured if Darrell Walker could make it 10 years in the NBA without a jump shot, I could make it one half."

Cartwright and Grant were often the objects of similar affection. The Bulls were getting ready to begin play in the 1993 playoffs when Cartwright, who sat out 19 games resting his back, saw only a few minutes of action in a blowout of Philadelphia. Jordan did not hesitate. "Yeah, I'm surprised he didn't play too much. I figured he needed to get out there and sweat off some of that gut he built up."

As the conversation continued and Jordan was asked what role Cartwright would play in the upcoming playoffs, he responded, "Don't you guys know this is what we've been saving him for."

Another night during the 1993 season, a fan named Don Calhoun came out of the stands at Chicago Stadium to participate in what was known as the "Million Dollar Shot" promotion. Standing at the foul line, he threw up a 75-foot shot into the far basket and won $1 million. After the shot went down, the Bulls broke their time-out huddle to mob Calhoun. Michael hugged him like he had just had a game-winning shot—a one-in-a-million reaction from MJ. When asked about the feat after the game, Jordan joked, "That guy made more on that one shot than Horace Grant makes for a whole year."

Over the long haul, the one guy Jordan prided himself in defending, the one guy he praised more than any other, the one teammate he considered to be a peer was Scottie Pippen. Pippen often caught the fans' and the media's wrath for, more than anything else, not being Jordan. Pippen went through two games at the end of the 1993 season when he made six of 23 field goal attempts. But the game before that he hit a three-point shot at the buzzer in an 88-87 victory at Atlanta. That came at the end of a five-game road trip. When the Bulls returned to Chicago, Jordan read the newspapers and vented the kind of feelings that usually well up only in support of a true friend.

"I wish everybody would realize that if Scottie had never stepped up, we wouldn't have won two championships," Jordan asserted. "You can't win with everything riding on one star. Here was the guy I had been looking for, the one I could have faith in. He took the pressure off me, he was so competitive defensively. I'm proud of the guy, the way he responded to all the people who said he would never be able to step up."

Pippen knew how to be Tonto, Lou Gehrig, or Ed McMahon to Jordan's Ruthian abilities. He never seemed to want Jordan's limelight or to be the guy who had to score like Mike. Those were the kind of teammates that Jordan wanted—guys who knew when to step up and knew when to stand aside. But it was tough water to tread for the supporting cast. With the exception of Pippen, if you tried to step up too much and be successful you were not being very helpful to the team, according to Jordan. If you did not step up when you were needed, you were not contributing. That is the way it came out in public.

Paxson became a successful teammate of Jordan's because he knew how to stay atop that balance beam. "I never needed the ball that much," was Paxson's company line. Translated it meant, "I knew to go to the corners and wait for Michael to find me if he needed me."

For Jordan, a near-perfect execution of his team concept came during his final game. The Bulls led the Phoenix Suns 87-79 going into the fourth quarter of Game 6 of the 1993 NBA Finals, when fatigue seemed to set in. The Bulls could not make any shots or play any defense, and the Suns scrambled to tie the game at 88 with 5:34 to play when Charles Barkley lumbered to the basket for a layup. Jordan ripped off the next nine Bulls points, all of which helped the Bulls maintain a two-to-four-point deficit. His last basket, which came after rebounding a Barkley miss and racing the length of the court to lay the ball in from high above the rim, cut the Suns lead to 98-96. Pippen then rebounded a missed shot by Dan Majerle with 14.1 seconds left, and the Bulls called time-out to set up a final shot for Jordan.

MJ took possession of the ball and passed off to Pippen. The play was designed for Michael to get the ball back. But Jordan was not open, so Pippen looked to score. He spotted Grant open under the basket. Grant had missed all five of his shots so far, including blowing an open layup moments earlier. So Grant passed off to an open Paxson, who nailed a three-point shot with 3.9 seconds left. The Suns had one last chance, but Grant blocked Kevin Johnson's shot as it left his hands. By the time Jordan made it to the postgame press conference he was in a frame of mind only winning and a few sips of champagne could induce. He was all over his teammates.

"Pax, I love Pax," he screamed. "I love Horace. We established so much faith in each other as a team that we never gave up. We always believed in each other's ability to get where we are. That's the sign of a great team."

What made it so difficult on his teammates is that such a reaction came out of Jordan but once a year. For three years. He was much more free-flowing with his frustration. He relished opportunities to come through in the closing moments like a dying man needed oxygen. But he hated to be forced into those situations or to put it more succinctly, Jordan hated to be left holding the ball.

He did not like situations like the opening night of the 1992–93 season. The Bulls had just come back from a 22-point deficit, trailed Atlanta by one point with 18.2 seconds to play, and had possession of the ball. Jordan tried to free himself to get the inbounds pass but got stuck in a triple-teaming defense. So he ran to the right side of the floor and tried to take the defender with him, hoping that would free Pippen for a shot. Pippen caught the inbounds pass and gave the ball to Jordan, who frantically dribbled onto the corner. No rescue came from the double-team. He was forced to try a game-winning shot that was blocked from behind as time ran out.

Those situations irritated Jordan. It left him with a hardened outlook on his teammates. "There I am, not in great shape, and the ball shouldn't have continued to pop in my hands," Jordan snapped. "Everyone should have been able to shoot the ball in those situations, not just me. Certainly the offense wasn't designed that way. I had a good memory for situations like that, though. You get in certain situations and you know what guys' capabilities are and that determined my actions. I knew Darrell Walker wasn't going to shoot the ball in a bail-out situation, so I would shoot before giving the ball to him. That's not a criticism. Those are the limitations of his game. If it came down to him or me, he wouldn't be mad if I took the shot. But not everybody should have been like that. And having to take those shots all the time, I didn't like that."

Jordan claimed that it was not fair and that his teammates needed to provide more than just obstacles to overcome in the closing minutes. If they could come through at that time when the team needed it and when Michael Jordan called on them, then he would come forth with that big-brother-is-watching nod of approval. As a teammate you were successful if you played the role that Michael cast you in.

At the end of Game 4 of the 1993 NBA Finals, Jordan completed a hanging drive-and-score sequence that drew a foul and fended off the Suns' last chance at victory. When the ball went down and the whistle blew, Jordan threw his hands up in the air and danced toward center court to take a bow. Armstrong came over to hug Jordan in a moment that usually causes athletes to rally around each other in support. Jordan nudged Armstrong away, which left B. J. confused. After the game Armstrong admitted, "You know you have to get out of the way sometimes and let Michael orchestrate." Perhaps B. J. did not understand at that moment that he was not being very helpful to the team.

FOURTEEN

The View from the Bench

June 5, 1991, Chicago Stadium, Game 1, NBA Finals. Phil had that look on his face again, the one where it was hard to tell if he was mad or frustrated. We were blowing out the Lakers, and because we lost the first game of the NBA Finals I felt like I could beat them all by myself tonight. Whenever I would get like that—all geeked up—Phil would give me the look like there was a conflict or something. Early in the game, the plan was to try and get everybody involved, so I did. But then my shot started falling. By the middle of the third quarter I hit 10 in a row, so the Lakers started sending two and three guys at me on defense. Phil raised those bushy eyebrows like he was getting ready to play another one of his mind games. What he was really telling me was that other guys were wide open and to look for them.

When I made a move, drew a crowd, and hit Pip or Pax for an open shot, he would walk back to the bench. Then, he'd see me dribble between my legs, fade away, and hit a jump shot and that would bring him out of his seat. You never would have known we were ahead by 22 points. In the fourth quarter, I pulled up on the break and gave it to Cliff, who was open on the left side of the basket. But he hesitated—Phil would have said he was "reticent to shoot"—then gave me the ball back as I was looking for a way to get to the basket and rebound. So I made that move, you know, the one where I went high with my right, switched to my left and laid it in. The one you see on ESPN every year and it's on all the highlight films. After it went down I turned around and Phil has this smirk on his face.

He didn't know which look to give me. It's like Michael get everybody involved unless you're hitting 13 shots in a row. But just don't forget we're a better team when you're getting everybody involved.

He used to say those kinds of things a lot. And it made me wonder if my ability to score or dominate or whatever and win games made him feel like it reflected badly on him as a coach. He used to say having Michael can right a lot of wrongs. But you wonder if he wanted things spread out more so we would look like more of a team. I never had a real problem getting along with my coaches. Loughery helped me learn all about being a pro, and he was entertaining. Doug helped me reach the height of my potential as a player, and Phil created a situation for winning championships. But sometimes it seemed like Phil wanted me to give up a few shots and few points for the sake of the team. That was hard because it seemed like it would hurt our chances to win. But he probably had a different point of view on all that.

Phil Jackson's eyebrows protruded like bristles on a broom, and he maintained a mad-scientist grin to form the I'm-about-to-give-you-some-secret-information look. The Chicago Bulls coach was about to explain Michael Jordan's genius after Game 1 of the 1993 Eastern Conference semifinals. Jordan bewildered two Cleveland defenders credited with being able to stop him in the past. He fooled Craig Ehlo first and then Gerald Wilkins by pulling up for jump shots when they thought he was going to drive. The next time he had the ball he changed directions three and four times to get past them when they came up to try and defend his jump-shooting.

During a three-minute stretch, Jordan lost Ehlo with a couple of nifty dance steps, took a pass from Scottie Pippen, and hit an 18-foot shot. He faked one way on Wilkins, cut back the other, and drew a foul. He made Wilkins run into teammate John Williams with a series of cutbacks and hit a 16-footer. Then he did the same thing to free himself for a shot from the top of the key. Jordan turned a 64-63 lead after three quarters into an 83-72 lead by scoring 16 of his 43 points in the fourth quarter of the 91-84 victory.

During any given postgame dissertation, Phil Jackson could recite from Plato, Shakespeare, Sartre, The Grateful Dead, and *Zen and the Art of Motorcycle Maintenance.* But now Jackson seemed to find it harder to explain Michael's plan of attack than it was for Ehlo and Wilkins to defend Jordan.

"A lot of it is him feeling the hot hand and taking it upon himself," Jackson observed. "When they were playing him with two defenders, he used the bigger guy as the screen on the quicker guy. He's always done that—use the bigger guy who doesn't have quite the lateral speed to create a block. Pretty smart, don't you think? It didn't take a whole lot of coaching. That's the way it was with him. Coaching was facilitating good plays."

Three days later, Jackson flexed his brow and wore the same look without the smile. He was about to provide his point of view on a game in which Michael Jordan made little impact in the first half because of an injury, yet pulled out victory in the second half by scoring 22 of his 32 points in the second 24 minutes. For Jackson the trick now was to explain how Jordan best contributed to this win.

"The further the [physical] deficit he's facing, the better team game and the better overall game he plays sometimes than when he's feeling buoyant and 100 percent. When he's not looking to have a [big scoring] night and he's focused on keeping everybody in the game and be a playmaker, we can be a [more] successful team."

Time-out. Didn't Michael Jordan just overcome an injury so imposing that he was scared to shoot and have the kind of night in the second half the Bulls needed to win games? One of the many decisions involved in coaching Michael Jordan that Jackson, Doug Collins, and Kevin Loughery, to a lesser degree, faced was how to use Jordan's talents most successfully. They had to balance the ledger between what he subtracted from the team when he added so much individually. And they had to find a way to tell him and make him understand he did not always know what was best. MJ could create so many ways to win that Jackson had to figure out which was the best or the most productive or the least damaging. He and Michael sometimes had different ideas about this, another element that made fitting Michael Jordan into the team concept a conflict and at many times a clash of wills. Coaching Jordan, just like being his teammate, was at once a hardship and a luxury.

There are those who argued that the most arduous task Phil Jackson ever faced coaching the Bulls came at the 1:48 mark in the first quarter of the first game of the 1993 NBA Playoffs. Michael had just hit his eighth shot in his last nine attempts, all of which came from a wide array of spots beyond 15 feet from the basket. On this last shot he faded away out of the reach of Atlanta's Stacey Augmon and fell out of bounds into the Bulls bench. Jackson, who was standing a few feet away, rushed over and helped Jordan up. A lot of times that's all it took to facilitate Michael's great play.

Arguing with Jordan about giving up his scoring for the welfare of the team concept was difficult if not pointless. For one thing, his stubbornness and competitiveness made it that way. But the facts and figures also were on his side. NBA teams average about 105 points per game. In Jordan's last four seasons the Bulls were an above average offensive team, averaging 108 points per game. Ideally speaking, no coach would want one player to score more than one third of the team's points on a regular basis. Risking or depending so much on one player would not seem to be the way to create a successful team.

But that was not the case with Jordan. In all the games he played during his prolific scoring period—which began with the 63-point output at Boston in the 1986 playoffs—Jordan scored 35 or more points 219 times. The Bulls won 157 of those games, when he scored one third or more of the team's points—a 71-percent clip. In the four years that Jackson coached Jordan, he topped the 35-point plateau 113 times in 322 regular-season games, and the Bulls won 88, or 78 percent, of those games. Overall, the Bulls won 73 percent of their games in those four years (240 out of 328).

Jackson said Michael's biggest nights left him with mixed emotions, not knowing whether it was a good situation or a bad one. It was the kind of turmoil he faced during his college days in the 1960s when his religious upbringing told him not to mess with recreational drugs such as LSD. But his rebellious, intellectual side made him curious enough to try them.

When Jordan scored 64 points against Orlando, Jackson did not exactly praise the effort: "When he's hot like that, we tend to stand around and watch. It seems to affect us when he scores a lot of points. We showed a lack of confidence in the end."

When Jordan's 55 points led the Bulls to a victory in Game 4 of the 1993 Finals, Jackson admitted Jordan was the team's strength but said his dominance had an adverse effect on the rest of the Bulls' ability to contribute offensively. When the Bulls came back from a 15-point, fourth-quarter deficit with MJ on the bench to beat Portland in Game 6 of the 1992 Finals and clinch the title, Jackson pointed out repeatedly that this victory was done the team way even though Jordan came back in the last two minutes to score 10 points.

Sometimes Jackson would come off a Jordan scoring virtuoso, like the one against Portland in Game 1 of the 1992 Finals, and say, "I marveled at Michael tonight. He really carried us." But nights like these would end with Jackson taking refuge in a corner of the Stadium's basement, smoking a cigarette, eyebrows raised, staring blankly at the final statistics, seemingly wondering what to make of it all. How could he ever reconcile this issue?

"The recognition was simply—when Michael and I sat down and talked when I was offered the job—that he hadn't been able to step up and win a championship," Jackson stated as he began this impromptu dissertation on the art of blending Michael Jordan into a team concept. "I pointed out that was because he never had people step up and offer him help. Not that he needed to be reminded, but as a consequence of him reaching down to meet the challenges, he always went 1-on-5, or 1-on-4, or one against the other team. I tried to make him understand that to win a championship he had to share the ball. He had to share the limelight. He had to share some of the glory and it would come.

"He was willing for that to happen provided his teammates were. But he had to understand that for his teammates to accept responsibility, he had to give them a chance to do so. When he did that, we were a better team."

If Jordan became a scoring monster, then credit Doug Collins with being Dr. Frankenstein. This, however, was more by necessity than design, according to Collins. When Collins coached Jordan from 1986–87 through 1988–89, MJ topped the 35-point mark 106 times, and the Bulls won 69 of those games (65 percent). Overall under Collins, the Bulls won 59 percent of their games. John Paxson was a major scoring threat on those teams, averaging 10 points per game. So was 6-foot-11-inch center Dave Corzine, an 11-year veteran who averaged nine points per game and as many beers afterward. Pippen and Grant came in Collins' second year, so Jordan was always the guy who had to score to make the Bulls competitive.

"Once that standard was established it was very difficult to break," said Collins, four years removed from the Bulls bench and perhaps a more astute observer of the situation as a television analyst for NBA games on Turner Network Television (TNT). "I always felt the Chicago Bulls with Michael Jordan could never be a balanced scoring team. You couldn't be because he was so great. I felt it came down to a coach's recognition to know you can't ask Michael Jordan to be something that he couldn't be. You couldn't say, 'Hey, Michael, we know you're great but we don't want you to be great.' He was great because he could score and the Bulls won because of that. He knew that, and he wasn't going to let anybody take that away."

In the end, Jackson fashioned a way for both parties to get what they wanted. He sold Jordan on the idea of becoming a decoy on offense, and Jordan offered that perspective as explanation for his sub-30-point games. "Sometimes I had to stand in the corner to keep the defense occupied and open things up for easy baskets," Michael explained. And Jackson installed the triple-post offense that assistant coach Tex Winter invented about the same time Dr. James Naismith nailed up the first peach basket at the YMCA in Springfield, Massachusetts, in the 1890s.

The triple-post, or triangle, as Winter explained it, predicated itself on player movement. So when Jordan moved to one spot, the other four players would move in sync on predetermined angles and hopefully create openings for shots. The triple-post took advantage of Jordan's ability to maneuver to the basket and create openings while creating scoring opportunities for players moving without the ball. "I never really understood it," said Jordan, who found it so frustrating the first couple of years that he would abandon it, making Winter and Jackson livid.

"But after a couple of years, I believed in it," Michael explained. "It gave us so many options I don't even think Tex knew all of them." Winter said that the triple-post was a sound offense because it took advantage of all the Bulls' resources. For Jordan, it was sound because it revolved around him. For Jackson, it was sound because it helped Jordan find a way to get others involved, and if Jordan did have a big night, well, the defense could not take everything away from such an ingenious offensive player. And Jordan's scoring was what the opposition decided to give up that night.

Jackson sat in a corner of the Richfield Coliseum with his reading glasses hanging off the edge of his nose working a *New York Times* crossword puzzle in May 1993. For him, this represented the same challenge Jordan found in the Pistons' Jordan Rules. Just as he asked aloud for a six-letter word meaning "the solution to all your problems," he was informed of the results of the 1993 NBA Coach of the Year voting. The Bulls lost 119 games during this season to player injury, meaning that injuries forced players to miss a combined 119 games. Each starter from the past two championship teams missed at least two games because of injury, except for Scottie Pippen, who missed his only game because of a suspension for fighting. But the Bulls still won 57 games, captured their third straight NBA Central Division title, and finished second in the Eastern Conference to the New York Knicks. These accomplishments would seem to have made Jackson a strong candidate to win the award or even finish among the top three. When he was told that the Knicks' Pat Riley won the award and that he did not get a single vote from the media members who select the winner, Jackson did not send up any cross words.

"When you have a Michael Jordan, your coaching is going to be overlooked," said Jackson in his raspy, professorial voice. Perhaps this was an attempt to confirm his perspective on coaching Jordan more than excusing the issue. "It should be. When you have a guy like Michael, it alleviates a lot of things you have to worry about. Sometimes, a spectacular effort can take care of a win. This guy made things a lot easier for me."

Jackson fought with his star, mollified his ego, and challenged Jordan intellectually. He baited him into arguments about who could play the game and who could not. Jackson was always trying to convince MJ there were guys in the NBA before 1980 who could play. Jordan tried to win every one of these friendly arguments with Jackson, and during his retirement press conference stated the thing that he would miss most about Phil was playing his mind games.

Jackson knew he was doing something special in coaching Jordan. He went out of his way to make others see that. When Jordan and Reggie Miller squared off in their boxing match in Indianapolis in February 1993, Jackson reprimanded the Indiana fans publicly for booing Jordan after Miller was ejected. He told them that you only get to see a Michael Jordan every once in a while so you should appreciate it. That's the type of relationship Jackson cultivated with Jordan, and it proved productive.

Jackson knew there were times to let Michael free-lance and live with it. When the Bulls were trailing the Pistons by two points with 4.1 seconds left in an overtime game at the Stadium in November 1992, Jackson called a play that was known as "Get the ball to Jordan." It was planned a little bit. But Jordan got the opening, got the ball, and buried it.

For the good of the Chicago Bulls, Jackson and his predecessors had to manage Jordan more than coach him. Doug Collins called it a matter of channeling him in the right way. Sometimes this wasn't always easy. During training camp prior to the 1987–88 season, the Bulls were in the midst of an intrasquad scrimmage. Jordan's team was trailing 4-3, or so Collins said, when Michael's competitive drive overwhelmed him. He insisted the score was 4-4 and stormed out of practice when Collins wouldn't agree. Jordan said the next day people may have thought of this as trivial, "but when you're a competitor and you want to win, nothing is trivial."

"One thing I had to make sure of," Collins said, "was that I stayed as competitive as he was." It was never easy having Jordan as a teammate. He demanded his teammates to be as good as he was or at least as competitive and as motivated, but there was no other player in the history of the game who could match Michael. That was also the return on investment for putting up with everything that went with playing on the same team as Jordan or coaching him. How many people who played pro basketball can say they played with the best ever?

PART II
His Life

FIFTEEN

How Did Life Ever Get This Crazy?

An off day during the middle of the 1993 season. In less-troubled times, shopping at the mall was at least possible. But after five or six years in the league, it turned into a situation where there had to be a significant purpose for me to leave the house. Forget running to the 7-11 for a quart of milk. Stealing early-morning breakfasts in a corner booth at Baker's Square or imposing on understanding downtown Chicago restaurant owners for late-night dinners became so tiring that eating out meant building my own restaurant.

How did life ever get this crazy?

Now, we're looking to buy a pair of shoes. You know how you would do it—go to a mall, look around, try on a few pairs. Maybe look in a few more stores, try on a few more pairs and when the shoe fits. . . . Well, we're in the mall, but there's no time for browsing. We—we also being my assistant George Koehler, who I need with me for protection whenever I'm out in public—go into one store, we find a pair of shoes, and we buy them. Then, we get ready to leave.

Only as we're walking out the door, two teenage girls scream, "That's Michael Jordan." Next thing you know 300, maybe 400, people have gathered outside and backed us into the store. George had to get the owner to lock the door. People are asking to come in to buy a pair of shoes, but as George will tell you, they just want to be in the same room with Michael Jordan. The owner can't even unlock the door. George looks for a back door. There isn't one, so we have to go out the front. George calls mall security, and a couple of guards come to the rescue.

They form a ring, put me in the middle, and we make a run for it. George says be careful not to hurt anybody, but they're all grabbing at me like a bunch of little John Starkses. People are asking for autographs, but you can't even think about stopping because it would turn into a mob scene.

When you put yourself in the limelight so much that your face is on television every five minutes you have to accept the lifestyle and make some sacrifices. I understand giving up some of the simple things in life, like taking your kids out for ice cream, driving your son to school, or Christmas shopping in public. And making the sacrifices never used to be a problem. But once in a while it would have been nice not to have to duck into a bathroom in the locker room to talk with friends after a game on the road.

I never thought my life would come down to needing somebody to go with me every time I stepped out of the house. George was the first person I met when I came to Chicago, and I figured I could use his limousine service every once in a while after that. But life got so crazy that I had to hire him. He became my only means of getting away from the crowd and handling the demands of the lifestyle.

Certain things I learned to deal with, like meeting all the different dignitaries and celebrities after every game. But I was standing there on the court in Phoenix before the start of the first game of the Finals, Glenn Campbell was singing the National Anthem, there were eight guys with TV cameras standing within a foot of me and I'm thinking, how did life ever get this crazy? At times like that, you wonder if maybe it wasn't worth all the cars, all the exposure, all the free Big Macs. I wonder if anybody realizes how the lifestyle caused me to walk away from the game so suddenly. I wonder if anybody realizes what my life was really like.

At some point, Michael Jordan found the postgame routine turning from comedy to misery. After every home game, he would endure the same remedial questions from reporters two and three times, provide every last answer, and wait until one of the Chicago Stadium security guards clad in a banana-colored nylon windbreaker would give him the sign that his car was ready. "My car is ready?" he would ask rhetorically, if not desperately. "OK, guys, I gotta go." That's when his life turned into a scene from "Mission Impossible."

One of the security guards, who were off-duty Chicago cops, picked up his bag and covered Jordan from the rear. Another cleared a path in front of him. A third shouted orders into a microphone tucked inside the lapel of his jacket. "We're coming out now. Which way is clear?" The entourage would lead Jordan out of the locker room. Then he had to deal with various friends, friends of friends, friends of people who had friends that did business with Jordan, and maybe pro golfer John Daly, gymnast Kim Zmeskal, or some other athlete or celebrity of Olympian proportion waiting for Jordan to drop a joke and a smile.

"Sorry, John, I can't play golf with you. You hit the ball too damn far, and I'd be hitting behind your ass all day," he said on the move as he always was at this time. "Kim, what have you been doing since the Olympics? Things falling into place for you?" If you caught him as he emerged from the locker room, Michael might stop one minute for photo opportunities. Then his bodyguards would steer him into the escape route chosen for that night.

During his nine years with the Bulls, security guards mapped out at least five exit plans to whisk Jordan safely out of Chicago Stadium. He would move out of the locker room door, up a back staircase, out a side exit of the Stadium where his Lexus or his Ferrari would be warmed up and ready to go. Chicago Bears defensive end Richard Dent, Ahmad Rashad, another friend, or sometimes his wife, Juanita, would be strapped in the passenger seat. Every time he walked through a door or climbed stairs on the way out, Jordan picked up another bodyguard. If it was really late after a game—say an hour or so—security felt comfortable enough to let Jordan walk the length of the court from the Bulls' dressing room to the players entrance and parking lot, where he came into this would-be mob scene five hours earlier.

That was the postgame ritual for Michael Jordan. More than one hundred of those each season could get exhausting. Michael found the whole ordeal somewhat amusing during the wonder years of his NBA career. He was very giving of his time to the public and the media then, which was like an injection of steroids into his growing fame. But the last two years of his career, he began harboring resentment for the constraints of life, like having to have secretive escape routes to get out of the Stadium without causing a riot. Ironically, he had given so much time to the media that he feared if he blew off just one interview it might cause a controversy. He worried that the image he created by making so many commercials and asking everybody to "Be Like Mike" was one he could not and did not want to live up to.

"You know that commercial I made for Nike about what if I was just another basketball player?" Michael reflected. "What if my face wasn't on TV every five seconds? Well, that wasn't done just to sell shoes. That's how I really felt. There came a time when I just wanted to be another basketball player. And you know, I couldn't."

Following Michael Jordan on one of his fastbreaks out of Chicago Stadium provided a glimpse of the maladies his high profile placed on the rest of his lifestyle. Michael would never have traded the way he lived his life during his NBA career, but he wanted people to know about what went on behind closed hotel-room doors. He wanted some privacy, but he also wanted a little sympathy. He wanted everybody to know just what his lifestyle consisted of and what he went through to handle it.

Jordan did not outwardly blame anybody but himself for the situation he lived in. But in retrospect, when he stepped away from the game and in turn the limelight, he could not help but wonder if he had not been a victim of the NBA. The league's salary cap, the rule that put a limit on the amount of money each team could pay its players, limited his earnings. To make money, to get rich, he had to sell himself and become the world's number one athletic endorser because the Bulls could not afford to pay him more than $3.2 million a year and build the championship team that he wanted even more than money. The NBA's star system, which gave heightened exposure to the best players in order to sell the game to network television and fans worldwide, added to Jordan's already saturated time in public view. Add in the 31 appearances on the cover of *Sports Illustrated* and similar coverage in every sports section of U.S. newspapers, as well as some foreign ones, and it got to the point where Michael only could have been more exposed if he posed nude.

"You know, I used to love to go to Paris," Jordan admitted during a rare quiet moment before a game in Detroit in April 1993. "They needed a little work on their basketball, so that's why I went over there. Then, they didn't know who I was. I could walk through the streets, I could sit outside at a restaurant and nobody would know who I was. I went back there, and I had to sign a few autographs and that was it. If that's the way it was now, I would still go there. But I can't even go there now. That was the last place, except maybe for Argentina. But Argentina nothing. I've been to South America. Went to Caracas [Venezuela] for the Pan-Am Games [in 1983]. They have kids walking around the streets with machine guns. I don't want to go out that bad to put up with that shit."

Despite the best efforts of Chicago Stadium security guards and despite the most carefully planned escape routes, Michael Jordan's exits after a home game often produced the kind of scene that greeted him after Game 2 of the opening round of the 1993 playoffs. As he walked out into a cold, drizzling spring evening in Chicago, Jordan was showered with attention. Security guards strained to keep people from closing in on Michael. As word spread outside about which exit Jordan had used, kids came sprinting around a corner in groups of threes and added to the mob. George cleared enough room for Jordan to get the door to his Ferrari Testarossa open and slip inside. He accelerated away to chants of "M-V-P, M-V-P."

At Market Square in Indianapolis, the Bulls team bus parked at the top of a ramp not more than five feet outside the entrance leading to the team's dressing room. In back of the bus was a four-foot-high concrete slab on the other side of which was approximately a 50-foot drop to the ground. Perpendicular to that restraining wall is a similar concrete slab on the other side of which is one floor of the arena's parking garage.

When the Bulls came to town, several hundred people frequently lined up behind the second slab after the game and waited to catch a glimpse of Michael Jordan. All anybody could see from that vantage point was a profile of somebody getting on the bus. Every time a person walked out of the tunnel toward the bus, the crowd shrieked the kind of pitch Ella Fitzgerald could have used to break the glass in the old Memorex commercial. When Jordan walked out, the last member of the Bulls traveling party to do so, the crowd shrieked and clapped as people boxed out for position to peek over the concrete. Michael was in view for about five seconds, long enough to wave and get on the bus.

At the Plaza Hotel in New York City, bellmen, doormen, and security guards had to form a human barrier along 59th Street from the back door to the Bulls bus. One by one, Bulls players filed out of the hotel and onto the bus. Jordan again went last to give the help enough time to beef up its chain of security. Some of the shrieks were not as loud as the cheers usually heard in the Bronx when Jordan walked out of the hotel. But the crowd was as frenzied as the one in Indianapolis.

As Jordan tried to leave after a game against the Cavaliers at the

Richfield Coliseum, a group of fans stopped him before he made it to the dressing room exit. He quickly autographed three basketballs, a poster, a replica Michael Jordan Olympic jersey, and two boxes of Wheaties before Bulls public relations director Tim Hallam escorted him to a corner of the locker room to film a public service announcement for television.

On the way to the team bus after a game against the Pistons in the Palace of Auburn Hills during the 1993 season, Detroit Lions defensive lineman Jerry Ball, a major star in his own right in this town, stopped Jordan to ask for autographs for members of his entire family.

When Jordan joked he was not going to watch his beloved North Carolina play Michigan in the championship game of the 1993 NCAA basketball tournament the morning of the game, it was the source of a significant news item in both Chicago metropolitan daily newspapers.

These were the calmer, saner moments and occurrences Jordan dealt with during the few seconds he stepped into public view away from the basketball court. At least that is the way it was when his career came to a close. Don't think for a moment that the idea of not having to deal with all of the hassles did not make Jordan want to quit.

He did not even want to participate in the NBA All-Star game his final year because of the exposure involved. The game, a chance to compete with the NBA's best players, the ultimate challenge for Michael, would not have been so bad if it were not for the hour-long media session the day before. "Hey, maybe I could get into a fight Wednesday," Jordan whispered matter-of-factly the day before the Bulls' game against Utah, the last one before the All-Star break. "That way maybe they would have to suspend me for the All-Star Game. I wouldn't mind that." He was only kidding. Or was he?

"He was always polite to the fans when we went out earlier in his career," Howard White said. "He would speak to everybody or smile at them. We would go to dinner, and people would just want to say hi or ask for an autograph. But then it started happening at the movies. Or we'd walk into a shopping mall, and there would be a crowd around him in a matter of minutes. At first, he would smile, and then later he would say, 'Let's just go.' There was a point where he said to me, 'I don't know how long I can keep this up.' "

If life did not get any crazier than George getting daily requests for Michael to appear at somebody's son's birthday party, MJ may have been able to keep it up a lot longer. But even four years into his NBA career, Jordan could feel the walls closing in. And the walls had arms and legs, reaching out to touch him and begging him for his autograph. Before the 1991 season, the Bulls did not have the luxury chartered plane that took them from NBA city to NBA city. That led to waits in airports for delayed flights. Doug Collins asked the Bulls organization to book as many 5:30 A.M. departures as possible because airport crowds were sparsest then. Imagine playing a game in Chicago at 8 P.M. after leaving another town that morning at 5:30.

"Sometimes I had to call better plays traveling than I did coaching," Collins recalled. "In certain arenas we'd have to send guys out one way and make people think we were all going that way. Then, we would sneak Michael out another way and pick him up down the street a block or two. I don't think rock stars had to deal with that."

Eventually, Jordan had to close off the entire outside world when he was on the road and vulnerable to the public. James Jordan said he could not remember the situation getting much worse than it did in New York during the 1993 Eastern Conference Finals. Michael was not even safe locked inside his hotel room because the telephone would not stop ringing. "We blocked all the calls, but they still found every way in the world to get through," James said one morning when Michael's lifestyle pissed him off so much that he decided to vent his feelings to a group of listeners. "I mean we had relatives calling, or at least people claiming to be relatives, saying, 'This is an emergency. I'm a cousin. I've got diabetes, and I've got to talk to him.' What are you supposed to do?"

What James did was take his son away. That led to the infamous incident when James, Michael, and friends rented a limousine the night between Games 1 and 2 of the series and went to Bally's Casino in Atlantic City. For Jordan, getting away from the craziness meant this: A two-hour limousine ride to play blackjack in an area roped off especially for him and other VIP gamblers in the casino. Word of his presence there leaked to the *New York Times,* which ran a story two days later reporting Jordan was there, how much money he lost, and how much time he spent there. It escalated into a full-blown controversy.

All of this happened because he wanted to *escape* from some of the craziness for a couple of hours.

"You know, I could have taken him to a triple-X-rated movie and somebody would have found a way to make something out of it," James said. "Michael went from one day to the next hoping he would be a little freer than he was the last. They will have enough stuff on me today. They won't need me tomorrow. But everybody always wanted more. He knew that. He couldn't control it."

The Atlantic City controversy may have pushed Jordan to the point of no return. Or he may have reached that point the preceding Christmas, when he went out shopping to buy presents for Juanita and the rest of the family. FAO Schwarz, the renowned toy retailer, had just built a new store on Chicago's One Magnificent Mile and displayed a 25-foot Teddy Bear in the front window of the three-story structure. If Michael could have bought that for two-week-old daughter Jasmine, then the shopping spree would have been a success. But it was near closing time, so he ventured into Chicago's Water Tower Place Mall to finish the job. Water Tower Place is a seven-story vertical mall across the street from the 100-story John Hancock center on Michigan Avenue, the main drag for shopping in Chicago's downtown. Two hours after the end of a business day, the mall usually clears out except for patrons at its six movie theaters.

"The mall should have been clearing out, but they still had to rush him into a private area in the back offices," Pops explained. "He did all his shopping by calling four or five stores, and the managers came running with armfuls of items he wanted and he had to pick one. He got to pick the best one of 10. There may have been 100 other things he might have liked. It would have been great to go from store to store, but that would have tied up the mall. So he's got to pick from what they showed him. Now that was a stupid damn way to Christmas-shop."

Doug Collins sat at the snack bar of the Multiplex, a suburban Chicago health club that the Bulls used as a practice facility until the 1992–93 season. That year, they moved across the street to the newly constructed Sheri Berto Center. The two practice facilities in a way represented what Jordan's life had become. The Multiplex was a public club where people exercised and could watch the Bulls practice when they finished. The Berto Center was a fortress that required all members of the Bulls organization to carry computerized cards to gain access. Visitors had to be identified by voice over an intercom before they were granted entrance. Collins was four years removed from coaching the Bulls, but he still liked to talk about the organization, and especially Jordan, to the Multiplex members. As he sat watching the people work out, he took a sip from his drink and blurted out, "You know, Michael Jordan could never sit here like you and I and have a diet soda. He could never look out at all those people and let the sound of those exercise bikes mesmerize him. Do you know that? He understands that. But can you imagine what it's like to live like that?"

Michael understood the limits of the lifestyle and invented ways and means to achieve a reasonable piece of normalcy or at least happiness. Mostly, it forced him to keep a small circle of friends. In such towns as Charlotte, where Michael moved his family after he joined the Bulls, the circle expanded to its largest at almost 20. They would all gather in his hotel suite, many of them who grew up in Wilmington with Jordan. Adolph Shiver was always there. He wore the title of Michael's best friend, the guy who would meet him on the road in a place where he did not have any close friends. On any big occasion, like the playoffs, Adolph was always there.

In some places, Jordan had adopted families. Tony Prather was an Indianapolis businessman who met Michael through a mutual friend in 1986. When he would go to Indy, Michael would hang out at Tony's house playing pool, staying up until midnight the night before a game playing with his four-year-old daughter Alexandria. The night Michael got into the fight with Reggie Miller, he answered all the questions about it, then darted out of the locker room and immediately picked up Alexandria, hugged her, kissed her, and made his way to the bus. That was how he could make basketball seem a world away.

"That's how he could get outside the arena and totally forget he was one of the most recognized people in the world," Tony Prather said as he smiled and watched Michael hold his daughter. "Michael's the kind of guy who, when he comes to a city, likes to have a family he can hang out with. He can sit there playing with my daughter, watching the basketball game, and be a normal guy. We'd just sit around and do dumb stuff. Stuff he could never do anywhere else. It was like being with any other friend I had, except that Michael liked it so much because he didn't have that many opportunities to be that way outside his own home."

Before he and Juanita married, when Michael needed to get away he would look up Howard White in Maryland and spend a couple of days in his apartment sleeping on the couch and watching television. On game days, especially the big ones in the playoffs, he surrounded himself with friends because, he said, "It helped me focus on the game during the day and kept me from thinking about all the other stuff that went with it." Because he could not go to movies unless he wanted to sneak in mid-week after the opening credits ran, entertainment became Sunday night dinner when friends and family would order in food and sit around teasing each other.

"His friends were his reality check, the way he handled all the craziness," George Koehler explained. "He had that good support system, and he didn't sway from it. That's how he kept his feet on the ground. That's the only way. If I looked in the mirror and I was making what Michael made financially and had all the power that went along with it, would I see the same guy? If you don't change just a little bit, it's not right. But Michael never changed. And that was because of his friends. People don't realize how important friendships were to this guy. When the Bulls won the championship, he had rings and pendants made up for some of us. Spent more than six figures of his own money just to say thanks. He wanted us to know we were every bit a part of the championship for him as he was for us. He gave me my ring in front of the whole team. I cried like a two-year-old."

Jordan did have to go to some extremes to keep from changing or at least keep the lifestyle from driving him away sooner than it did. One of those extremes was having Koehler, who served him with Lassie-like loyalty and efficiency. When Jordan was drafted in 1984, he flew into Chicago to start training camp. He stepped off the plane with no ride into town. Koehler, who ran a limousine service, had missed the person he was supposed to meet at Chicago's O'Hare Airport. He saw that Jordan looked a little lost and asked him if he needed a ride.

Koehler drove Michael to the Hyatt Regency Hotel in the Chicago suburb of Lincolnwood, where the Bulls were housing their players during training camp. He left Michael his business card and told Michael to call if he ever needed a ride. That was his standard business procedure.

A week or so later Koehler's telephone rang. "I answered and the voice said, 'George, this is M-J.' I said, 'I don't know any M-J.' He reminded me about giving him the ride and asked me if I could pick his parents up at the airport. I started working for him. The first week I made the mistake of calling him Larry Jordan. That was a guy I played high school ball with. Funny, isn't it?

"Here I am having to fight crowds and all the craziness and the only job I can think that would be better would be chaperone on 'The Dating Game.' I used to look at all those crowds and think people were just using him to get to me. Seriously, though, I think it was my destiny to work with Michael. I was able to help him. How many people were able to help him?"

When Jordan lost control of his public life, such simple pleasures as eating dinner out were taken away as well. He could pick and choose certain restaurants in Chicago, but in order to dine out at will he built Michael Jordan's: The Restaurant. He even put in a private dining room enclosed in glass. Here was more proof of how crazy life had become. Jordan knew that attraction of the restaurant was his presence. So he voluntarily put himself in the fishbowl. That way people could come and eat there and watch him, but he did not have to be bothered by them. And at least he could enjoy the best seafood pasta and macaroni and cheese in town. Those were two of Michael's favorites, and the macaroni was made from a special recipe Juanita created.

But the game-night stress only worsened. To accommodate a television crew from Japan, Michael sent a message to the people of that country. "I've heard a great response from the people but until they get a Concorde I won't get over and see y'all," he said. "I just don't think I can deal with the 20-hour flight."

Jordan faced so many requests for interviews that he could not do all of them. But he feared outright refusal and had to develop a plan to politely give media members the brush. When he did not have time for an interview, he would tell them to contact Hallam. "That meant that he wasn't going to do it," Hallam confirmed. But those adjustments merely kept things from getting worse rather than enable Jordan to regain control of his lifestyle.

This was one thing about Jordan his teammates never envied. Scott Williams said there was not enough money in the world to deal with what Jordan had to deal with. Pippen said seeing what happened to Jordan made him realize that he never wanted to be in the position of being the NBA's leading scorer.

"You take it for granted, but the one thing he wanted was to be a regular guy, a normal person," Will Perdue observed. "My rookie year for the team yearbook, they asked me, Who would you like to be for a day? and I said Michael. After I spent all that time with him, I take it back. I never would want to be in his shoes. Everybody wanted to be separated from him because he was watched so closely. He couldn't even have car trouble without an article appearing in the newspaper the next day saying Michael Jordan was seen fixing a flat tire."

He eventually let signs that it was starting to get to him slip out. On February 17, 1993, Michael celebrated his 30th birthday by skipping out on the media after a defeat of Utah at the Stadium and getting an early start on the All-Star break, which began the next day. By that time of his career, the first chance to dash off into a few days of relaxation made him move faster than an open-court breakaway. Before the game he discussed his feelings about turning 30 with a select few members of the media who dropped by just to wish him a happy birthday.

"Hey, I felt like I turned 30 a long time ago," he admitted. It was easy to believe this because of his hairline. "My image was projected to be more matured, or whatever. I feel 30 now because the back-to-back games are harder, and I don't dunk in warm-ups anymore. It just seems like I'm so much older because being in the public view made me have to mature so quickly."

His life as a prisoner of the public may have angered Michael. He admitted it trapped him. But it never scared him until April 30, 1993, the day the NBA playoffs began. Earlier that day Monica Seles, the top-ranked women's tennis player in the world, was stabbed in the back by a fan during a tournament in Hamburg, Germany. The man who got to Seles was a self-proclaimed Steffi Graf fan who hated to see

Seles ranked ahead of Graf. It set Jordan to thinking about the price of fame.

"That kind of incident is one of the things you really think about, especially when you're in crowds or arenas where you're not well liked," Jordan admitted. "I mean, you can go into a tunnel maybe after a game where you beat the home team and some nut fan maybe didn't like the way you played. You feel vulnerable to it. You start looking around and say that can really happen to you. You go about thinking about it and try to prevent it then you really alter your normal life and your relaxing life. If they wanted to get to me, they could get to me."

When he started thinking about an untimely ending at the hands of tragedy, Jordan realized the lifestyle became too much to handle. During the 1993 NBA Finals, Michael experienced the transformation from idolization and suffocation to persecution. During his 10-day media embargo, a story surfaced about more high-stakes gambling. Supposedly, he lost $1 million playing golf to a San Diego businessman named Richard Esquinas. Finally, Michael had to give in. He let Ahmad Rashad interview him for a national television audience so he could dispel reports that he had lost more than $1 million gambling on golf. Cliff Levingston, who was working for a Chicago television station as an analyst covering that series, watched his old friend go through this and realized he had enough of this kind of life. "He once told me that he would give a million dollars if he could walk down the street one time without anybody recognizing him. And at the same time he knew he could never do that. That was hard for him to accept."

As Jordan announced his retirement, he repeatedly said that it was the first step in getting his life back to normal. Or as normal a life as he could ever have. As he looked out at a crowd of more than 500 media members gathered at the Berto Center for his farewell press conference, he pointed out, "This is the first time I've had this many people around without a scandal." He went on to charge that because people ran out of things to say about his basketball they started picking into his private life. And he said he just could not look at all that and motivate himself to play basketball anymore. Not that Michael would ever be able to go to the mall and buy a pair of shoes, but retiring from basketball meant that he would never have to deal with how crazy life had become.

SIXTEEN

Money: It Is the Shoes . . .
and the Underwear

*January 31, 1993, Super Bowl
Sunday, Salt Lake City, Utah.* Somebody once asked me if co-star-
ring in a commercial with Bugs Bunny made me feel like a real
celebrity. Bugs was a great teammate. Came in handy when it was
time to play Marvin the Martian. Never thought we'd share the
stage at halftime of the Super Bowl. That commercial was a lot of
fun.

Funny thing about commercials. You know, you sit at home,
watch television, and say, 'I can do that.' But after doing a shoot
and seeing how involved and technical and perfect these directors
and producers had to be and how much time was spent sitting
around waiting for them, it's hard to believe I did so many that I
was on TV more often than Bugs Bunny.

193

It never felt like I got a million dollars every time I said, "Drive a Chevy" or "Better Eat Your Wheaties." Making those commercials could be such a pain in the butt. You have to tie your shoe 200 times to see which way the laces would usually fall and then try to make them fall the same way every time on camera. You had to pick up a french fry and hold it the right way. Like there's more than one way to hold a french fry? Sometimes it seemed like we had to shoot 17 million takes to get the one line right while the logo was facing up. For any 30-second commercial it took us four to six hours of shooting, and that was hard to deal with. Why did they need so many takes? In my game, I only got one shot at it.

Falk put together this great marketing plan, and when he came up with the Air Jordan thing I never thought it would make 200 million a year. The whole endorsement package kind of just followed out of my skills and personality. But if Falk wasn't as competitive as I was, we never would have had all those deals that made all that money. Sometimes, I used to look at those commercials where I just sat there and smiled or nodded my head while my father did all the talking and wondered what made them so popular. You wonder what it is about you that made all those people walk around Chicago, New York, and Japan with my face on their T-shirts. Got to admit, though, the stuff was comfortable to wear. If it wasn't one of those custom-tailored Italian suits, give me some Air Jordan warmups.

After five or six years, the endorsement thing got kind of tiring. I didn't want to use all my free time during the season making commercials and appearances, so I scheduled a lot of it during the summer. But then I was working harder than during the season, and there was no time for golf. So we had to figure a way to cut back. We told any company that made a proposal we wouldn't look at anything for less than a million. And the offers kept coming.

Finally, we had to write agreements into contracts that anything I did would last no more than four hours. You can imagine what I was like sitting around waiting for somebody to put up a different set or rewrite a script. I couldn't deal with that shit.

It probably didn't hit me how commercial I had become until I announced my retirement and all my products started selling even faster and became more valuable. A couple weeks after I quit, I was watching television, and I saw that somebody stole this jersey I donated to a museum in Chicago. Took it right off the wall. How did Michael Jordan merchandise get to be such a sought-after commodity? You know, I used to give away that stuff all the time. Like my shoes. For every game, I wore a new pair of shoes and used to give them away when people asked.

One time we were playing Golden State, Tim Hardaway was guarding me, and he was hacking all over me. Real physical stuff. After the game, he asked for my shoes for a charity thing he was doing. I gave them to him because I didn't think they were worth anything. But I guess Michael Jordan stuff was worth something, because right after I hit the shot to beat Cleveland in the playoffs in 1993, Mike Sanders came up to me and asked me to autograph his Michael Jordan basketball cards.

The best part and the worst part of the endorsement aspect of my life were the commercials. There was a lot to put up with. But I got to make one with my dad about underwear. That's something I'll always remember about him. Every time a new commercial came out, somebody would ask me if this was the best one or if I got paid more than Bugs Bunny. To be honest, the best one was the one with Larry Bird. You know, where we played a game of HORSE for a Big Mac. I would like to have tried that shot over the river, off the expressway, nothing but net. . . .

JORDAN
195

When Michael Jordan was named the Most Valuable Player after the Bulls beat Phoenix in the 1993 NBA Finals, Jeep/Eagle hosted a reception at Chicago's Sheraton Hotel to award him the customary car that went with the honor. His vast experience at these corporate functions made Jordan fully aware of the commercial obligations associated with the presentation. He posed with Jeep marketing executives, posed with his new white Eagle-TSI parked in the Sheraton Ballroom. He even posed holding up the keys to the car. "Nice keys," he said.

After the photo opportunities, he conducted a press conference where he was asked about a mishap the day before. When the triumphant Bulls landed at the airport on the return flight from Phoenix, Jordan could not get his car started. Nothing about his life was secret anymore, and everybody wanted to know what happened with his car.

"Well, my wife changed the security code, you know how they have those on the Chevys," Jordan began. Then he stopped in mid-explanation. "Wait a minute, I can't talk about a Chevy at a Jeep ceremony. I'll tell you about it later."

He smiled and laughed briefly with head hanging and shaking, the kind of reaction most people make out of embarrassment. He did not care about hiding his trouble, "But I didn't want to make the Jeep people mad by talking about Chevy," he said. "Sometimes, it's hard to keep all these companies straight."

At that moment Michael Jordan wondered how much longer he could hold the company line. After nine years, basketball had put excessive strains on him, mentally and physically. He could deal with that because he still loved the game. But he had become a product unto himself, a prototype for the American marketing icon. And now it did more than take time away from his private life or make him so overexposed that he had no private life. It made him worry about what he said in public.

This was not the idea when David Falk, an up-and-coming agent from a sports management company called Pro-Serv, developed this grand plan to make Jordan an unprecedented corporate point guard in 1984. Falk parlayed Jordan's revolutionary athletic skill and down-home country wholesomeness into a cottage industry. So much so that

Michael Jordan the endorser topped the *Forbes* magazine list of the 40 highest-paid athletes each of its first three years (1990–92) by pulling in $32.5 million a year through commercial ventures.

For the most part, Michael endured or even enjoyed being a walking, talking, breathing, dunking billboard. Wearing Hanes underwear, eating Wheaties and Big Macs, and drinking Gatorade was easy. But as he stood atop the Sears Tower, 110 stories above Chicago, with Larry Bird at his side, preparing to attempt the shot over the river, off the expressway, nothing but net, even he may have wondered how the commercial side of Michael Jordan had grown to such legendary heights.

David Falk was no more than an advisor when Pro-Serv landed a skinny-legged kid from North Carolina as a client in 1984. Actually, when Jordan decided to hire the sports management company to represent him, Pro-Serv president Donald Dell was the front man. Dell negotiated Jordan's first pro contract for $6.3 million over seven years. Falk accompanied Dell to the first meeting with Jordan, and after cutting the deal with the Bulls, Dell stepped aside to spend more time tending to the tennis stars who made Pro-Serv most of its money in those days.

Falk moved into a relatively unknown area with a relatively unknown player. Basketball had not produced many endorsement deals for its stars at the time. Jordan was coming off a starlight performance in the 1984 Summer Olympics in Los Angeles, but he was not the first or even the second player taken in the NBA draft. And he was going to a team that drew little attention. But Falk put together a plan to harness Jordan's personality, acrobatic style of play, and Olympic participation. The idea was to take a chance on what he perceived as a growing marketplace.

Falk and Dell had just negotiated a deal with New Balance to pay another North Carolina star, James Worthy, $1.2 million per year to endorse the "Worthy Express" basketball shoe. That was the first shoe contract of such magnitude in pro basketball, and one of the first high-profile shoes marketed especially for the game. Soon after, Falk called all the athletic shoe companies and opened the bidding for Jordan to become a spokesman.

"No one had seen even a glimmer of what kind of dollars were out there," Falk explained. "There was no precedent. Dr. J didn't have it. Larry Bird hadn't done it. It was beyond the imagination what was possible, so we decided to set it up to let them sell us and not us sell them on Michael."

Nike was one of seven companies to make a bid. The Beaverton, Oregon, company was a step behind Adidas in the escalating shoe wars but made the best offer for Jordan with a deal that guaranteed him $7 million plus incentives. Nike wrote a clause into the contract specifying if Jordan did not make the NBA All-Star team at least once in his first three years, the deal could be terminated. On a balmy August afternoon in 1984, Falk sat in his Washington, D.C., office with two Nike executives trying to brainstorm a name for the line of shoes Jordan would wear. Nike had just come up with its "Air" insole, a fluffy, pillowy-like design that seemed to add spring to the step, and had a shoe on the market called "Air Force." Falk swished various ideas around his mouth like fine wine before hitting on the vintage: "Air Jordan."

The first Air Jordan came out in 1985 and recorded $100 million in sales. By 1991, Air Jordans led a product line that grossed Nike more than $3 billion worldwide. The most popular gym shoe in history enabled Falk to put his plan into action. He pitched ideas to Coca-Cola and McDonald's. That was the key.

If he could get those companies to sign Jordan, then the work was done. The rest would see the contiguous air time for Air Jordan on television and want to cash in on the exposure.

By 1988, Jordan had deals with eight different companies. Only one did not prove to be a success. A watch deal with a Canadian company called Excelsior for "Time Jordan" was a bust.

In 1991, Jordan also got out of the cola business and switched to Gatorade, because that's really what he drank after games and practices. Citrus cooler was his favorite flavor, and he went through two cans after every game. He was also becoming more health conscious, so Gatorade was more like Mike than Coke. He even ate at McDonald's less often, too, but he had a deal with the company that lasted through 1994.

Falk's plan reached its absolute pinnacle in 1991 when he negotiated a new deal with Nike for $20 million, the most lucrative endorsement deal ever for an athlete. None of Jordan's other deals topped $3 million per year, but the total in 1993 came in at $32 million. With his annual salary, he was the highest paid athlete in the world according to *Forbes* magazine, more than $7.9 million ahead of the next highest grosser, boxer Evander Holyfield. Auto racers Ayrton Senna ($22 million) and Nigel Mansell ($14.5 million) were next, with golfer Arnold Palmer fifth ($11.1 million).

Falk completed his plan to make Jordan a commercial giant when he tailored his deals to a group of core companies during Michael's last year in the league. Hanes agreed to put Jordan in underwear until his 40th birthday, and he had similar 10-year renewals with Gatorade, Nike, and Chevrolet. When he retired from basketball, he was also doing work for Sara Lee's Ballpark Franks and signed on with Fleer to produce a commemorative basketball card.

Jordan figured Falk's plan worked because he was very committed to it. Michael once called the relentless Falk the Rick Mahorn of agents, a guy you would not like unless he played on your team. Mahorn, of course, was one of the Detroit bruisers who used to beat on MJ. Falk said after he made the first few deals, the commercial gusher was all attributable to Jordan.

"If you were to create a media athlete and star for the 90s in the age of TV sports, spectacular talent, midsize, well-spoken, attractive, accessible, old-time values, wholesome, clean, natural, not too good with a little bit of the devil in him, you'd come up with Michael Jordan," Falk explained.

That description did not exactly account for Jordan's unprecedented market saturation, so Falk considered the question again. This was long after Chicago Stadium had cleared out but while the aroma of Jordan's 54-point outburst against the New York Knicks in Game 4 of the 1993 Eastern Conference semifinals was still fresh. "Well, maybe it's an intangible mix of many things: his ability to play, his ability to communicate, to come across as a genuine individual. It's a whole combination of factors, and if you broke them apart and put them back together you would lose the synergy. He's a classic example in marketing of what we call synergy. The whole is just much bigger than the sum of the parts."

Clearly Jordan's ability to electrify on the court combined with his magnetic personality and just enough pop-culturish charm—the solid gold number 23 earring in his left lobe, for example—gave him commercial appeal. His appearances in public in high-fashion suits and the way he handled his fame enabled Jordan to break the barriers of race, age, and gender.

The classic example of his appeal is how Gatorade used Jordan. He had come to symbolize everything the public loves about basketball, according to the *Sports Marketing Letter,* a monthly newsletter that charted the sports sponsorship business. As a result, Gatorade commercials showed Jordan hanging out with playground players after a game in an effort to tap that market. Other Gatorade spots show him playing with kids, which taps what Nova Lanktree, president of Lanktree Passport Celebrity Network, a sports talent consulting company in Northbrook, Illinois, described as Jordan's "charisma and singular distinctive personality."

Consider the results after Nike exploited such qualities. The first advertising campaign featured Jordan on a lifesize billboard set on the outskirts of Chicago's downtown area known as the Loop. That was in 1984 when a pair of Air Jordans sold for $64.95. In January 1994, the Nike commercials featuring Jordan as Johnny Kilroy formed the advertising highlight during Super Bowl XXVIII at a cost of more than $3 million. At that time a pair of Air Jordans sold for more than $120.

Freelance writer David Breskin explained why Jordan had become such an advertising icon in an article he wrote for the December 1989 issue of *Gentleman's Quarterly.* Wrote Breskin: "People are not only awed by Michael Jordan, they like him. They believe him. Somehow he manages to be both the downest brother and whitest bred at the same time. That Jordan reconciles the opposites within his own character so smoothly has made him the most admired, idolized, and moneyed team-sport hero in the entire American-hero worship business. In fact, for some folks he has come to represent America—as in, we may not make cars or televisions too well, but we turn out a helluva Michael Jordan."

What made Jordan's selling power special was the way he moved merchandise. You could actually see this happen much in the same fashion fans would flock to a music store when their favorite artist released a new album. Except with Jordan this happened every day, sometimes in the strangest places. Before Game 2 of the 1993 Eastern Conference Finals series against the Knicks, John Napierowski, a 35-year-old Long

Island resident, brought his young son into Gerry Cosby's sporting goods store at Madison Square Garden in New York. Napierowski figured that he had spent more than $1,000 on Michael Jordan merchandise the past few years, but here he was dropping another $39.99 on a souvenir Jordan jersey because that's how his son wanted to remember the first NBA game he would ever see that night.

The same feeding frenzy broke throughout Manhattan that day. Jordan's latest video at the time, "Michael Jordan: Air Time," was outselling all sports videos except for one about the Knicks, history at a local video store. At Paragon Sporting Goods in downtown Manhattan, Michael had the edge: his stuff outsold that of hometown hero Patrick Ewing of the Knicks.

Jordan beat the local favorites one-on-one worldwide. After the 1993 season, a newspaper in Australia conducted a survey among high school students as to who the most popular athlete was. In Australia, the local version of pro football stopped activity in the country on Saturday; everybody either attended a game or watched on television. Local pro basketball drew crowds of no more than 15,000 fans. But the *Sunday Mail* in Brisbane reported Jordan won with 1,375 votes, while footballers Allan Langer (1,054), Wally Lewis (798), and Willie Carne (726) followed. Golfer Greg Norman, Australia's only true international hero, finished 12th.

Some fans were so hot for Jordan paraphernalia that they did not care what it cost. After Michael made his first commercial with Bugs Bunny in 1992, Nike introduced a leather bomber jacket with "Air Jordan" and "Hare Jordan" embroidered on the back. Priced at $180, they were hard to keep in any of Nike's outlet stores. Some fans did not bother to pay for stuff. During his last year with the Bulls before retiring in 1993, Michael reported that the "Champs" license plates on his Jeep Cherokee had been stolen.

Make no mistake. Jordan knew how to cash in on his popularity. In spring 1993, he and a limited group of partners opened Michael Jordan's: The Restaurant and attracted people with a $350,000 video wall in the bar, a roomful of Jordan memorabilia, including all 30 of the *Sports Illustrated* covers on which he appeared through 1993. If you stood in line for three hours, you could get a seat in the main dining room and have a chance to look at Michael eating with friends. Three hours before tipoff for Game 3 of the 1993 Finals, an overcast Sunday in Chicago, more than 100 fans lined up outside the restaurant. By game time, the line stretched to well over 2,000.

Jordan was such a marketing phenomenon that the content of his commercials almost seemed irrelevant. Chevrolet actually aired a spot with him leaning on a Blazer, talking about his uncontrollable tendency to stick his tongue out while playing the game. Michael knew his value as a promotional tool, but it was one aspect of life that made him feel used. Other people were profiting by using his face to sell T-shirts and other merchandise. He figured putting an end to that maybe would limit his overexposure in the market place. Falk figured that if T-shirts and other merchandise bearing Jordan's likeness would continue to be in demand, then MJ should be the one who profited. He filed suit to keep the NBA from producing and selling merchandise with his picture on it. That whole controversy made Jordan seem selfish or even greedy. But that is also when he realized the return on investment of being a commercial puppet dwindled below an acceptable rate.

"All the companies wanted more of my time, more of my days," he said. "After a few years, my time was more valuable to me than money could ever be."

Marketing Michael had some upsides for Jordan. He made a lot of money. He had an impact on a lot of people. He made commercials with Bugs Bunny. But it also led Jordan into many situations like one that took place after a home game in December of 1992. A television crew from the Netherlands was in Chicago to shoot film for a special on Jordan. As he was about to leave, one of the members of the crew pulled him aside for a short interview. "Michael, we've seen all the commercials in Holland," he began. "Now tell us, can you really fly?"

By then Jordan was sure of what this marketing monstrosity had done. It had turned his life into a media nightmare. Every time he made a new commercial, it gave members of the media one more thing to ask him, one more reason to pry into his life. After the first commercial with Bugs Bunny, somebody asked him if being on television with Bugs made him a real star. How did he ever put up with this treatment?

 SEVENTEEN

You Guys

December 12, 1992, Bulls Locker Room, Chicago Stadium, After a 95–89 Defeat of New Jersey. This writer who has been following me and the team the last couple years cornered me as I was about to leave. He was from some foreign country, France, I think. "Michael, do you mind if I ask you a couple of off-the-wall questions?" he asked. Why did they always come off the wall with their questions? Every night it seemed like they came from another country. France, Holland, Japan, Germany. Did they ask anybody else off-the-wall questions?

He said nobody wanted to know what the other guys think. A win over New Jersey, 38 points, and the perfect night should end with dinner with my wife. But since he came all the way from France, I'm impressed enough to humor him for a few minutes.

"What's you favorite movie?" he asked.

"*Ghost*. Ever see that?"

"How much money would you give for a drink that would make you invisible?"

"A lot," I said, "like right now."

"Do you know how much money you have?" Questions about money were personal, so I joked with him by checking my pockets. He wanted to know all together, not right now.

"Ask my wife," I told him.

"Do you tell bedtime stories to your kids? What is your favorite?"

"Well, that depends on what their favorites are, not what my favorites are. But usually the Turtles."

He said two questions. That's five, but why stop now?

"Are you curious whether there are aliens out there in outer space?"

"I don't know, are you?"

"Michael, have you ever been in contact with the Mafia?"

Couldn't keep from laughing on that one. "I don't know," I said. "I don't think so."

"Would you like to see a woman in the White House?"

This was about as far as I could go. Had to give him a reason to stop asking questions. "There are lot of women in the White House. Women run the White House. Women run all houses. You been married? Doesn't your wife run the house?"

Dealing with the media was part of the job and sometimes you had to make it fun. "You guys" was kind of like a nickname I used for reporters. I was like that with all my friends, calling them by their initials or something but never by their names. Sometimes it seemed like I spent more time with them than I did with my teammates or my family. Like I said, it was part of the job, and I never really had a problem with any of the beat writers. Occasionally, a columnist would piss me off, but I always let them know when I liked what they wrote. I used to read it all, you know.

Maybe that was the problem. Maybe I gave those guys too much time, and they started taking advantage of it. Sometime during my last year—probably the time when the Atlantic City thing happened and my gambling became an issue—I felt betrayed. You have to put up with what they say or write about you, because if they never said or wrote anything I probably never would have got to this level. Some things like being called a goat in one of the papers during the Knicks series I could understand. Some of it I couldn't take anymore, like when they started questioning what I did in my private time. The way they reported my involvement with gambling and playing golf for money and some of the things that were written about my father's death caused me so much distress that one of the best things about retiring was leaving "you guys" behind.

So many times Michael Jordan joked with the media the way children teased one another. Before a mid-winter game during the 1992 season, he sat and discussed the recent breast implant controversy Dow Chemical was having and asked a female reporter if she ever considered trying them. He offered to foot the bill for a pair of implants, as Michael said laughing, "to see if they really did any good." Oftentimes he found this conversation relaxing if not comforting and amusing.

The day after Game 1 of the 1992 Finals, three reporters lingered around at the end of the formal media session that players were forced to deal with for 30 minutes. This was three out of more than 600 media members from 110 countries. Jordan likened his three-point shooting the night before to what most people experience playing on a Nerf hoop and admitted the best practice he had to prepare for the exhibition was playing with his kids and their "Jordan Jammer" miniature basket in the basement.

When he was at ease talking in public, Michael could ramble on indefinitely. And he often did. Two days after staying around to talk for more than 45 minutes after the overtime loss to Orlando on January 16, he was asked why he did that. Why did he do that when everybody would have understood if he had bolted after 15 minutes. "Always feel like I have to pay my respects to you guys," he said. "Stupid questions and all."

The day the Bulls started their Eastern Conference Finals series against the New York Knicks, the day before he made his infamous trip to an Atlantic City casino, he had challenged members of the media to probe him. Jordan sat beneath the hook that held up his clothes in a dressing room half the size of most of the closets in his house and offered, "Don't y'all want to ask me some questions?" When the questions were all answered, he swapped stories about basketball, golf, and Atlantic City. Michael seemed to have no problem enduring these nightly sessions, which was why the NBA beat writers voted him to the All-Interview team in each of its six years of existence through the 1993 season.

"I understood what dealing with the media was all about, and learning that was part of my education and maturity," Michael related shortly after his last formal meeting with the press as a basketball player concluded. "Sometimes, I wished I wasn't the only one on our team who did most of the talking. But sitting with the media was just my nature, part of my personality. I never wanted them to think of me as a rude type of guy. It took a little bit of experience to understand matters.

"They all had a job to do, just like I had a job to do. But they didn't have any sympathy for normal people sometimes. I didn't appreciate that. I didn't appreciate the way things were reported. I never minded them printing the specifics, but opinions the columnists used to have bothered me sometimes. Those were the guys who had no sympathy. You couldn't have paid me enough to do their job."

Imagine spending a day traveling in a rainstorm that would not let up. You come in out of the rain, dry off, and go back outside when it seems to be clearing up. Except here it comes again, and you never get completely dry. There's always enough dampness to provide just a little itch and irritation. That's what Jordan's life with the media was like. He would talk for a half hour after practice, and one more person would come up with a few more questions. "Don't abuse the privilege," he would say, then spend another 15 minutes providing answers or long enough for a third person to want some time.

It was like that after every Bulls game. The double-wide size stall he had in the Bulls' locker room in the Stadium was not much bigger than a telephone booth. So many people tried to cram in to talk to him after a game that the scene was almost comical. One group would surround him, making the second tier lean in waiting for those in front to finish. When a space opened up, the action was reminiscent of Charles Barkley and Rick Mahorn bouncing off each other's butts battling for a rebound. People holding cameras would turn to move out and hit other reporters in the back of the head. Jordan said he would have found the whole ordeal funnier than the Three Stooges if he had not had to answer the same questions two and three times after every game.

Jordan could deal with persistent requests to be the subject of a cover story for *Mondial* basketball magazine in France because he understood the publication's circulation skyrocketed with his picture on the cover. "Almost 12,000 per issue," according to Christopher Derollez, founder of the magazine. When *L'Equipe* sports newspaper in France selected Jordan as the best sportsman in the world in 1992, the issue sold out completely, quite a phenomenon, according to *L'Equipe* writer Pascal Coville. Picking up a copy of the *New York Daily News* during the 1993 playoff series against the Knicks and seeing a caricature of his face affixed to Superman's body on the back cover did not bother Michael. Picking up *New York Newsday* after Game 1 of that series and being called "the goat of the game"—he knew it just meant more questions for him to answer.

He was the first to admit that he was good copy. He could not explain why two days after he scored 54 points in Game 4 against the Knicks in that 1993 series, *Newsday* would run a picture of Madison Square Garden on its front page with this inscription: "Michael Jordan, In Concert Tonight at 9, Madison Square Garden, 33rd Street and Seventh Avenue: Mr. Jordan will attempt an encore of his Monday performance." Likewise, he could not explain why the same newspaper would run a complete shot-by-shot account of his performance that night and not those of Patrick Ewing or John Starks, the hometown heroes.

Up until a point, Jordan obliged all the media requests. Toward the end of the 1993 season, a reporter from ESPN solicited an interview by saying, "This one comes out of left field." That was pretty normal compared to some of the off-the-wall requests. The story was about the Bulls and the Pittsburgh Penguins, the two-time defending champions of the National Hockey League. The Penguins, like the Bulls, were chasing a third straight league title. The Penguins, like the Bulls, were led by the game's best player. What did Michael think of Pittsburgh's Mario Lemieux, who had just overcome Hodgkin's disease and returned to lead his team in the playoffs.

"Mario, huh. We played golf together," Jordan said, then provided all the details without being asked a single question. "We both came into the league the same year, we both won championships the same year. He's shown he has a love for the game that helped him overcome some of his personal problems. I admire him for that. Winning is our common denominator. Our styles of play—we're very creative players—are similar. We both try to include everyone, but we try to carry the load when no one else is there to carry it. That's probably one of the reasons I admire him so much. That, and he's a two-handicap."

That's what it was like for Michael. Because Jordan was such a marketable commodity, the NBA scheduled the Bulls to play on Christmas night and on Martin Luther King's birthday. After the latter, he had to answer questions from *Ebony* magazine and the Black Entertainment Television (BET) network about why he would play on such a day and if that showed any disrespect to Dr. King. When the riot broke out in Los Angeles over the verdict in the Rodney King police brutality trial in 1992, Jordan was asked to comment on the issue.

Jordan, who grew up in a community that was 60 percent white and 40 percent black, responded by telling a story about what happened when he was in ninth grade. That was in 1978 when the television miniseries "Roots," based on Alex Haley's book, had recently been aired. A girl in school called Michael a nigger, he said, so he threw ice at her and was suspended from school. "I didn't care about getting suspended, I just felt I had to express my displeasure for using that word. I was always aware of (prejudice) from that point on. I felt it was us against the world."

Then Michael lashed out at Jim Brown, who criticized Jordan for not being more active in the King situation. "When something like the L.A. riot happens, I'm asked to comment on it. People tend to expect me to do more, be more opinionated, more vocal. They make it sound like Magic Johnson and myself are the only wealthy black people in America. Where are the Eddie Murphys, the Arsenio Halls, Bill Cosby?"

The year forced Jordan to become more guarded in his dealing with the media. The season started with controversy that made Jordan think in retrospect: "They couldn't find any flaws in my basketball, so they started attacking my private life."

That 1991–92 season started when Jordan did not accompany the Bulls on their trip to the White House to meet President Bush. Two days later, he showed up 45 minutes late for the annual media day gathering. Then a month later, Jordan encountered his first major scandal. Reports showed that a $57,000 check he wrote was found among the belongings of convicted cocaine dealer James "Slim" Bouler, who had been arrested for money-laundering. Jordan said the money was a loan to Bouler, who was trying to build a golf driving range. Further investigation revealed another $108,000 in payments was made to murdered North Carolina bail bondsman Eddie Dow. What's more, the checks were dated the time when the Bulls were visiting the White House, the time Jordan said he spent relaxing with his family and friends.

Jordan was subpoenaed to testify at Bouler's trial a year later. Since Jordan was the source of so much hard copy, Chicago's newspapers sent their Bulls beat reporters to cover his testimony at the Bouler trial. Jordan said the $57,000 was payment for a gambling debt. The legal end of the world was satisfied with his explanation. The media side of the world wanted to know why he lied. Jordan said he was "embarrassed, caught off guard, ashamed of what I had done." The questions about the $57,000 came up during a news conference Jordan held with Nike officials in October 1992 to announce $100,000 in donations to the Chicago Public Schools. The school corporation was raising money to save its athletic programs, which provided opportunities for predominantly black students, and there was not enough money in the budget to do so. Jordan was trying to help the black community, and the media jumped on him for something else.

"I really thought all my troubles were behind me at that time," Michael said. "I didn't want to talk about any of the gambling stuff anymore. I tried to keep people from asking me about it by telling them I thought my troubles were behind me. I tried to get them to focus on what I was doing on the basketball court."

On the basketball court, there was not anything new to write about Michael. How many different ways were there to describe his nightly romps as the best player in the game? When he bailed out the Bulls with 20 fourth-quarter points and led the comeback from 17 points down that ended with a 96-92 win over Utah, the headline in the *Chicago Tribune* the next day read: "Jordan rescues Bulls again." But the smallest piece of gossip could outdo his on-the-court acrobatics and heroics at this point of Michael's career. The scuttlebutt after this game came out of a casual conversation that Jordan had with friends two weeks before the game at Utah. Salt Lake City was the site of the NBA All-Star game, and Jordan commented that all there really is to do in Utah is ski. Because his contract and all NBA contracts prevented players from skiing, he wondered if the All-Star game would not be better off held in some warm climate more conducive to playing golf. "Jordan criticizes Salt Lake City," headlined the local newspaper the next day.

Utah governor Mike Leavitt tried to intervene by inviting Jordan to play golf with him in the southern part of the state where there was no snow or skiing. Jordan declined that offer, having already made plans to play golf in Las Vegas with friends during the All-Star break to attend a 30th birthday party being thrown for him there. More than 300 people reportedly called Leavitt's office to protest the red-carpet treatment for Jordan and that made news as well. Charles Barkley said at the same time the All-Star Game should be held in Orlando every year because that was the best climate. Nobody bitched and moaned about what he said, Jordan noted.

"Big headache," is how Michael described dealing with the media after such an incident. "I always paid my respect to those guys. Tried to make their job easy. All I asked was that they try to make my job easy. The reality of life is that I was just as human as any other player, but somehow I wasn't being treated that way."

From that point, Jordan merely co-existed with members of the media. Those he trusted, he obliged. But he trusted fewer and fewer people, and the change was easy to see. He would do off-day interviews wearing sunglasses as if to say he was never going to let anybody get inside his head or even close to him. He was not going to open up.

"The way the Slim Bouler thing was handled really made him retreat," Cliff Levingston observed. "He talked to me about it a lot, and he said I was one of the only people he felt he could talk to about it. That was the point where he decided he couldn't really talk about the things that were on his mind because everybody was so caught up in the Michael Jordan thing. He felt as though nobody ever thought of him as a real person. You know he hurts, he bleeds, he cries just like everybody else. But he had felt like he had to start looking at everybody very carefully, like under a microscope. I wasn't with him the last season, but he told me he wasn't having any fun anymore."

If the night in the locker room talking nonsense with the French reporter was a turning point, then Michael's attitude toward the media went off the wall, over the sink, and down the toilet . . . nothing but net. His forays into the gambling world only made things worse.

How much the public had a right to know about what Jordan did with his private life became an issue for debate. Jordan contended nobody had a right to know about what he did with his free time. Nevertheless, when he was spotted at Bally's Casino in Atlantic City Monday night between 5:30 and 11 P.M., everybody knew about it because the *New York Times* reported the incident in its editions on Wednesday, May 26. *Times* sports columnist Dave Anderson quoted an anonymous source who claimed Jordan was playing blackjack at Bally's until 2:30 A.M.

On May 27, Jordan faced a crowd of more than 80 media types and explained his side of the story. This was a Michael Jordan many people had never seen before. He was defiant and accusatory. "If one person says I was there until 2:30 A.M., show them to me and I will certainly lay a lawsuit on them." His voice, normally a sub-baritone, the kind that could echo through a drain pipe, reached a high pitch. His voice cracked, the way some people get when they're holding back tears. "Show me these people. Show me. Where? Where?

"I'm just trying to get away from the city of New York, instead of sitting in my hotel room listening to the media hype up about the first game, my mistakes, Michael Jordan didn't play well. I didn't have my golf clubs. If I did, I would have went golfing, and you guys probably would have criticized me for that. That's enough. If my life comes to the point where it's scrutinized to what I do on my free time, then there's no need to even talk to you guys."

That point was about to come. Jordan admitted he went to Atlantic City, admitted he was there between 5:30 and 11 P.M., and admitted he lost money. He said he came forth and addressed the issue because "I wanted to tell the truth so you guys would quit hallucinating and taking it further." It did not work. A Chicago television reporter, not one normally assigned to cover sports, asked Jordan if gambling was his regular pre-game routine. He wanted to know if Jordan made regular visits to Joliet, a city 30 miles south of Chicago that operated a riverboat casino. He wanted to know, in the wake of the Slim Bouler issue, if Jordan had a gambling problem that was escalating.

As the TV reporter pressed for answers, Jordan walked away, turning his back on the media world. If Mike Wallace or Morley Safer had been asking the questions, Jordan's exit would have made a perfect segment on "60 Minutes." He was the subject of an investigation who walked away angry after a probing barrage of questioning.

Michael figured if the order of the day turned from reporting sports to compiling dossiers, then that was not news. That was "A Current Affair." That was "Geraldo." That was the *National Enquirer.* He stopped talking publicly then and did not start again for another two weeks.

He even played nasty tricks on the media. Two days after the initial walkout, the Bulls beat the Knicks in Game 3 of the Eastern Conference Finals. In the 20-point victory Jordan scored 22 points and had 11 assists but made just 3 of 18 shots. Afterward, Bulls public relations workers reported that instead of meeting the press corps of more than 500 at the usual spot, a podium set up in a spot that doubled as the media dining room, he would be available in the locker room. As the usual crowd jockeyed for position in front of the empty chair where Jordan normally sat, Michael was sneaking around behind closed doors to his car. He never did show.

His silence only created more problems. A week after the Atlantic City junket, more reports about Michael and gambling surfaced. San Diego businessman Richard Esquinas alleged in a book that Jordan had lost more than $1.25 million to him during a 10-day period in 1991 wagering on golf. Esquinas said they played rounds in which $300,000 was bet on a single putt and that putts for $100,000 were frequent.

Michael's temporary vow of silence allowed the media to speculate about his gambling activities without benefit of denial or verification from Jordan. The question never really addressed during the next week was whether his gambling was a problem because it was reported or whether it was reported because it was a problem. The way it was reported—one Chicago newspaper, for instance, published stories asking experts to evaluate whether Jordan had a gambling problem— seemed to indicate the former to Jordan.

Jordan finally issued a written statement through David Falk's office the day after the Esquinas book was released. He said that he did play golf with Esquinas and that they did wager. He said he did not keep records but that the amount wagered "was substantially less than the preposterous amounts reported." He even thanked the members of the media who "had the courage and independence to report this incident and the coverage for what it was: an embarrassment."

That statement came out the same night the Bulls finished off the Knicks in Game 6 of the Eastern Conference Finals, a colossal victory that put the team in the NBA Finals for the third straight year. Guess what grabbed the next day's headlines? Jordan's statement and Madonna's attendance at the game at Chicago Stadium.

When Jordan did decide to go back on the record, it was in an interview with Ahmad Rashad on NBC during halftime of Game 1 of the NBA Finals. Maybe this was his way of saying, "This is a guy I trust, so he gets the story from me." Michael was that upset about the whole ordeal. Anyone who has talked with an ex-wife or ex-husband during a nasty divorce settlement knows the tone Jordan used when he started talking again. This was the day after the Bulls 100-92 win in Game 1. The night before, he explained about the gambling. Then, after the game, he dug in on the reporters the way a hungry person goes after a steak. His nasty, confrontational viewpoint only hardened in the months after the incident."

"I understood it (how it was reported)," Michael admitted the next day after taking time to evaluate the situation. "But they (the media) didn't understand it from my point of view, from a humanistic side, from the reality side of Michael Jordan. They saw it as a role-model image, a certain purist image. I felt like that was unfair to me because I hadn't broken a law. I felt the way they were treating me—I felt like a criminal when I really wasn't. I wanted them to understand no matter how high they put you on a pedestal, we are people and we have a life to live. You want to keep things positive in the public's eye. But that doesn't mean you've got to live a purist life. And it didn't mean you were a criminal when you didn't.

"The way I felt, if the only thing people could say bad about Michael Jordan was that he was competitive and he gambled, that's far better than a lot of situations other people have faced."

If Jordan had not walked out of the America West Arena after talking that day following Game 1, he may have harbored a lasting disdain or contempt for the media. After Michael finished, NBA commissioner David Stern and deputy commissioner Russ Granek held a press conference to comment on Jordan's gambling. When Stern stated that betting on golf and going to Atlantic City did not violate any NBA rule or any rule the NBA planned to enact or any rule the NBA thought it was wise to enact, it touched off a scene that combined the most dramatic elements of "L.A. Law" and "The People's Court."

The national media assaulted Stern and Granek with the following line of questioning. "Is it fair to say," the commissioner was asked, "that if one of the NBA players was consorting with people who's image might be harmful to the game that you would tell him not to do so?"

"Would it be wrong, Mr. Commissioner, to say that a person losing money playing golf could compromise the integrity of the game?"

"Are you worried, Mr. Commissioner, that if a player loses large sums of money gambling, that he might be putting himself in a compromising situation that might lead to his considering fixing a game as a way to pay off the debt?"

The Jordan gambling issue never did die. Stern said that he would conduct an investigation into Jordan's relationship with Esquinas. Jordan said that he had no worries about it and that he had hired his own private detective agency to check out all perspective golfing partners in the future. Michael's feeling was that he was hustled into losing money to Esquinas. The day after Jordan announced his retirement from basketball, Stern announced that the NBA's investigation into Esquinas turned up nothing to be acted upon.

But for Jordan, the damage was permanent. During his farewell press conference he blamed the media for that. During the 45-minute question-and-answer session, Jordan took shots at the press as if it was one big Gerald Wilkins.

When asked if he would continue to live in Chicago, he said, "I would like to, as long as you guys stay away from my house so I can have some peace and quiet." He emphasized that he would never let the media drive him away from the game, but he added that the members of the press were not people he would miss.

"I'm capable of relaxing," Michael asserted. "I'm capable of hiding from you guys. Sometimes you guys have gotten on my nerves. Sometimes I've omitted that and sometimes I've admitted that. But I have no regrets about walking away from the spotlight."

Just before he got up to walk out, Jordan was asked what his special contribution to the game was. "My special contribution was the tongue. You never saw anything like it and you may never see anything like it again." A legitimate question produced an off-the-wall answer. Michael Jordan had the last laugh on the media, perhaps his way of getting even with them for ruining his life.

EIGHTEEN
Fore-Peat

Thursday, July 15, 1993, Stone-bridge Country Club, Aurora, Illinois. The last time any competition made me this nervous was my first pick-up game at North Carolina. Back then, I was trying to show a few of my future team-mates that I could play on their level. But golfing with Arnold Palmer in a pro-am with thousands of people watching made me so hyped that I basically missed the ball on my first drive off the practice tee. Barely got the top of it, and after it bounced off the tee one of the other pros in this senior tournament yelled at me, "Better get a little more air time on it." After that, J. C. Snead came up to me with a few pointers. Figured I better listen to him. His father, Sam, invented the game.

Never thought I would get to this level. Had a chance to play golf all over the world, but even playing for big money never could compare to the feeling of playing with Arnie. He's one of my idols. I heard somebody call him the Michael Jordan of golf. I would be lucky to be called the Arnold Palmer of basketball.

It would be great to forget all of that now, because even though this is a pro-am in the Ameritech Senior Open, it's still a competition. And you know me, I want to win, no matter what the stakes are.

Good thing I have my lucky hat on. If you see me wearing that straw hat, you know I'm ready for some golf. Just wish I could have stepped up to the first tee and both sides of the fairway weren't lined with people all the way to the green. That's 570 yards of people on both sides. As it is, when I stand over the ball and get ready to tee off, you don't always know where it's going.

Whenever I played golf, I expected to play well. That was just my nature. But in tournament situations, I learned to expect embarrassing moments. Just wish the first one in this tournament wouldn't have come on the first hole. Didn't have anything to mark my ball, so I had to borrow a nickel from Arnie. Figured if I paid him back with a dime it might make up for it. Must have made him feel lucky because he went out and knocked in a 25-foot birdie on the next hole.

Do I get an assist on that?

You know, if I never live to see another round of under-par golf, I will remember this game with Arnie. After nine holes, I had the man beat. Put that 10-foot birdie on the eighth hole down just like I was shooting over Gerald Wilkins. I'm one up on him making the turn to the 10th hole, somebody is playing that music they always played at the Stadium where we were rallying, and with the third title still fresh in my mind I'm thinking Fore-Peat. After 13 holes we were still even.

Then, Arnie turned into the Knicks. Or I turned into the Timber-wolves.

No point in talking about the drive out of bounds on the 14th hole, the three-putt on the 15th hole or what happened on the 16th. Golf taught me a humility basketball never did. It also taught me frustration.

When you hit a shot like the one on the 16th that flew out of the bunker and over the green, you have to learn to keep on fighting. The Pistons taught me that. So I put an X down on my scorecard under the 16th hole and tried to save face. Especially if I couldn't save par.

The score is not what I loved about golf. The challenge of playing against somebody like Arnold Palmer or playing against a course is why you play. And the game teaches you something. It was the closest sport to basketball in terms of providing the competition and mental stimulus. Some of the things I learned on the golf course made me a better basketball player. The feeling of hitting the ball solid off the tee was almost better than going up for a dunk. I felt having golf would ultimately make it easier to give up basketball.

─────────────────────────────

Michael Jordan sat at the podium following the Bulls' victory over Phoenix that wrapped up the 1993 NBA championship with a cigar in one hand and a bottle of champagne in the other. He was just about finished answering questions and his words had begun to slur, the obvious effect of a little bit of bubbly on a man who rarely imbibed. The final question was put to Jordan: "What's next, Michael?"

In the context of NBA playoff press conferences, such a question would prompt a player of Jordan's stature to provide historical perspective on what he had just accomplished, the third straight title that neither Magic, Larry, nor Isiah ever won. But Jordan already said he would put that off until a later date, one after he retired from basketball for good.

What's next could also have been a request for his views on the chances of the Bulls' four-peating, or winning a fourth straight title. But when the question of what's next came up, Jordan stood up and barked out, "Golf, golf, lots of golf." Then he raced out of the room as if he were late for a tee-time.

Michael Jordan could never get enough golf. One time during his rookie season, the Bulls were on a road trip on the West Coast, where the weather was usually ripe for golf. But a game-day shoot-around and the game that night did not leave enough time to play. So Michael grabbed teammate Rod Higgins, and they played 18 holes of miniature golf.

Once, he manufactured a scheme to get away from an NBA Finals off-day press conference early in order to get to the course in time for 36 holes. What was the attraction for Jordan that even when an injury made him think it was better not to play golf while in Portland for the 1992 Finals he got in a golf cart and rode around a local course? His 54-hole binges on two-day layovers in NBA cities with year-round warm climates were legendary. But was he any good? Was he as good as he thought he was? Was he good enough to ever give a professional career a shot? And did golf really provide as much of a challenge or stimulus as basketball? Were there similarities between the two games that made Michael think he could be as good at golf as he was at basketball? How did he keep golf from being another aspect that added complications to his already complicated lifestyle? Why did he love golf so much?

"I'll never forget the summer of '84," Jordan said with the smile he flashed during private moments. "I came out of college and Davis Love got me started playing golf. He thought it would be a good way to get away from basketball and relax. It was a couple days after we lost to Indiana in the NCAA tournament. I made a par, one par, on my first 18 holes. You know how golf is, one good shot keeps you coming back. From that point I was hooked."

Until his success on the 1992 professional golf tour, Davis Love's claim to fame was being the man who got Michael Jordan started. When the PGA Championship was played at Kemper Lakes Country Club in the Chicago suburb of Hawthorn Woods, Love could not step up to a tee without hearing something like, "Look, honey, that's Davis Love. He's the one who taught Michael Jordan how to play golf." Every time the PGA tour came to Chicago, which was at least once a year for the Western Open, reporters flocked to Love to ask him questions to do the story about the man who started Michael Jordan playing golf.

When the good shots were few, the opportunity to play with the game's best players kept him coming back. Whenever Michael played in an event, such as the Ameritech Senior Open Pro-Am, he could count on a dozen or so pros giving him lessons. But golf was the one opponent Jordan could never beat—not consistently anyway. And that's why he played it so relentlessly.

"Golf was a different challenge every day you stepped on the course," Michael explained. "For me, it was something I could never conquer. Maybe you would get a hold on it for a little time. But if you feel like you can conquer a game every day, then it's boring. Golf soaked up some of my competitive juices. For me, it was something that always had a challenge. It was a driving force.

"When you're a competitor like me, you need a driving force all the time. Basketball couldn't be there all the time, so golf filled in when basketball wasn't there."

And to think Michael called golf his way of getting away from basketball, his relaxation. Funny how some people relax. Jordan using golf as a method of relaxation was like turning to chewing gum to give up smoking and then turning to coffee to give up chewing gum. But golf did the trick for Jordan because it consumed his bottomless supply of energy. Jordan professed to need challenges, but he also confessed to a need to simply be occupied. Howard White used to recount how Michael talked of the many nights when he would lay on the couch at home watching television because he could not sleep. The pent-up energy of the game of basketball left him that way, so he went channel-surfing, especially during the winter months in Chicago when he could not play golf. When Michael noted that he slept soundly the night before he officially announced his retirement, it was the first time anybody who knew him could remember his talking about being able to sleep.

For Jordan, Bulls practices got to the point where it took only so much energy to whip everybody's butt. He vented it on golf instead. That was one reason the game became such a passion.

"When I was playing with Arnold, I noticed he was at peace with himself," Jordan reflected. "That means a lot, because then you can start to deal with the things surrounding you. I learned that as I matured and got older. I knew I needed to be at peace with myself before dealing with the things surrounding me. That's something you can get on the golf course. That's why I put smiling faces on my golf balls. Golf was a way to remind me to keep a positive attitude."

Two weeks after announcing his retirement, Michael Jordan shot a career-low 69 at a course near his home in the Chicago suburb of Highland Park. He had the ability to score on the golf course and was quite the player, considering what he had to overcome. His long arms forced him to fight high club lag on his backswing. As any golfer knows, the straighter the backswing and follow-through, the better you strike the ball. When you're 6 foot 6 inches tall, your golf swing has a greater radius. Jordan's high club lag meant he had to control his swing for a longer time than somebody of average height, which in turn left him less margin for error. This is why there were never many 6-foot-6-inch golfers on the PGA tour.

Additionally, his strong forearms and right wrist, super-developed from shooting, caused his ball to hook off the tee. When he got into trouble—the 14-15-16 stretch playing with Arnie at Stonebridge, for example—it was because of his hook.

Jordan believed the strength of his golf game was the short game— the shots within 100 yards of the green. Obviously, there are parts of the game that require the most intense concentration. After making a game-winning shot with time running out, Craig Ehlo in your face, and elimination from the playoffs hanging in the balance, a 20-foot putt would seem easy to focus on. Similarly, the short game exploits execution and repetition, something Jordan drilled into himself during his daily, after-practice shooting sessions with Doug Collins during the middle of his career.

"Michael swings the club very well," Palmer said after his round with Jordan. "He has a lot of potential as a golfer. I was pleasantly surprised. He hits the ball very soundly, and he hits it very long."

When golf was a hobby or a distraction from basketball, Jordan was never as good at the game as he thought he was. In April 1993, he declared himself a five handicap after being told that Mario Lemieux of the Pittsburgh Penguins was a two handicap and admitting that Lemieux bested him during their last meeting on the links. In June, Jordan said his handicap had risen to a 10. That admission came in the wake of his confirmation that San Diego businessman Richard Esquinas beat him out of a substantial amount of money, $500,000 by Jordan's estimation. For his match with Palmer, Jordan checked in at an eight-handicap and said in passing, "I'm the only guy who cheated in terms of having a handicap lower than higher."

In competitive situations, he was not very competitive. He finished the round with Palmer at 81. Starting in 1992, he competed in some events on the ten-stop Celebrity Golf Tour (CGT). The CGT was a made-for-television competition pitting athletes, former athletes, movie and television stars, and occasionally an ex-president in three-day, 54-hole tournaments. During his first year, Jordan carded a pair of rounds in the 80s and one in the 90s. After the 1993 basketball season ended, he put up a pair of 80s in his only tour stop but came back with a 71 on the final day. In his only other prestigious competition, Jordan was granted an entry to play in the 1990 Western Amateur. The Western Amateur is played in Benton Harbor, Michigan, and is considered one of the top five amateur tournaments in the country. Players go through 72 holes of stroke-play competition to determine the 64 who qualify for the one-on-one match play phase of the tournament. Jordan, who was a member of the Western Golf Association Board of Directors, was criticized for being granted entry through a sponsor's exemption, one of the spots reserved for tournament sponsors to choose players they want to put into the field. Some of the players argued that he was in the tournament as a drawing-card. He was paired with then U.S. Amateur and NCAA champion Phil Mickelson and failed to break 80 in either of his two rounds before missing the first cut.

Despite such competitive air balls, Jordan fielded questions about playing professional golf once or twice a week. Many people figured this was an easy way to get Jordan to talk to them. In fact, golf turned into kind of a pick-up line for many of Michael's followers. He would be sitting in the locker room at Madison Square Garden before a game with the Knicks when somebody would walk up to him and utter, "Winged Foot," the name of a famed golf course in nearby Mamaroneck, New York, that hosted several U.S. Open tournaments. Jordan would smile and say, "Now, don't get me started thinking about that when I have a game to play."

There were times when he was asked if he ever thought about playing golf in the winter in Chicago. He would look at the person who initiated such a question with a perplexed expression, then admit, "I've been asked more off-the-wall questions."

He never confirmed that pro golf was his goal, but he never completely dismissed the idea either. When he announced his retirement, he was asked again about giving pro golf a shot. He said for now that was a hobby, his relaxation. For now.

"It was another driving force for me, a reason to go out on the course and be competitive in addition to enjoying myself," Michael said after retirement, when he had actually had some time to consider the prospects of a pro golf career. "I don't know if I could ever get good enough to play pro golf, but you know me. I would never jump into an arena I'm not good enough for. But you know me, I'd love to do it. That's just the competitive attitude I have."

Golf was never a game to Jordan. He wanted to win whenever he played, and he felt he could beat anybody. "He was as driven in golf as he was on the basketball court," Doug Collins recalled. "He wouldn't go out and hit a bucket of golf balls at the driving range like you or me. He would be out there for five hours."

That desire caused Jordan to get into high-stakes games of golf with Slim Bouler and Richard Esquinas. But it also enabled him to be up one shot on Arnold Palmer after nine holes of the Ameritech Senior Open Pro-Am. That tournament was played under a four-man, best-ball format. According to such rules, each player tees off, and the rest of the members of the group hit from the spot of where the best tee shot lies. Then they each hit from the spot where the best second shot lies and so forth. The others in the Jordan-Palmer foursome that day included Bill Weiss, chairman of Ameritech, and John McCoy, chairman of the Banc One Corporation. The total net worth of that foursome might well have been more than $500 million. Jordan's foursome tied for the low score at 15-under-par 57, and his shots counted on 6 of the 18 holes.

The best moments on the course for Michael were those when he could be on the first tee at sunrise, play 18, eat lunch, and then play another 18. He was the kind of guy who could land in Orlando with the team on Sunday night and squeeze in 54 holes before tip-off on Tuesday. That happened frequently but most recently in January 1993, when Jordan also took time during a round to knock on Shaquille O'Neal's door.

The Orlando rookie, whom most experts rated as the megastar to carry the NBA when Jordan retired, lived in a house on the course. O'Neal declined an invitation to play golf, perhaps opting to focus on his inaugural meeting with Jordan that night. Perhaps if Shaq had picked up a club and lost to Michael, maybe Jordan would not have blocked his first shot that night. Not likely, though.

The two games, golf and basketball, went together for Jordan the way he loved his macaroni and cheese. He wanted to play in more tournaments to test his ability "to focus on the game while people were cheering in the background," as he put it. And to Michael the feeling of making a birdie could only be described by invoking the kinds of success he knew best.

"Sinking a birdie putt was more thrilling than a three-pointer or a dunk shot because I did those all the time," Jordan explained. "When I made birdies, I felt good about the game. When I hit three-pointers, I felt like I could do that all the time. It was my job. The difference between golf and basketball was that I had to learn to be as conservative as possible. My nature was to be more aggressive. But this game (golf) teaches you to be humble and not so aggressive. The similarities caused you to evaluate a putt or how to play a hole the way you evaluate how to approach a game. All of it happened in angles. The challenge in both was to figure out the angles."

The golf course was the last safe place for Jordan to avoid invasion on his privacy. Was. Between Games 1 and 2 of the 1993 Finals in Phoenix, it was an average day in the desert—103 degrees with very little oxygen to breathe. But it was a perfect day for Michael to play 18 holes. Then again, anything short of snow was a perfect day for Michael to play.

Throughout the 30-minute interview session following practice he must have answered the question 20 times if he was going to play golf with Charles Barkley that day. Michael started Barkley playing golf, and it proved just as addictive for Sir Charles. He had one good shot that round and kept coming back. After practice, Michael booked a tee time at a local course. Midway through the round, a helicopter flew over him with a camera sticking out. That night on its news report, a local television showed the film it shot of Jordan playing golf with a rotund-looking black man. The station reported it was Charles Barkley. Actually, it was Quinn Buckner, the NBC television basketball analyst.

That was easy enough to live with. What happened during a late Saturday round in the spring of 1993 was not. Jordan was playing with some friends at the Evanston Golf Club, an intimate private country club in the Chicago suburb of Skokie. When Jordan hit the 18th green, his presence came to be known to guests at a wedding reception being held on the premises.

All the guests rushed out to get a look at him. The family asked if Jordan would take a picture with the bride and groom. He finally consented, then had to duck behind the caddy shack for the photo opportunity.

Because the golf course sometimes could not even provide privacy, he wound up purchasing memberships at courses and country clubs all around the country. After retiring, he would get on an airplane and fly to the course he wanted to play.

The lifestyle that Michael Jordan led made the privacy of golf important. When his lifestyle left him no chances to go out in public without creating a mob scene, he retreated. When his face appeared on television every five minutes or was on a billboard in every U.S. city and many foreign countries, he retreated to the first tee. When the media pestered him relentlessly, he walked away. But for Jordan there was always golf to provide an escape. The last few years of his basketball career Michael was always looking for the escape that golf and time with his family could provide.

NINETEEN

The Family

May 2, 1993, Chicago Stadium. Everybody knew about how I would check the box seats in that corner section of the Stadium right before every game to see if my family was there. Usually, I was looking for my father and sometimes my mother because I just didn't feel right, didn't feel like the game would be right unless they were there. My father didn't miss many games, and like I said, the one bright spot in his passing and my retirement was that he was there for my last one.

But this game was different, and not just because it was a playoff game against Atlanta. It was a Sunday afternoon, and that meant my wife and kids could be there. My sons, Jeffrey and Marcus, only were able to come for the afternoon games; they had already been to a couple of games this year. When I looked into those seats in the corner there, I saw Marcus standing on his chair, looking around checking everything out. He's such an independent person, just like his mother. Jeffrey was there with my mother, probably waiting for B. J. Armstrong to do something because B. J. was his favorite. That was good too, because my sons really only knew me as their father more than some basketball star.

Then I looked over at my wife and sitting on her lap was my daughter. Named her Jasmine after the princess in the *Aladdin* movie. I could only see the pink headband she was wearing but I knew it was her.

It gave me a good feeling to have them at the game, because I always worried about whether I was being a good father and husband. I always promised Juanita that was something I would continue to try and improve on. Sometimes, my wife would come to games, and we would go out for dinner afterward. But with three kids, it was hard to get away—all those diapers to change. My mother and father were such good parents that it made me want to be just like them. Mom never used to say much about my basketball, but when she would say things like she saw me relating to my boys the way she used to relate to me, then I knew she was proud of me. In a way, a lot of what you saw in me on and off the court— the outgoing personality and the serious side—came from certain genes I adopted and just being around my mother and father.

I never tried to put on a show when my family was at the game. Actually, once the game started there was never any time to think about them. Maybe sneak a look up there to see if they're watching. But this was a playoff game, so I was thinking if I put my mind to it and we can win another 14 of these, I can be with them on a full-time basis. And this was a game that demanded my full-time attention. After beating the Hawks by 24 points in the first game of the series, they came back with a more committed effort. I think Dominique was trying to show me up in front of my family, and with time running out in the first half we were only leading by four points.

With about three seconds left in the half, Will pulled down a rebound on a missed free throw and threw me an outlet pass. I took two dribbles and threw up a shot from halfcourt that bounced off the backboard, over rim, nothing but net as the halftime buzzer went off. Just before I turned around and headed off to our locker room, I looked at where my family was sitting. Five empty seats. I guess they went out for cotton candy or popcorn or something. They missed the shot. But that really didn't matter, because to them I just wanted to be a husband and a father more than anything else.

Deloris Jordan loved to walk into the grocery store, pass by the cereal counter, and see her son's picture plastered on the front of the Wheaties box. She thought the picture of Michael holding a spoonful of flakes smiling a playful grin made him look just like Pops, the way most of the world affectionately referred to James Jordan.

Michael Jordan's family life appeared to be just like everybody else's except that not everybody could have his mom walk into the store and see his face on a box of Wheaties. But as hard as he worked to be superhuman on the court, Jordan made just as devoted an effort to be a normal guy at home. And he was. Though he rarely traveled without his father at his side, Michael wondered if people knew just how much of a family man he was.

A look into his wonder years in Wilmington reveals that Michael was little more than a kid who enjoyed a mouthful of cereal every morning for breakfast and whose most outstanding qualities, other than his athletic abilities, were that he once played the trumpet in the school band and that he never really held a job. He was just like everybody else in the sense that he always proclaimed himself to be just like his mother and father.

Before there was Michael Jordan, there was simply Mike, a guy who cut his hair so short and neat that his friends in Wilmington called him "Baldy." Before there was Mike Jordan or any of his four brothers and sisters, there was James Ray Jordan and Deloris Peoples.

James and Deloris met in 1956 after a high school basketball game, when James gave her a ride home and before dropping her off told her in true Jordanesque style, "Someday I'm gonna marry you." Deloris was 15 at the time, but James lived up to his promise. When on leave from the Air Force a few years later, he found Deloris had returned to the Wilmington area after becoming homesick at college and he married her. James was in the Air Force long enough for him and his wife to have five children in order: James Ronald, Deloris Chasten, Larry, Michael, and Roslyn.

The three Jordan brothers were a study in diversity. Ron drove a bus and worked at Shoney's before joining the Army. Larry, like Pops, had mechanical talents but was more introverted. Michael had the outgoing personality, could never sit still, according to his mother, and never had a job. He used to bribe his brothers into doing his chores at home.

James Ronald, known as Ron, was perhaps most like his father. He became an Army sergeant specializing in communications. Young Deloris turned out most like mom, becoming a homemaker and moving to Philadelphia.

Larry and Roslyn were the other members of the family to garner some celebrity status. Larry, at 5 foot 7 inches, played for the Chicago franchise in the 6-foot-4-and-under World Basketball Association in 1987–88. But during his two seasons, he never played more than two minutes at the end of games. He suspected he was part of that team only becuase he was MJ's brother, so he left that world to help run Michael's companies.

Roslyn, who may have been the smartest of all the Jordan children, skipped a grade in high school to accompany Michael to North Carolina. She had her dose of fame singing the national anthem at Chicago Stadium before a Bulls playoff game in 1993.

Michael was born while his father was still in the Air Force and the family was living in Brooklyn. After finishing his stint in the Air

Force, James moved the family back to North Carolina. Although he had grown up in Wallace, he settled the family 40 miles south in Wilmington, where he built a house on six-and-a-half acres in the Weavers Acres neighborhood halfway between downtown and the beach. James had more land than anybody else in the neighborhood, so he built a basketball court in the backyard, and all the rest of the kids came to play there. With the court in the backyard, a Baptist church across the street, and the ocean three miles away, Michael's home was about as much a part of Americana as something that was not made for television could be.

James worked his way up from being a ground-floor mechanic at the General Electric plant in Wilmington to a supervisor of three departments. But he never had much time to work with Michael on his basketball game. "So I concentrated on teaching him values, the values any family would teach their kid," James noted. "Michael was a good learner. We tried to teach him to be himself. Always like people and never put yourself above anybody. But never put yourself below anybody. Always look people eye-to-eye."

Deloris was the stern parent, the one who had to punish Michael. She never gave in to him. When he was suspended from school one time for cutting class to leave and get something to eat, she made him come with her to her job at United Carolina Bank and study all day. She always said Mike was not the easiest to bring up. When Michael and Deloris got together, even when he was eight or nine years into his pro career, she would always ask to make him something to eat. And she would always remind him to throw out the garbage.

"You know, when I went off to college, my mother wasn't too happy about it," said Jordan, rubbing his chin and smiling widely, the way youngest sons smile when they talk about their mothers. "She understood I had some dreams for myself, but she heard a lot of people were advising me not to go to North Carolina because of disappointment that I might not get to play. I threw something back in her face that she always taught me. She used to say, 'If you have dreams, you got to work hard. Even though you may fail at least you tried and you can't go about life saying I never took that opportunity.' Once she heard that, she knew she had taught me well.

"She was also opposed to me leaving school a year early to turn pro. She was always very family-oriented. She always was attached to the kids. She hated to see them leave. A lot of the things she taught me, and the way she treated me, helped me with my kids. As a parent, I always think about steering my kids down the right path because my mother did with me. And I think she did a heck of a job."

When Michael Jordan was interviewed, which was more often than he was home, it was easy to see his mother's influence, her personality. The seriousness of his answers, the straightforwardness, the politeness—those were her best qualities. For Michael, being in the public eye was his business, and because he got his business sense from his mother, he was able to excel in that arena. Deloris worked a full-time job at a bank while raising five kids. She advanced from teller to an executive position. When Michael started accumulating his wealth through endorsements and investing it in business ventures, the first person he hired to oversee those operations was his mom.

She also played a major role in running the Michael Jordan Foundation, Jordan's non-profit fund-raising organization. When Michael announced his retirement in October 1993, Deloris did not find out about it until a day later because she was in Africa leading a mission for kids made possible through the foundation.

Television stations and newspapers forever do stories about the mothers and fathers of famous people for Mother's Day and Father's Day. In 1993, Jordan participated in the annual piece on his mother for Chicago's NBC affiliate. After revealing that his mother could tell some stories about him he really did not want anybody to know and refusing to tell those stories himself, Jordan looked into the camera and said, "Happy Mother's Day, Mom. I love you so much." Then a tear rolled down his cheek. It was the kind of tear sons shed when they miss their mothers.

Sons like that usually wind up marrying women with all the best qualities their mothers had. But even before Michael realized that he could turn the financial side of their relationship over to Juanita, perhaps he knew that he had found the woman of his dreams. Discount the fact that they had a baby together 10 months before they married, and Michael and Juanita had a storybook romance.

So many times when the Bulls were on the road, the FTD man would ring the doorbell at Juanita and Michael Jordan's house. Another bouquet of flowers would come from Michael, a ritual he started when she was still Juanita Vanoy—the model from the south side of Chicago whom MJ started courting when he was 22. Four years into their marriage—Michael's last season on the long and grinding road of the NBA—the romance was even too mushy for a crowd-pleasing episode of "Love Connection."

The day after the Chicago Bulls won their first NBA title (June 13, 1991), Juanita Jordan celebrated her 32nd birthday at a championship love-in with one million fans at Chicago's Grant Park, on the shores of Lake Michigan. Earlier that day, Michael had given her two presents. One was a chance to hold the NBA championship trophy that he had hardly released since the Bulls won it 12 hours before; the other, a gold Cartier watch adorned with a band of rubies and diamonds.

Later that day, Michael took her to a downtown photographer to have a portrait of them taken. While waiting for lights to be adjusted, film to be loaded into cameras, and actually sitting still for a picture, Michael hugged and kissed his wife continuously. Their relationship was not without its scenes from a Harlequin romance novel.

This was not so unusual a courtship and marriage. Michael met Juanita Vanoy in February 1985, midway through his rookie season. This was a time when he was thinking marriage or an extensive relationship would not happen until the last year of his pro career or after retirement. He had dated Robin Givens, who moved on to marry Mike Tyson. That made him think that some girls were more interested in investing in a corporation than marrying a man. "It was hard for me to trust a woman's alleged affections because it was difficult to know whether she liked me for what I had or who I was," Michael commented. "I realized it was hard for many people meeting me to separate me the successful player from me that man."

Once Michael and Juanita started dating, rumors spread that this was the woman who threw herself on the ground in front of his car while he was leaving the Stadium. Actually, a mutual friend introduced Jordan to Juanita, who at the time was working as an executive secretary at the American Bar Association. The same friend invited them both to a party, and that's when Juanita remembered Michael "asking how he could get in touch with me."

Juanita, a onetime model who had worked for the same advertising agency that handled some of Jordan's endorsements, was a very striking woman. Light-skinned, she was a high-fashion dresser—lots of elegant suits highlighted with gold jewelry—which matched Jordan. But as they developed a relationship that transcended their four-year age difference, looks were not a major part of the attraction for either one.

"She always was very independent," Michael began when asked to describe his wife. "She knew how to work and provide for herself, which is what I loved."

"I was a little apprehensive about dating him at first because he was an athlete and he was younger," Juanita admitted. "He proved his maturity to me, and he had this big heart. The more time we spent together, the more our personalities just clicked."

When dating turned into a lasting relationship, Jordan tried his best to keep his lifestyle from invading their relationship. In fact, even after they were married the most memorable moment he shared with her in the public eye came in 1991 when the Bulls won the championship.

As Bob Costas of NBC interviewed Michael after the Bulls polished off the Lakers with a 108-101 victory in Game 5 of the series, he noticed a woman to Michael's left. "Is this your mother?" Costas asked. "No, it's my wife," Michael cried out as he hugged her with one arm, clutched the trophy in the other, and stained all three with his tears. A similar moment came during his retirement press conference, when he said the main reason he was able to sleep the night before was because "I had a great roommate," then grabbed her hand and walked away from the game with her arm-in-arm.

Only their wedding was a novelty act. Michael had proposed to Juanita on New Year's Eve in 1987 over a plate of seafood pasta. They called the engagement off for a year, and when they resumed their marriage plans Juanita discovered that she was pregnant. In December 1988, Jeffrey Michael Jordan was born.

At 3:30 A.M., September 2, 1989, Michael and Juanita strolled into the Little White Wedding Chapel in Las Vegas to get married. No, the minister was not dressed as Elvis, but the bride wore blue jeans and so did the groom, with loafers and no socks. One of the two groomsmen wore a pair of shorts and Nikes. Jordan was in Las Vegas playing in a celebrity golf tournament, and he whisked Juanita off to LaCosta, California, for a honeymoon that included the first "Michael Jordan Celebrity Golf Tournament" and a birthday party for Deloris. He gave Juanita a five-carat diamond ring worth about $25,000.

Jordan played in an era when professional athletes were known for sordid, short-term relationships with women. His good friend Magic

Johnson had so many sexual relationships that he contracted the virus that causes AIDS. His college teammate James Worthy was arrested in Houston for soliciting prostitutes. Wilt Chamberlain, the player Jordan's scoring extravagance was always measured against, claimed in a book that he had slept with more than 20,000 women during his life and after-life as a professional basketball player. Rumormongers used to spread stories about Michael being seen crawling out of the backseat of a limousine with a local television personality late one night after a home game.

But the attention that he gave his wife, as well as the jewelry and clothes he bought for her and the repeated mentions of her birthday and their anniversary, made it hard to doubt that Michael was faithful and loving to Juanita. His attitude toward being a husband made it easy to dispel those rumors. "I tried to do more for her because that was what she expected from me as a husband," Jordan said during a 1991 conversation about love and marriage and how they got together. "She expected to be taken out to dinners, movies, on vacations. She is more the stern side of the relationship. And I love that."

Juanita was the one who always had to say no when Michael's generosity and loyalty would not let him. Juanita said that she was probably perceived as a bitch at those times, but it did not matter because "that's how I protected what we had." And she never worried about protecting Michael from other women. He did that. "I considered it somewhat of a compliment and then somewhat of a pain," Michael revealed. "When they got too outrageous, my wife would put them in their place. Magic said his wife demanded to be treated with respect when she was out in public with him. I demanded other people to always treat my wife with respect."

Michael offered up the fact that Juanita was chief of finances in the household as proof that, outside the public arena, his marriage was just like anybody else's. They basically did normal things. "We would sit down and argue about what she did with different foods," Michael said when asked to give an example of their everyday life. "She put sugar on grits, I put salt and pepper. I put coleslaw on barbecue; she couldn't believe I did that. We just did lots of things differently like everybody else. She put salt on watermelon and peaches, I told her I couldn't understand why she would take natural fruit and turn it into potato chips. We argued about stuff like that all the time."

In all his years as a basketball player, Michael never knew a double-team like this one. Four-year-old son Jeffrey coming from one side, two-year-old Marcus coming from the other, showing Daddy they knew how to play physical. The boys would jump on him every time they pulled out the six-foot basket in the playroom, the same kind of "Jordan Jammer" millions of other kids across the United States played with in their basement. When Jeffrey and Marcus would try and take the ball to the basket, Michael would show them what it was like to play against the Pistons. "He beat on those kids, and they loved it," said George Koehler, who oftentimes was MJ's two-on-two teammate against Jeffrey and Marcus. "They used to get right down on the rug and climb all over each other. Michael loved it, too." The game, however, ended when Jasmine wanted to sit on Daddy's lap because when he was home she would not let anybody else hold her.

Two days before his 30th birthday (February 15, 1993) Michael again faced one of those moments when he was asked to put his life in perspective. If life were a basketball game, Jordan would still have been early in the second quarter at that point. Nevertheless, the moment commanded some profound recollection. Were the 20 points he scored in the fourth quarter at Utah two weeks ago the same type of personal achievement as scoring 69 against Cleveland in 1990 or 63 in the playoff game at Boston in 1986?

But when Jordan was asked to determine his greatest accomplishment, he said with hesitation, "My kids. That's the biggest product I can enjoy now. That's my escape. I love my kids to death."

When Michael came bouncing out of the bathroom in the Bulls' locker room on Christmas night of 1992, he had a big smile on his face. Was it the 43 points he had just scored helping the Bulls come back from a 10-point halftime deficit for an 89-77 prime-time network win over New York that put him in such a mood?

Not.

"My kids just had the greatest Christmas," he said. "They really loved it. It was just a joy to watch this morning."

For a guy who spent up to sixty nights a year on the road playing basketball, Jordan was an attentive, if not a compulsively conscientious, father. He constantly spoke about wanting to be there for his children and about the way his parents provided the support system that enabled him to become Michael Jordan. When he made his infamous, supposedly irresponsible, trek to the Atlantic City casino during the 1993 playoff series against New York, he took time to call home and check on his sons.

Marcus James Jordan was born right before Christmas in 1990 with the looks of his father and the personality of his mother. By the time Jeffrey was four years old, he was demonstrating the same athletic tendencies as his father, and he used to join Michael during his daily weight-training session at the gym in their house. Jasmine Jordan, born in December 1992, and brought into the world with a bevy of television cameras watching from a waiting room at Highland Park (Illinois) Hospital, had her mother's looks, her father's nose, and Michael wrapped around her little finger.

After Jasmine was born, Jordan was asked what he liked about his daughter. He said she was a good sleeper. "And that was good," he continued, "because if she got up in the middle of the night, my wife would have to get up with her."

He also recognized life would change with a daughter. "It made me a little more sentimental," he said. "But I was a sentimental father already. Having a daughter meant I couldn't just spoil my wife anymore. She could have been a little jealous of that."

Michael focused on fatherhood as intensely as he worked on winning a championship. "I wanted to be there to instill discipline and guidance for them," he said when discussing how retirement would affect him as a father. "I wanted them to learn patience and understanding. I wanted them to be very loving and sharing people, able to give."

Michael was proud to be able to give his family the nicest house on the block. Actually, the house that Juanita and Michael began building in 1993 was the only house on the block or the seven acres of land. That was the same type of plot the house in Wilmington was built on. But this one had 22,000 square feet of living space, an indoor, full-court basketball court, indoor-outdoor pool, Jacuzzi, sauna, and enough driveway space to park his dozen cars.

Being able to share all this with his family made Michael realize that if they missed his halfcourt shot it was not really important. He wanted his family to watch him play basketball whenever possible. But as long as one member of his family was there, that's all that Michael wanted. And that was Pops. Clearly, there was something special between this father and this son.

TWENTY

Pops

Sunday, May 18, 1992, Highland Park, Illinois. We had been debating all morning, my father and I, about how to approach this game. Game 7 of the Knicks series was one of those fatherly advice type games. I was a little nervous because it was a one-game series now. The Knicks had been beating me up to tie the series at three games all, and if we didn't get out of this Eastern Conference semifinal series our season would be a total disappointment. Should I come out aggressive or should I come out passive? Should I try to evaluate how the other guys are playing and try to get them all involved? I didn't want to sit back and think about making it happen. I wanted to make it happen.

When I needed answers like that, I always turned to Pops. This was not just my father, but the guy everybody in the neighborhood knew as "Pops." He was the guy with all the answers, the guy who was everybody's friend. I had this close friend when I was growing up. His name was David Bridgers. We played Little League baseball together and used to ride our bikes around the neighborhood. His parents got divorced, and his dad moved away. Pops became his second father, and it didn't even matter that David was white.

Having Pops with me on the road the last few years of my career was maybe the only thing that kept me from going out of my head. He knew when to tell me to shut up, and he would deal with the phone calls when some long-lost relative was trying to get tickets for a game. Nobody knew what it was like to be me except for him, because he was me or I was him. Same hair. Same tongue.

The game against the Knicks was about five hours away, and it was time for Pops to give me the word. We were bouncing around this issue for quite a while, when we did what most friends would do. We played out the game. Pops, you be Gerald Wilkins and I'll be Michael Jordan and let's see what happens if I come out aggressive. Now you be Michael Jordan and I'll be Gerald Wilkins, and we'll get the other perspective.

In the end, his advice was to be aggressive. He told me to go and do it, make it happen. They'll take your lead. That's exactly what happened. On the first play of the game, I drove right by Gerald Wilkins, and Oakley fouled me. Then I hit three straight jumpers, we took the lead early in the first quarter and never gave it up. If Scottie doesn't come up with a triple double in that win, Pops would have been the most valuable member of my supporting cast.

After we finally beat Phoenix to win the third straight title, my father suggested afterward that I go into the chapel at the America West Arena. He figured it was the place I could get away from everybody and enjoy what I had just accomplished. Right up until the end of my career, he knew exactly what to do. Pops had all the answers.

The lobby of the Plaza, the lavish New York hotel that caters to the lifestyles of the rich and famous, is quiet. This does not at all look like the place that served as the set for the movie *Home Alone 2*. No bellboys are bounding after little boys. There is barely any activity, in fact, except a few Bulls fans checking in before heading to Madison Square Garden for Game 5 of the 1993 playoff series against the Knicks.

Suddenly the quiet breaks when a bald black man bursts through the front door. Two beautiful blonde women rush at him to hug and kiss him. Pretty soon a crowd of ten has gathered around, and people are asking him what he thinks of tonight's game. "You can count on me not to miss a shot," he says. "Won't make any fouls either."

James Jordan could light up a room, even if it was the lobby in the Plaza, faster than Michael Jordan could light up a basketball game. He was fun-loving Pops, the guy who pumped the fun back into life for Michael Jordan when the demands of his legend drained it out. Their relationship was significant because James was the one person who could make Michael feel human, feel ordinary, feel normal. They shared more than the same hairstyle. Getting to know James was like getting to know Michael.

Then on August 12, 1993, just when he was becoming almost as popular a father to America as Robert Young or Danny Thomas, James Jordan was found murdered. He was taken away—he left as Michael described it—at the height of his popularity.

Maybe Michael leaving at the peak of his own popularity was no coincidence. When Michael said the best thing about retiring was that it meant his father had seen his last game, we finally began to understand: This was one very special father-son relationship.

The treatment that he received in the media over his trip to an Atlantic City casino during the 1993 playoff series with New York made Michael Jordan upset and angry. Now that Michael was not talking publicly, Pops stepped up to the microphone. Actually the microphone came to him, while Michael and the Bulls were practicing the Sunday between games 3 and 4 of that Eastern Conference Finals series. The impromptu press conference could not have been more impromptu when two media men in search of a reason why Michael Jordan hit just three of 18 shots in the Bulls' 20-point win the day before asked his father.

"Well you can ask me, but I ain't got much to say," Father Air responded. An hour-and-a-half later, he was talking to a group 40 times as big as the original. He even asked them all outside the Bull's practice facility in Deerfield, Illinois, to have a cigarette with him in the midst of a steady drizzle. By the time Pops finished his stand-up, those around him realized just how overblown the coverage of the gambling junket had been.

"Did you ever stop to think that Michael was just the same guy, and everybody else around had gone crazy?" Pops said. "I mean, I talked him into going to Atlantic City, and I looked at it as a situation to get away and eat a hamburger. Let's just get away. We didn't go down there to win a lot of money. Hell, I lost $50, and turned around and found a way to eat it all back. Had a $42 meal and with the [free] drinks I broke even. The limo ride was free. If we went to an R-rated movie, everybody would have said Michael's daddy carried him to a dirty movie. We should have taken the whole team with us. Maybe they would have played better the next night too."

A Chicago sports writer dubbed him "Father Air" because Pops needed a stage name. He was the kind of guy who commented on the increasing ticket and money requests that Michael received from alleged relatives by saying, "Our family has grown by 5,000 members year by year. There's only one way we can tell who belongs. When we get a group of them together, if the tongue don't hang out, we put them right out."

When Michael was seven years old, he explored his competitive side by playing pool with Pops. Pops would never let him win, and after beating him would pick on Michael. "I'd talk some trash. Used to get him so mad." James knew how to get Michael to use that to his advantage at the end of games. When being in the stands at the game was not enough to put Michael in the right frame of mind, they developed a new ritual. Before every home game, James would stand at the bottom of the long, steep staircase leading from the basement of Chicago Stadium, where the locker rooms were, to the court level.

When Michael would come out with his teammates, Pops would be waiting with a cup of soft drink. Michael would down a few sips. "Hey, even Popeye had his spinach," James said of the routine.

James Jordan said that when he used to get frustrated he would vent his anger by working. He would get up at midnight, go to the office, and work it away. He said that was the biggest similarity between him and Michael, and that was his explanation for why Michael played the game so intensely. That, and the magnetic personality, were what Pops and his son shared.

James Jordan loved to live the high life. He figured growing up the son of sharecroppers and working his way up from laborer to supervisor at the General Electric plant in Wilmington entitled him to do so. Before every Bulls game the last two years of Michael's career, it was rare not to see James talking with a handful of people. And it was rare for some of those people to not be strikingly attractive females, often members of the Chicago Luv-A-Bulls, the team's dance and cheerleading group.

James was not without his flaws. In 1985, during his time as a supervisor at GE, he pleaded guilty to accepting a $7,000 kickback from a contractor while in charge of inventory control. He received a three-year suspended sentence and was fined $1,000. Some of his friends argued that the plea was an attempt to cover up for fellow workers. When Michael turned pro and moved his family to Charlotte, James changed his lifestyle. He began to live a more separate life from Deloris and went for days at a time without contacting members of his family.

But he really lived for one thing—to be with Michael. It was July 22, 1993, when he decided to go back to that job after spending the previous few weeks attending to business. He attended the funeral of longtime friend and co-worker Willie Kemp on that day in Atkinson, North Carolina, about 20 miles north of Wilmington. He left Wilmington about midnight and headed for Charlotte, where he was going to fly to Chicago to be with Michael. Freewheeling in the brand-new red Lexus Michael had given him, James was at the peak of his life—or so it seemed. He tired on the drive to Charlotte and pulled over to the side of Route 74 in North Carolina to rest.

More than three weeks later, nobody had heard from James Jordan.

A report that he was missing hit the news. The next day, reports of his death surfaced. On August 3, a body was found in a creek near McColl, South Carolina, just across the state line. Two days later the red Lexus was found on the outskirts of Fayetteville, North Carolina, 50 miles north of McColl, stripped of all of its valuable parts. On August 6, a South Carolina coroner ordered the cremation of a body that an autopsy showed was killed by a gunshot wound to the chest. On August 13, a check of dental records revealed that body was James Jordan.

During the 15-minute eulogy that Michael gave for his father at the funeral August 15, he cried and he laughed. He said, "Pops taught us a lot, and Pops would want us to carry on." Michael walked out of the church arm-in-arm with Deloris. He was smiling. Pops left him that way.

Less than two months earlier, Michael Jordan had talked about how his father helped him realize how to carry on when things were going bad. James had reminded Michael not to worry about the expectations or standard others set for him, and that it was OK to be whatever person he wanted to be. This came after Pops served as his voice when Michael was not talking to the public world.

The traits Michael always said made him the player he was—competitiveness, a goal-oriented approach, the need for new challenges— left Jordan fans thinking that Pops's death would inspire Michael to his greatest professional season ever in 1993–94. With nothing more to prove as a champion or an individual, the challenge for Michael would be to excel when life was most adverse. And Pops would want him to carry on that way.

When he announced his retirement, Michael said that he made the decision as soon as the 1993 season ended. A few minutes later he said, "Being an optimistic person, the best thing I can take from my father's passing was that he got to see me play my last game." The message was obvious. Michael said that he no longer felt the desire, the motivation to go through all the things necessary to excel in the NBA. But with nobody to make life fun, with nobody to talk trash to him, with nobody to make his shaved head look good, with nobody to help him relieve all the hardships that went along with life as a basketball star, Michael Jordan just could not carry the load anymore.

TWENTY-ONE

I Must Work Like Hell

June 20, 1993, America West Arena, Phoenix, Arizona. When it got to this point two years ago, I cried in front of everybody. That's when I finally felt that feeling inside—in my chest—the difference between being a winner and not being one. Last year, I jumped up on a table and danced and shouted—kind of like a big in-your-face to the world to tell them the first one was no fluke. But now that we had just beaten Phoenix to win our third straight NBA Championship, I wanted to be alone.

Everything was just so crazy out there. Including me. The excitement and few sips of champagne went to my head, and I couldn't help letting off some steam about how winning a third straight title made me feel. Everybody started talking about who had the greatest team ever, and I had to point out that the Celtics never won three in a row when there were 28 teams in the league.

I figured everybody would turn the whole debate on me, so I went ahead and did it for them. I wanted them to remember that Magic, Bird, Isiah—they never won three in a row and how much that meant to me. I stopped short of saying I was better than all those guys in terms of continuance and consistency. Were they waiting for me to declare myself better than those guys? Certainly, they had to think this third straight title put me right up there with Magic, Bird, Isiah, and all the others. I thought it put me a step above them, and I said so.

So I had to be alone for a few minutes after that. Actually, there was a time after every championship when I wanted to be alone. You're happy for the team and you want to celebrate first with your teammates. But chasing championships became such a component of individual measurement for me.

After the first one, I'm thinking now, it's OK, now they will put me in the same class as Magic and Larry, even though I felt like I belonged there before I ever won a title. The second one came after a year of more adversity than I had ever faced in my life off the court, and I guess it was a test to prove I could handle trying to stay on the pedestal and come back and do it again. That's what everybody seemed to judge Magic's and Larry's greatness on.

And the third one, well, that was the one that meant the most because it put me on top. It made me feel like I accomplished everything I could in the game of basketball, and it separated me from all the others.

Maybe I got caught in one of those periods of pro basketball when I couldn't just be Michael Jordan. I did all these things—individual things—and all I heard was talk about how I measured up to

Magic and Larry. Then Isiah won two titles, and I had to measure up to him. Didn't like that much because Isiah and I never really were very good friends.

In the first Finals we played in, everybody was comparing me to Magic. The second one was me and Clyde. During this series against the Suns, it's all about me and Charles, and they're comparing us both on and off the court. Every time I made some kind of athletic move they would put it on videotape and see if it was as good as Doctor J. Doc was the one who started all of the high-flying stuff, and I never felt like I could be compared to him. So they also measured me against Dominique because he came into the league a couple of years before me and was doing all that "Air" stuff. And he scored a lot of points too, so he was always a measuring stick for me.

All this stuff was building up in me after we clinched that third title, and I wanted to get away and put it all in perspective. Pops suggested I go into the chapel at the America West Arena. Maybe I should ask God what he thought. Everybody else had an opinion.

It's not like I was campaigning to be the best player in the world or even to be better than Magic or Bird. Everybody played different in different eras. But we won three titles in a row, and I was the leader of that team. That meant a lot to me. It meant that I was a champion.

The moment all the made-for-television partying over the Bulls 1992 championship win against Portland concluded, Michael Jordan led his teammates on a sprint out of the locker room. The rest of the Bulls followed him up the Stadium stairs, and at the same speed he used to fill the lane of a fastbreak he headed for a table at courtside. He jumped up on the table.

Jordan dancing atop this table, holding out two fingers, was the end of the line as far as the viewing public was concerned. After about 20 minutes, however, he headed downstairs continuing the same pace and raced around the basement of the Stadium until he found a private corner. There he sat, popped the cork off a bottle of champagne, shook it up and like a homeowner watering his lawn, sprayed it all over the few people who managed to stay with him on this jaunt.

"This is for all you nuts who said I couldn't do it," Jordan yelled as he turned his bottle of champagne into a fire hose and sprayed a steady stream. "I've never felt anything so joyous in my life. This was much more joyous than the first. I wanted this one so bad."

In victory or defeat, Jordan was usually reserved, as emotionless as a corpse. So many times after a game he sat straight-faced, just another day at the office. The night that he hit the last-second shot to beat Cleveland in Game 4 of the 1992 Eastern Conference semifinal playoff series, he talked in a monotone. No smile.

But after beating Portland in six games to win a second straight title, Jordan revved up emotion like a drag racer waiting for the green light. Each championship compelled him to show rare signs of human frailty. He cried after one title, twisted and shouted after the second, and prayed after the third. Was that his way of showing just how important a championship—and a second and third—were?

All season, every season, Michael downplayed the individual accolades. Except when the championship was won, then he put himself in the spotlight. Selfishness? Perhaps. But as John Paxson said after he hit the game-winning three-point shot to drop Phoenix 99-98 in Game 6 of the 1993 Finals, "Michael is the one who deserves all the credit, all the attention right now. He carried us tonight just like he carried us all year, just like he's carried us his whole career." Perhaps winning championships had extreme individual significance for Michael. Because everybody insisted on comparing him to Magic Johnson, Larry Bird, Isiah Thomas, Julius Erving, Charles Barkley, and Dominique Wilkins, Jordan wanted the ultimate measure to be in terms of championships. Nobody really knew what the championships meant to Jordan. He knew there was more empirical data to support his being the champion of champions, but he also knew that would separate him from all the others.

*   *   *

Michael Jordan dashed out of a Bulls preseason practice in October 1991 and paused briefly to polish the vanity license plate beaming "Champs" on the front of his white Jeep Cherokee. The sky was gray, providing a somber setting that also seemed to describe Jordan's mood as he tried to make a fast getaway. But a request to discuss how winning his first NBA championship, which came with a defeat of the L.A. Lakers four months earlier, compelled Michael to put on the brakes momentarily. He was not smiling as he began to convey his thoughts. He actually hung his head as if this championship was becoming a burden.

"You know I can't have any off-nights now," he said as he sat there, motor running, clutching the steering wheel, perhaps attempting to get a grip on life. "That's the challenge now. Where am I going to find the passion to play with every night? You work so hard to get to this level, so now you have to show people how tough you are. If I don't win a second one, the first one may not mean a whole lot."

The lasting feeling from winning his first NBA championship should have kicked in the day after the Bulls finished off the Lakers. Returning to his Highland Park home, Jordan found a crowd of more than 100 friends and neighbors forming a welcoming committee that made him feel like a head of state.

Posters and signs were attached to his front door. Balloons adorned the house. All the flowers and plants people sent made his front porch look like an arboretum. It was then that the feelings of "I'm never gonna win," and all the little doubts that he had about it were alleviated. And the whole scene enabled Michael to feel such personal achievement and satisfaction that, in retrospect, he admitted: "The championship in the minds of a lot of people, the way I perceived it, was a sign of greatness. They could say that about me."

When Jordan returned for training camp the next season, Bulls assistant coach John Bach noticed a more serious MJ. The elation, the celebration seemed to pass quickly through him. Bach reasoned that Jordan was now even more focused on being known as the greatest player ever and finally winning a championship made MJ more uptight than relaxed. As Jordan turned over the ignition on his Jeep, he contemplated what lasting impact the championship would have on him. "It means," he observed, "I must work like hell."

"Hell" and "work" most accurately described the 1991–92 season for Jordan. First he had to deal with the fallout over his not accompanying the team to meet President Bush in October. Then, the published reports depicting him as a selfish, dictatorial teammate and the news of his losing large sums of money through gambling with convicted felons may have left Jordan *needing* a second championship rather than just wanting it. The night that the 1992 Finals began, Michael came out of the training room adjacent to the Bulls' locker room and barked out, "Don't ask me no questions. Leave me alone to think. I'm all geeked up."

Those Finals could have been the crowning moment in his career. Already during the playoffs, he had provided emphatic closing arguments in the final games of series victories over the New York Knicks and Cleveland Cavaliers.

Then, of course, there was the three-point shooting frenzy in Game 1 of the Finals. To that, he added 46 points in the Game 5 must-win situation with the series tied two games apiece. Jordan capped off his second straight NBA Finals MVP performance with his most dramatic effort of the playoffs. He scored just two points in the first half and was watching from the bench in the fourth quarter when the Bulls made up a 15-point deficit. But in the final 8:36 of the game, he scored 14 points, including the final four of the 97-93 win over Portland.

Michael did not remember that second championship season as the one that put him on an even keel with Magic and Isiah, whose teams had each won back-to-back championships in 1987–88 and 1989–90 respectively. The feeling was not of accomplishment but of relief and vindication.

"I felt like a lot of weight had been lifted off my shoulders in terms of what I had to deal with personally," Michael observed. "It was a good ending to an educational story. What I realized (after that championship) was that it's very difficult to be something for everybody. Things I was saying or said were being taken advantage of. When you get taken advantage of, you start fighting back. You start fighting back, and you take more hits. So you fight back a little harder. That's the way it was that season. The championship capped off for me a maturing season. I said it many, many times that it was something that I hopefully learned from. I just wanted to move on after that and move on in a very, very positive way."

The third championship provided finality for Jordan, an ending— finally a happy ending. Throughout the season, he said that he was playing for history, for that third title that would put him a step above Magic, Bird, and all the other players of his era. He used that phrase, "a step above Magic, Bird, and Isiah," over and over during the season as if it had become a mantra.

The season was not a pretty one. He struggled with his shooting, finishing at 49 percent, the first time since 1987 that he had shot below the 50 percent mark he obsessively coveted. He also took more than 2,000 shots for the first time since 1987. Despite his hope that the Bulls would become a more balanced team, he led them in scoring 69 times in the 78 games that he played and averaged just less than a third of the team's total points with his highest scoring mark in four years (32.6).

The third championship provided a reason for Michael to move on as much as move up. By his estimation, winning a third title made him the greatest winner in the game's current era. "Once that was done," Michael said, "I knew right there I had nothing left to prove or accomplish. Winning the third title meant it was time to walk away from the game."

Retirement day led to judgment day. In 1993, Michael Jordan became the only player to ever be named the most valuable player of the NBA Finals three years in a row. His scoring average of 41 points per game was a Finals record, and he became the third player to score more than 30 points in every game of a Finals series—Rick Barry and Elgin Baylor were the others. He became the first player to score more than 40 points in more than two straight Finals games. He did it in four straight games. Measure that against what Magic, Bird, Doctor J, Isiah, Barkley, and Dominique had accomplished and understand Jordan's view that there was nothing left to prove.

The slam-dunk contest during All-Star weekend in 1988 came down to one last jam session for Michael. He trailed Dominique Wilkins by 48 points, and was tapped out on his creativity. "I didn't know what to do," he remembered. "Then I saw Doc sitting at courtside. Doctor J was the one who started all the dunking. I figured I could go back to his roots." Several years earlier, Julius (Dr. J.) Erving bragged that he could then complete a dunk in which he took off from the foul line,

15 feet from the basket. Slowly, silently, Jordan began to take big steps backward from the foul line at one basket all the way to behind the far baseline, more than 94 feet away. The capacity crowd in Chicago, which hosted the 1988 All-Star festivities, joined Jordan's silence. As he reached the baseline and stopped, the crowd combined for one huge gasp that sounded like helium being pumped into a balloon. Jordan started his run, accelerated to full speed at half court, and catapulted off the foul line like Carl Lewis hitting the springboard at an Olympic long jump competition. As he floated toward the basket, he flexed his right arm, then reached out to complete the dunk. The maneuver drew a perfect score of 50 from the five judges and gave Michael the slam dunk contest championship.

Shortly after landing, Jordan downplayed the spectacle of his move. He directed the credit to Julius Erving, the one player Jordan did not want to be measured against. "I couldn't hang with the Doc in his prime," Jordan reasoned. Erving had his best years as one of the first superstars of the old American Basketball Association (ABA), when he was a three-time MVP and had one season in which he averaged 31.9 points and 15.7 rebounds per game.

Overall, however, Erving could not hang with Jordan. Michael averaged more points (32.3 to 24.1), more assists (5.8 to 4.1), and more steals (2.7 to 1.8), and he was a better shooter from the field (.516 to .507) and the foul line (.846 to .777).

In addition to coaching MJ, Kevin Loughery coached Erving in the ABA when he played for the Nets. He had Erving from 1974-1976 when the Doc was the ABA's Most Valuable Player each year. During the 1993 season, Loughery was coaching the Miami Heat when he brought his team to Chicago for a game in April. He was easily dragged into a discussion about Jordan's accomplishments and asked to compare him to Erving. He did not even hesitate. "Competitiveness, talent, flying through the air like nobody else can—that's what I think of Michael. He was better with the ball than Doc was. He was just better."

Comparisons between Erving and Jordan were inevitable because of their athletic abilities. Michael faced the same thing with Dominique Wilkins his whole career. He knew that Wilkins was never the winner he was—just three times did Wilkins lead his team past the first round of the playoffs, and never beyond the second—and he knew

Dominique could not compare statistically. In scoring, rebounding, shooting, steals, and blocks, the 6-foot-8-inch Wilkins edged the 6-foot-6-inch Jordan in only one. He averaged 6.9 rebounds per game through the first 11 years of his career; Jordan averaged 6.3 per game.

Yet whenever they faced each other, Jordan seemed compelled to prove Wilkins did not measure up. Whether it was a last-second blocked shot to preserve a victory or outdueling Dominique when they turned the game into their personal one-on-one, Jordan usually got the best of Wilkins. On the last night of the 1987 season, Wilkins hit a last-second shot to give Atlanta a win in Chicago. But that was the night Jordan scored 61 points to become the second player in NBA history to top the 3,000-point mark.

"We always pushed each other to another level," Wilkins said. "He would just get into those streaks where it seemed like he would never miss. He always reacted any time I got hot. You play against Mike, and you realized he recognized that. And he had to do something to keep it going. We had a lot of great nights together. Sometimes he won. Sometimes I won. Mostly, he won, unless I got lucky."

When the Bulls drew Atlanta as a first-round opponent in the 1993 playoffs, the postseason hype zeroed in on the series being a machup of Jordan and Wilkins. Phil Jackson appraised the matchup before the series started by wondering why anybody would put Wilkins in the same class with Michael.

"You think Michael and Dominique are equal threats?" Jackson asked. "Michael's assists are higher (5.8 to 2.5 over their careers). There are a lot of other things I don't need to enumerate. They both have the explosiveness, the dynamic kind of assault on the hoop. Dominique was looked on as a once-in-a-lifetime player when he came into the league. Everybody went 'Wow, that's incredible what he did. No one can do that kind of thing.' Michael came along two years later and was doing things even better or more stupendous.

"But that's not why there's no comparison. Do you wonder why Chicago Stadium has been sold out every time Michael put on a uniform the last six years? Why can't Atlanta do that? Don't they have a player of equal magnitude?"

Michael was never the type of player who would come out and say that he was better than somebody, though he liked to hear others say it. But after he and Dominique had their shootout in February, the press was on. Michael gave Dominique the edge in three-point shooting but called himself a better ball-handler and driver-to-the-basket. He added jumping was a toss-up. So who was better? "I can't judge," he said, "because I hate to sit here and pull my own chain."

Rarely a night passed during the 1993 season when Michael Jordan did not talk about motivation, Magic Johnson, and Larry Bird all in the same context. "That's what I'm chasing," he would say as if those guys had a legacy that was a ghost haunting Michael. "If I can catch them, I can make history."

Long before he made history, though, the chase was over. Jordan averaged more points for his career than either Johnson or Bird. Bird was the best rebounder. Johnson dished out the most assists. Each won three Most Valuable Player awards. Magic won three NBA Finals MVPs, Bird won two. Jordan won three in a row. Magic won five championships, Bird and Michael won three. But Jordan never had a Kareem Abdul-Jabbar and a James Worthy to pass to nor did he have Robert Parish and Kevin McHale on his side—All-Stars each. And Jordan won three in a row, which neither Magic nor Bird accomplished. Jordan created new units of measure, such as becoming the first player ever to record 200 steals and 100 blocked shots in a single season. And he did that twice. He was the NBA's defensive player of the year and its leading scorer in 1988. Magic and Bird never accomplished either of those. Bird made the NBA's all-defensive first team once. Jordan made it six of his last seven years. It was no contest.

In 1987, when Magic's Lakers were preparing to play Larry's Celtics, Johnson sent up the famous line about who was the best player in the game. "Everybody says there's me and Larry," the Magic man said then. "Really, there's Michael and there's everybody else."

"Michael was the most exciting out of all of us," Magic said when he took up the appraisal between Games 4 and 5 of the 1993 NBA Finals while working as an analyst for NBC. He held court on this topic for more than an hour, debating every aspect of Jordan's game as compared to his and Bird's. "I don't think there was any question he was the most exciting. Larry and I could never score two points and leave the crowd going crazy like it was the greatest move you ever saw. We couldn't leave you with your mouth hanging open like Michael could. Larry got the most out of his talent, which is why I rate him right behind Michael.

"We also could never take over the game like he could. I tried to get him on winning, telling him I had five championships. But he would come back and say you never got three in a row. He got me there."

Jordan said the most rewarding part of being named the Most Valuable Player is that it put his name alongside Magic and Bird. He never felt competitive with Magic in terms of ability.

Jordan thoroughly outplayed Johnson when the Bulls won the 1991 championship over the Lakers, and Magic admitted as much. When Magic made the 1992 All-Star team even though he had retired from the game because of being HIV-positive, he wanted one last shot at guarding Jordan one-on-one. Michael set him up, drove to the baseline and missed on a pull-up, fade-away jumpshot from about 15 feet. Magic wound up being named the MVP of the game for scoring 25 points. Afterward, Jordan said to him, "Just remember, I could have dunked on you if I wanted to." Magic just nodded his head and conceded superiority.

Jordan had more of an admiration for Bird than a friendship. He called the McDonald's commercial he made with Larry his best ever. When the question arose as to who would win that game of HORSE they began to play in the McDonald's commercial, Jordan smiled and said, "I'd love to take him on in a real game of HORSE." Jordan explained that Bird was the one player whom he competed with in the mental aspect of the game.

"People used to say Larry was cocky, but being in that same situation I never considered it cocky, but very highly confident type of talk. Cockiness would be to say something and then go out and not do it. Confidence would be to say something and then go out and do it. That's the kind of person I thought Larry Bird was. He went and backed it up. The man was very confident about his skills, and in many ways I wanted to be respected like that when I retired."

When Jordan finally had the third title, he figured there was one more venue to one-up both Magic and Bird. "Every player wants to go out on his own terms," he explained. "You could tell leaving the game was something Magic had to deal with. That's part of the reason he wanted to come back. Larry thought he could play until he was 40. When you quit, you want to be the one who makes that call and not let it be because of some illness or injury. When I left, I made my own decision, left on my own terms content with having accomplished everything I could."

The afternoon before the Bulls eliminated the New York Knicks from the 1993 playoffs and advanced to their historic third straight NBA Finals, Michael Jordan made an important telephone call. Charles Barkley was taking a nap when the phone rang with Jordan on the other end. "Hey, I thought we were coming to Phoenix," Jordan charged. "Looks like we'll be going to Seattle if you don't start taking the ball to the basket."

Barkley had struggled with doing just that in Game 6 of the Western Conference Finals against Seattle the day before. Using Jordan's words of inspiration, he took over Game 7 with 44 points and 24 rebounds to set up the Bulls-Suns, Jordan-Barkley Finals.

When Charles Barkley was named the NBA's Most Valuable Player after the 1993 season, Michael welcomed him into the elite class. He now had somebody new to compete with, and Jordan simply loved to match wits, handicaps, and drives to the basket with Barkley, his best friend among NBA stars.

Barkley was the one player in the NBA who claimed to be as competitive as Jordan. He clearly was not the golfer Jordan was, yet kept challenging him to one more round of 18 holes because he thought this was the one he was going to win. Their friendship started when they tried out for the 1984 U.S. Olympic team. Jordan made it. Barkley was cut. Michael has gotten the best of Charles ever since.

"We had a relationship where we could joke about what's at stake, yet when we're on the court we could be at each other's throats," Jordan said. "We loved to compete each against each other. We were always having conversations about having confidence in your team and your organization to get the right people to get the job done. We'd be on the golf course, and he would be talking trash about his team. I knew I couldn't talk trash about my team, because you couldn't win with him. He was a great comic, and he was always going to get the last laugh. He would try and joke and attack my mental approach to the game. But that would never work. We always talked about retiring from the game together. But he still had some things to accomplish, and the problem was that I was always standing in his way."

Barkley would make fun of Jordan publicly to help him not take life so seriously. When Michael had to deal with the accusations that Richard Esquinas made about his gambling addiction and compulsion to bet large sums of money on golf, Barkley jumped on it.

"I'm trying to get my handicap down so I can get in some golf games with Mike," he said. "You know, Michael offered to let me use his Ferrari Testarossa before I could afford one. I think they go for one hundred and some thousand, maybe two hundred, two-forty. That's just a couple of rounds of golf." Barkley pointed out his friendship with Jordan has nothing to do with basketball.

Barkley called Jordan a great player, and during the early part of the 1993 NBA Finals he added, "I don't want to say any basketball player is better than I am." But Barkley clearly realized not even he compared to Jordan when he said, Michael, "is the one guy I will accept losing to if I have to lose."

Barkley conceded second-tier status to Jordan. Magic said that Jordan could do so many things that he and Larry could not, including winning at a pace they never knew. Julius Erving and Dominique Wilkins exhibited the same physical or athletic style Jordan played with, but they never won on his level.

The day after Michael scored 55 points in Game 4 of the 1993 NBA Finals, his place in history was imminent. So was retirement. That seemed an appropriate time to ask Jordan whether he thought he was the best, the greatest to ever play in the NBA. As always, he would not answer.

TWENTY-TWO

The Greatest?

May 25, 1993, Madison Square Garden, New York. Everybody had their own different value to a team. But how valuable are you in getting your team from one level to the next? If you take yourself away from that team, how would that team respond without you? There's an argument you can make for consistent numbers, but what about the attitude and effort you bring to the court and how that affects your teammates?

Stats is stats, and unfortunately that's what a lot of people base things on. Do the people who choose the most valuable player or the greatest player think of all these other things when they cast their votes?

Every year this time, it was the same debate. A group of people have crowded around me. And they're not only asking me who the most valuable player in the game was but what should determine

MVP. And then it would lead to discussions about whether the Most Valuable Player and the best player were two different things. And that would lead to different conversations about which players were the greatest or which one was the greatest. I always said it was hard to compare players from different eras, but I would tell Phil and Jerry Krause that nobody who played before 1980 could compete in my era or Magic's or Bird's.

This comparing players controversy really started back in 1987 when I scored the 3,000 points and became the first player other than Wilt Chamberlain to do that in one season. Seems like I was always finishing second to Wilt. We went from 30 wins the previous season to 40 wins that year, and I finished second in the balloting for MVP to Magic. When I didn't win—which I probably shouldn't have—I heard it was because my game was too one-dimensional, too much scoring to be rated as high as Magic or Bird. But I was playing with Granville Waiters and Earl Cureton, not Kareem and James Worthy. I had to score that many points just for us to be competitive in every game. I bet if you look back and check, you will find that there were only four games of the 40 we won that season where I scored less than 30 points.

But you know how it is. You hear that you score too much and you think maybe that's a knock on your defense. So I went out the next year and led the league in scoring and steals, and they named me the defensive player of the year. Then, they named me the MVP. But then people are saying to be a truly great player you have to make your teammates better to win championships. So I did that. And we won two titles, and I got two more MVPs, and then it gets to be a question of whether Michael Jordan is the greatest player of all time.

I'm happy I set a high standard for myself, and I was happy I could meet that high standard. That's something 20 years down the road—when someone comes and breaks my records or passes my point totals or whatever—to hold in the highest esteem. Actually, it's a feeling that you get when people say you changed the game. For people to say you have a uniqueness that changed the game, that's something to be proud of. But I never went out each season to prove I could be as great as this guy or the next guy. I wanted to equal what I had done the year before, and if I surpassed it, great, If I wasn't the MVP or the greatest player in the game, I could accept that. But then you get to a point where you think, well, what do I have to do to open people's eyes? Average 38 points, seven-eight rebounds, three steals?

Every player, or every great player, gets into a mode where they want to leave the court every night thinking they were the best in that game. And they want everybody else to think that too. That's what makes players great. Magic, Bird, Wilt, Kareem, Oscar Robertson, Bill Russell, myself—we were all like that.

So if it comes down to picking one of these guys and separating them from the rest of the group, how do you do it? Do you judge by winning? Attitude and effort? Making your teammates better? Impact on the game? Stats? Is it a certain intangible?

When I came to Chicago and started to have some success, people started to compare me to Walter Payton and Ernie Banks and Bobby Hull. Here they are comparing me to great players in other sports in Chicago, and I still couldn't figure out how you compared players from the same sport from different eras.

Was I the greatest? I don't know. How do you determine that? How in the hell do you determine that?

The conversation took place in a bar in a section of Cleveland known as "The Flats," just down the road a piece from a place called Dead Man's Curve. The subject was Michael Jordan's legend and how he was currently redefining his standard of excellence. The debate included several Chicago reporters who realized Jordan was in the process of providing new fuel to settle the question of who was the greatest basketball player ever. Mike Greenberg, a Chicago radio reporter, asserted that this was a rare time of Jordan's playing career. Here, he said, was the greatest player of his era, playing his greatest at a time when he absolutely had to. Greenberg noted that his return from the ankle injury a week earlier in Atlanta and the 14 points he scored afterward made him feel like what Jordan was doing would have historical significance. That Jordan was never playing better than he was during these playoffs. After another shot and a beer, several reporters raised the question as to whether Jordan's feats would compare to the home run that Bobby Thomson hit to give the New York Giants a victory over the Brooklyn Dodgers in the 1951 National League playoff game. The home run that became known as the "shot heard round the world." Would it, the conversation continued, become part of sports history like a Babe Ruth home run?

This all came to pass after Game 3 of the 1993 playoff series against the Cavaliers, before he hit the last-second shot to win Game 4 of the series and knock the Cavs out of the playoffs.

That game against Cleveland was not the last or definitive word on whether Michael Jordan was the greatest to ever play professional basketball. In fact, when MJ scored 54 points to crush the New York Knicks with a 96-88 victory in Game 4 of the Eastern Conference Finals, the argument resumed. Then when he single-handedly delivered victory to a Bulls team fatigued beyond despair by scoring 55 points in Game 4 of the NBA Finals, Jordan left the naysayers searching for ways to argue that the other great players in the history of the game measured up to him.

The search eventually revealed that no other player compiled a list of superlative achievements and accomplishments like Michael Jordan. Doug Collins tried to diffuse the argument by asking any doubters to walk down the street of any major city in the United States at midday and count how many Michael Jordan T-shirts, hats, and other attire you see in a one-hour period. By Collins' reckoning, no other NBA player, past or present, had the impact on the game on and off the court that Michael did.

Kendall Gill, the high-flying guard of the Seattle Supersonics, was a junior at Rich Central High School in Olympia Fields, Illinois, a suburb 20 miles south of Chicago, when Michael Jordan was drafted by the Bulls in 1984. Gill was pretty much of a basketball phenomenon on his own level, and a year later he would carry the Olympians to an appearance in the Illinois Class AA state basketball tournament championship game. It was a meaningless mid-January game against an opponent Gill could not remember seven years removed from the scene, but he finished off a breakaway with a spinning dunk, throwing the ball down with two hands and his back to the basket.

Because he wore a wrist band halfway up his left forearm and because he made such a move, Gill read comparisons of himself to Michael Jordan when he picked up the newspaper the next day. During the next few weeks, he perfected an ability to walk like Michael Jordan did from the court to the bench. He already stood six feet, five inches and had a body sculpted similar to Michael's: rippled biceps, thick shoulders, skinny legs. He even wore his basketball pants long and baggy. He passed on the shaven head and the tongue thing, but Gill knew the impact Jordan had on him and the game of basketball.

"His presence in Chicago added to my zest for the game," said Gill, realizing that moment led to a current point in his career where he was putting on a Charlotte Hornets uniform in November 1992 and getting ready to match up with Michael Jordan. "All of the sudden, everybody wanted to be a high-gliding dunker, and suddenly everywhere you looked around where I lived, 12-, 13-year-old kids are playing basketball. I guess the label of being like Mike was tagged along with me. There could be worse compliments, right?

"But he just electrificed Chicago when he came here. The year before they finished last. But he came and they had this slogan: The Chicago Bulls, a whole new breed. I became a basketball fanatic. He rekindled the fire Chicago needed in basketball."

One player having an impact on one city. Not unusual. Doug Collins was conducting a basketball clinic at Marquette Park, a depressed area deep in the heart of Chicago's inner-city housing projects during the summer of 1992. Marquette Park had basketball hoops with no nets, bent rims, and cracks in the pavement. And that was on the good courts. Collins brought his son Chris, who was named the outstanding high school player in the state of Illinois in 1992 and went on to become a sharp-shooting guard at Duke University in the mid-1990s, to help with the clinic.

Chris Collins put on a shooting exhibition in which he hit 11 straight shots from the high school and college three-point distance (19 feet, 9 inches) and farther out. The tepid reaction to that display made Doug Collins realize the impact that Michael Jordan had made on basketball in Marquette Park and nationwide.

"All they said when Chris was finished was, 'Can you dunk?' That was the statement. If you turned on the NBA highlights on ESPN, it was all dunks. And it was mostly Michael Jordan. So everybody wants to dunk like Michael Jordan, because they believed that's how you could be successful in a game. And when one guy did it, they said he was the next Michael Jordan. Magic had all that until Michael came along. They stopped wanting to be like Magic and wanted to be like Michael. Michael Jordan actually changed the way the game of basketball was being played. People looked at him, and his size wasn't abnormal, so they figured they had a shot at becoming the next Michael. He changed the way the game was played. How many other guys can you say that about?

"You know, the guy was so good he changed the whole television package in the NBA. The superstation (WGN in Chicago) sued so they could put Michael on more. That hurt me, because if it came down to watching the game we had on TNT or Michael on another channel, they're going to watch Michael. If we went head-to-head with Michael, we were dead."

In October 1993, WGN's suit against the NBA finally went to court. WGN charged that the NBA was in violation of antitrust laws by dictating how many games a superstation, with national distribution that was contracted with a team, could televise. Originally, the restriction was 20 games, which was expanded when the suit was first filed.

But WGN could never complain about losses suffered with Michael as the focal point the way the Cleveland Cavaliers could. Four playoff series defeats to the Bulls in six years between 1988 and 1993? Two of those coming on last-second, acrobatic shots by Jordan in the final game? Seven days after he hit the shot in Game 4 of the 1993 series, Cavs coach Lenny Wilkens resigned. This one guy shook up an entire franchise. Who else had that kind of impact?

When Utah coach Jerry Sloan brought his Jazz team to Chicago in February for its only appearance in 1993, he spent most of the 20 minutes that players used to warm up to watch the crowd come into the Stadium. Sloan was the leader of the great Chicago Bulls teams of the 1970s, including the one in 1975, the only team in franchise history to reach a conference finals series without Michael Jordan.

As he noticed fans packing the place for one of the 241 consecutive sellouts between 1986 and 1993, he realized the greatness of Michael Jordan. "Just to give you an idea," Sloan explained, "we won 50 games four years in a row here, and we couldn't draw 10,000 people. But the Bulls were drawing 18,000 every night when they won 30. An entire franchise survived on one player."

For this one player, the Chicago Bulls devoted four pages of their 1993–94 media guide to chronicling his accomplishments. Four pages. Four times as much as any other Bulls player. And he did not even play that season.

Michael said that he never played the game for individual accolades, but what he achieved made him a category in the record books unto himself. You hear or read some of these things and you share Cleveland center Brad Daugherty's sentiments after Jordan hit that high-rise jumper over Craig Ehlo to squeeze out a 101-100 victory in the fifth and final game of the 1989 opening-round playoff series: Simply unfathomabull.

Jordan accomplished much during his professional basketball career. Among his achievements:

- He retired with a 32.3 points per game scoring average, the highest of any player in NBA history.
- On April 16, 1987, he scored 23 consecutive points—the

most ever by an NBA player—in a 117-114 loss to the Atlanta Hawks.

- His 131 blocked shots in 1988 were the most ever by a guard in NBA history.
- He was the only player in NBA history to record more than 200 steals and 100 blocked shots in a single season. He did it twice: 1986–87 and 1987–88.
- He was the only player in NBA history to be named the league's defensive player of the year and win the scoring title in the same season.
- He was the only player in NBA history other than Wilt Chamberlain to score more than 3,000 points in a single season. He had 3,041 in 1986–87.
- He scored his 15,000th career point on January 9, 1991, reaching that plateau in 460 games, faster than any other player in NBA history except Chamberlain.
- He scored his 20,000th career point on January 8, 1993, reaching that plateau faster than any other player in NBA history except Wilt Chamberlain.
- Between 1987 and 1993, he won seven straight scoring titles. The only other player in NBA history to do that was Wilt Chamberlain.
- He scored fewer than 10 points only once in his career—eight points against Cleveland on March 22, 1986. It was his first game back from a broken foot that had kept him out 64 games. He played eight minutes that night.
- He was the only player in NBA history to win the scoring title and make the league's All-Defensive team six consecutive years (1988–1993).
- He scored 40 or more points 135 times. Only Wilt Chamberlain topped 40 points more times (271).
- His streak of 575 consecutive games scoring in double figures was longer than any other player's in NBA history except Chamberlain's.
- He was the only player in NBA history to win consecutive NBA Most Valuable Player Awards and NBA Finals Most Valuable Player Awards in the same season.
- He was the only player in NBA history to win two consecutive NBA Finals Most Valuable Player Awards.
- He was the only player in NBA history to win three consecutive NBA Finals Most Valuable Player Awards.
- He led all players in votes for the NBA All-Star team seven straight years (1987–1993).
- His scoring average of 41 points per game in the 1993 NBA

Finals was the highest ever in a championship series.

- In 1993, he became the third player in NBA history to score more than 30 points in every game of an NBA Finals series. Elgin Baylor and Rick Barry were the other two.
- He is the only player in NBA history to score more than 50 points in seven playoff games. Wilt Chamberlain scored 50 or more in four playoff games.
- He scored more points in one half of an NBA Finals game than any other player in NBA history. He had 35 in Game 1 of the 1992 NBA finals against Portland.
- He scored more points in an NBA Finals series than any other player in history, with 246 in 1993 once.
- During the Bulls' three championship seasons, the team lost more than two consecutive games once.

Could these 23 points of interest be reason enough to declare Jordan the greatest ever to play the game? Perhaps Wilt Chamberlain could take issue with that. So would Doug Collins. Not because he didn't think Jordan was the greatest. He just thought so for an entirely different reason.

"I think Michael was probably as great as any other player because of the way he single-handedly carried a franchise," Collins said as he concluded two hours' worth of comments on the life and work of Michael Jordan. "But there is one thing that was never talked about. He was the reason the Bulls were allowed to be patient, trade away draft picks, go with mediocre players, and build a champion. With Michael's greatness, the Bulls always knew that they would sell out the building and be competitive. You were never going to be awful.

"He kept the Bulls competitive so they could trade off draft picks down the road and get a (Scottie) Pippen and a (Horace) Grant. Think about it. The first year I was coaching, he took the team to 40 wins with Granville Waiters, Earl Cureton, Gene Banks, and Steve Colter. And the building was sold out every night. Then you add Pippen and Grant, and you're at 50 wins. The next year you add Cartwright, and you're in the Eastern Conference Finals. Then you add B. J. and a bench, and you win championships. He allowed that organization to be patient and build."

If it came down to all of the above, Jordan would stand a good chance of standing alone when compared to the NBA's other legends.

Offering Michael a chance to play them each one-on-one would be the surest way to settle the issue once and for all. And that's probably the only way he ever would have participated in the debate. But take Magic and Bird, Bill Russell, Oscar Robertson, Kareem Abdul-Jabbar, and Wilt and match them one-on-one with MJ. What do you get?

Magic joined a good team and made it great; Jordan carried an average team to three titles. And if his assists do not compare with Magic's and Bird's in the much-too-hyped "making your teammates better" category, remember Jordan had to give up assists for points because that was the only way for the Bulls to win. When he did decide to get his teammates involved and the teammates delivered, the Bulls were 20 points better than any of the challengers of the era. (For reference, see Game 3 of the 1993 Eastern Conference Finals when Jordan dished out 11 assists and the Bulls won 103-83.)

Bill Russell was the 6-foot-9-inch anchor of a Boston Celtics team that won 11 championships in 13 years between 1957 and 1969, including eight in a row. But during those years, the Celtics played a total of 17 series. In their three championship years, the Bulls played 12.

In winning the title in 1959 the Celtics won both playoff series over a pair of teams with regular-season losing records. Russell also dominated in an era when the talent was significantly lower. He played with five other players who were inducted into the Basketball Hall of Fame. Bob Cousy was the point guard on those Celtics teams and one of the Hall of Famers. Even *he* picked Jordan over Russell.

"As far as I'm concerned Michael was Nureyev against a bunch of Hulk Hogans," Cousy said once the Bulls captured their third straight title. "His talent was that far above everyone else's. Russell was the most productive center I've ever seen, and he complemented the talent we had. But you can say he wasn't as good a shooter as some other people. Jordan didn't have any area like that."

Oscar Robertson had what was probably the greatest single season in NBA history in 1961–62 when he averaged 30.8 points, 12.5 rebounds, and 11.3 assists per game. He averaged a triple-double; 79 games worth. Jordan had 27 career triple-doubles. Oscar loses impact, however, because of the quantity of talent and because his 6-foot-5-inch frame was big for that era of the NBA, whereas Jordan's 6-foot-

6-inch height was average in his era. And did Oscar's 1961–62 performance have the same magnitude of Jordan's 1987–88 campaign when he was the game's best offensive and best defensive player?

Kareem would seem to be one player who would tower over Jordan. He played 20 seasons, more than any other NBA player, and he holds career records for points, field goals made, defensive rebounds, and blocked shots. These records may never be broken. He led the NBA in three major statistical categories—scoring, rebounding, and blocked shots—at one time in his career. He won six championships and the same amount of Most Valuable Player Awards.

He did not, however, make the NBA All-Defensive team as many times as Jordan. And he played alongside Magic and Worthy. Jordan had to create his own shot, often spending precious energy and eluding squadrons of defenders to do so. Magic put Kareem in point-blank position to score, and his presence kept opponents from sending two and three defenders at Kareem like they did to Jordan. No team ever devised anything known as the "Kareem Rules."

"Just like Wilt had trouble with Russell, Kareem had trouble with Chief (Boston center Robert Parish)," said Danny Ainge. Ainge played in three NBA Finals against Kareem and two against Jordan. He picked his way into this debate in March 1993, when somebody asked him to compare Jordan and Charles Barkley. Ainge quickly dropped Barkley, his Phoenix Suns teammate at the time, and moved Jordan in against the legends of the game.

"The difference between Michael and Kareem and everybody else was that he can score on anybody, and he can score in a lot of different ways," Ainge remarked. "He can hit for three, he can dunk. His combination of speed and strength, nobody else had that. Couple that with a great shooting touch and a great confidence level. His mental approach set him above everybody else. He can shoot over you. He can go around you. There aren't very many guys who can do that."

Not even Chamberlain. He was 7 feet 1 inch tall, and he could score over people because there was nobody in the game with his height and strength. His scoring feats made Jordan look like a 20-points-per-game man. Wilt scored 100 points in a single game. He averaged 50.4 points per game in 1961–62. He led the NBA in scoring seven times. He led the league in rebounding 10 times, and he even led the NBA in assists once. Make a case for Jordan over Wilt, however, because he led the league in scoring just as many times, and he did it while being only average height and facing better talent and more complex defenses designed specifically to stop him.

But does Wilt compare to Jordan in the all-important realm of winning? Chamberlain won two NBA titles. One with the Philadelphia 76ers in 1967 and one with the Los Angeles Lakers in 1972. In Philadelphia, he played with three Hall-of-Fame caliber players in Chet Walker, Hal Greer, and Billy Cunningham. And Cunningham came off the bench. Yet that team won but one title. In 1972, Wilt was a role player—albeit a big role player—on a team that had guards Jerry West and Gail Goodrich dominating the scoring.

Throw out all that criteria and consider that no other player had the experts of the game lining up to praise him as Jordan did. Rarely 20 minutes passed without somebody uttering some kind of superlative in regards to Michael Jordan. Larry Brown, who has coached for five NBA franchises, once said that he would pay money to see Michael play and he would pay to see him practice. Brendan Suhr, who served as Chuck Daly's assistant in Detroit, then moved to New Jersey with Daly in 1992, could not believe any other player would be voted more valuable than Jordan. "The MVP should be named the Michael Jordan Award," he quipped. "Don't put any other players in a contest with Michael. He's the best player in the universe."

And these last few words from Donnie Walsh, president of the Indiana Pacers, who stopped in Sacramento while on a scouting trip just to see Michael Jordan play the hapless Kings in 1993: "He's the best I've ever seen. The reason is that he's blown all the myths we used to believe about the game. We always said a team dominated by a guard cannot win a championship. And we always said a guy who plays that many minutes, he's going to wear down. But he gets better. Oscar Robertson, Jerry West, they couldn't do the things Michael could. When you really think about it, yeah, you've got to say he's best ever." That was a night when Michael scored 3ʎ could that be what ultimately set Jordan aᵣ great ones?

Chuck Daly was sitting courtside at Chı 1992 watching Jordan practice before a ₂ some general opinions when Jordan made a ı flash back to the time he spent coaching Jordan with the U.S. Olympic basketball team the summer of 1992.

"In the semifinal game against Lithuania, Jordan guarded Sarunas Marciulonis so perfectly that Marciulonis could not drive because Jordan was playing off of him. But he also couldn't shoot from the outside because Michael was too close. I never saw anything like it. He was playing perfect defense. It was one of the most intriguing things I had ever seen a player do. He had overall skill, he had a will, he had determination. But because of little things like that, I think you'd have to say he's No. 1."

If it is possible to settle this debate, then perhaps it is necessary to turn to the questions Jordan himself raised about how to determine the best player. Based on all the preceding information, which player is more valuable to his team in terms of getting it from one level to the next? If you take that player away, what would happen to the team? In the seven years after Jordan missed 64 games with a broken foot (1986) he sat out seven games. The Bulls won once. Statistics are statistics, and Jordan's numbers put him at the top, if not on top, of the aforementioned group. As for attitude and effort, is there any one thing that made the Bulls a champion more than Jordan's competitiveness and willingness to answer challenges? And is there any one player who hit so many acrobatic, game-winning shots?

The question of who is the best player in the history of the NBA will be asked forever. But there may never be a better answer than Michael Jordan.

EPILOGUE
Looking Ahead

November 6, 1993, Chicago Stadium. This was a weird point of view: sitting courtside, watching the Bulls struggle to score against the Miami Heat, a team that beat us maybe once during my career. A few minutes ago my family was watching and everybody was cheering when I got my third championship ring. Now everybody is booing because my former teammates can't even score six points in one quarter. And I'm hiding my eyes because I can't bear to watch Will put up another air ball. I think subconsciously I grabbed Jeffrey and held him in my lap to keep from getting up and trying to play when the Bulls fell behind by 17 points.

In the third quarter, everybody saw me get up and yell at the officials over a call they made against B. J. Right then, it probably looked like I was missing the game. I'm sure some people were thinking I was gonna go downstairs, find that old No. 23 uniform, get my old locker back from Scottie, and return just in time to bail out the team. But when I needed to bring two security guards with me to go to the bathroom in the second quarter, I remembered why that wasn't going to happen. So I stayed until the final minutes, long enough to make sure the Bulls weren't going to get any closer than 20 points. People cheered when I walked out at the end.

Sometimes you think about the cheers as one of the things you miss about playing. Could that be a reason to come back? Then you see Shaq score 42 points on Orlando's opening night and hear him called the next coming of Michael Jordan on ESPN. Could that be a reason to come out of retirement? You sit there looking at your championship ring and think the team probably could have won another one if I hadn't quit. Everybody else figured the way I was so competitive, I couldn't resist another chance to win. And if that was the case, then why did I ever bother to quit?

I heard all these different speculations that money could bring me back. Somebody asked me the other day if Jerry Reinsdorf had offered me a hundred million dollars to come back for another two years, would I take it? I would have thought about it. But I wouldn't have done it. When I was standing there at center court a few minutes ago, holding my third ring, so many cameras were going off. I knew right there that I was walking away from the game on top, on the absolute top.

When I retired, I made sure to let all the fans and the media know the word *retire* means you can do anything you want. If I had the desire to play again, maybe I would. Maybe that's a challenge I would need someday when golf and vacuuming and washing dishes couldn't fill the void. I didn't believe in never.

I wasn't going to close the door on coming back. I couldn't really say for sure if I was going to stay retired. I knew at the time I didn't have the mental drive to push myself to come out and play for a certain focus. But I also said, if the urge came back five years down the road, who knows?

The question everybody in the United States, perhaps everybody in the world, wanted to ask beamed across the cover of *Sports Illustrated*'s October 17, 1993, issue. "Why?" in big bold type was set at the bottom of a picture of Michael Jordan walking away.

Why would he retire from basketball at a time when he was the game's best player and nothing was there to keep him from maintaining that status the next few years?

Why would he quit when a chance to win a fourth consecutive NBA championship seemed better than the one the Chicago Bulls had at winning a third?

Why would he retire when he could still go out and show that giving the 1993 NBA Most Valuable Player award to Charles Barkley was, in words he may have uttered, "a joke"? Jordan revealed clues to the answers to these questions after his retirement.

"There was nothing more for me to prove as a basketball player," Michael asserted. "I had done it all. I went to (Bulls coach) Phil (Jackson) before I announced my retirement and asked him if there wasn't anything left for me to prove. He hesitated for a moment, and that's all I needed. If there was, he would have told me real quickly.

"I lost the sense of motivation," he continued. "I went through all the different stages of getting myself prepared for the next year and the desire was not there. I was always in touch with what was right for me as a player and a person to deal with the circumstances. With the circumstances, it just wasn't worth it anymore. I didn't want to go through that scenario again."

The answers to "why?" in retrospect are really pretty obvious. Less clear was what was ahead for Michael after retirement. What would he do with his new-found free time other than play golf? Would he play basketball again? Would he play in the NBA? Would he play for the Bulls? What would bring him back?

Perhaps Magic Johnson knew that he had seen the last great scoring soliloquy from Michael Jordan. This was when Michael scored 55 points in Game 3 of the 1993 NBA Finals, the 111-105 victory over Phoenix that put the Bulls ahead three games to one. The next day, Magic advised everybody to cherish this performance. "Now that he's all but got that third title, ain't nothing left for him to prove, you know. Now that's he got me and Larry beat, there's nothing there to push him. Me and Larry had each other, and then we pushed him. But who's here now to push Michael? Ain't nobody. Charles is the closest. And he isn't even close. No reason for Michael to stay around."

If that was a reason Michael retired, then that would be a reason for him to come back. Charles Barkley's bumping, banging, and foul-mouthed soliloquies were not enough to make anybody forget Michael Jordan, were they? Besides, Charles said before the 1993–94 season tipped off that it was going to be his last. So he might not be around long enough to make people forget Jordan.

But if Shaquille O'Neal scoring 78 points in the first two games of the season actually had people saying, "Here comes the guy to replace Michael," Michael probably would notice. Was he so competitive that Shaq, Alonzo Mourning, or Larry Johnson supplanting him as a marquee man in the NBA might make Jordan want to come out of retirement? Probably not, but the first time anybody said some guy was making his team a winner just like Michael Jordan, that might have had an effect on Jordan. When he retired, however, Michael said in so many words he did not see that kind of player coming.

"Maybe 10 or 20 years down the road, but that is not one of my fears," he remarked. "When I was playing the game, I believed in myself as a basketball player and a person. Hopefully, there will be another guy who someday comes along and has the impact that Magic, Larry, Dr. J, or myself had. A lot of people tried to make me out as the star who carried the league. I don't believe one guy can do that now. I mean, there were some rising stars when I quit, but nobody in a big market."

It's not as if Michael needed the money, even $100 million, to come back and play for two years. Even after he retired, he was still the leading commercial endorser among professional athletes. He confirmed that one of the things that would occupy his time would be giving more time to the products he endorsed. Jordan was almost more visible commercially after retirement. Not bad for a guy who said that he was quitting to get out of the spotlight.

A month after he announced he was walking away, the door to coming back remained opened. Not just unlocked or open a crack, but propped open with a door stop. Michael waited an entire month before officially filing a letter of retirement with the NBA. Those official papers meant that he would have to sit out for a year unless the NBA's board of governors unanimously approved his appeal to return. All Michael ever talked about during that month was that he was definitely out for the year and "probably done for good." When he announced his desire to play pro baseball for the Chicago White Sox, he said, "I'll probably never play basketball again."

The Chicago Bulls, on the other hand, announced no plans for a farewell night at the Stadium like the one the Boston Celtics held for Larry Bird in February 1993. Bulls owner Jerry Reinsdorf said, "It's a good bet nobody else will ever wear No. 23 again for the Chicago Bulls." But didn't we know that long before Michael won his first title?

Michael, however, continued to make plans for the future. If he did have a thirst to play basketball competitively, he would slake it by playing exhibitions. He decided to take part in a made-for-television one-on-one with Sheryl Swopes, the 1993 NCAA women's college basketball player of the year. In leading Texas A&M to the 1993 NCAA championship, Swopes was called the female Michael Jordan. Did she realize by playing Michael she would receive the same treatment as Billy Owens?

Otherwise, Michael knew there was no coming back even before he walked down the red carpet leading from the Bulls' locker room to center court at the Stadium on November 6, 1993, with a searchlight marking his path through the darkened arena. Michael stood at center court, under a spotlight, holding a microphone to his lips for more than five minutes without saying a word. The fans would not stop cheering long enough to let him talk. After receiving his championship ring and posing for pictures with NBA commissioner David Stern, Jordan performed in the spotlight one last time. These are the moments that make for great endings to movies as well as careers. "Thank you, Chicago," Jordan screamed out, "for a great nine years."

The cheers that shook the Stadium for the next five minutes came from more than 19,000 representatives of basketball fans everywhere who wanted to leave Jordan ringing with one final thought:

Thank you, Michael.

AFTERWORD

A Whole New Ball Game

February 1994, Ed Smith Stadium, Sarasota, Florida. You want to know my birthday wish? I'm working at it. I'm working at my dream. I thought about playing baseball two years ago. I wanted to walk away from basketball and still have my physical skills to do something like this. I've always dreamed about playing baseball.

Once I retired, I knew I was doing this. It's no gimmick. I'm not out there in a White Sox uniform because of my name. That doesn't help me. I've taken some hits, and I understand that. Some have come from former players. I know it's a hard game. But I see it as a challenge. Standing in the batter's box trying to a hit a 90-mile-an-hour fastball or a curveball may be the ultimate challenge. That's why I'm here.

C hallenge. The word flashes through our minds in big bold type. Again. Why? Why would Michael Jordan want to play professional baseball? Why would he want to do something that threw him back into the public eye and once again made him the object of media scrutiny? Weren't these the headaches that pushed him out of basketball? But in December 1993, he began pursuing a career as a baseball player.

Why he must do this tells you why Michael Jordan became the greatest basketball player and greatest athlete of our time. He needed the challenge.

Jordan was headfirst into his winter baseball workouts when the challenge finally surfaced. The indoor batting cage at Comiskey Park, where the Chicago White Sox play, provided his initial practice venue. As he became more serious about playing baseball, and word of his activities leaked to the public, Jordan moved across the street to the Illinois Institute of Technology on Chicago's South Side. IIT's Keating Sports Center—a high school gym with offices—had a batting cage and additional space to work on fielding and throwing. It was the same place Bo Jackson had executed his workouts in an attempt to make the White Sox the year before.

The Keating Sports Center also permitted IIT students to watch Jordan. In fact, his workouts had to end by noon because the Keating gym was needed for a recreational basketball league.

One day a pair of students watched Jordan finish batting practice and then began talking to him. They questioned whether Michael really could take off from the free-throw line and dunk as he had done to win the 1988 slam-dunk contest during the NBA All-Star weekend at Chicago Stadium. Jordan debated momentarily, then ordered, "Go get a basketball." He accelerated down a full-court runway, took off from the foul line, and slammed easily.

Just two months after retiring from basketball, he found his life devoid of challenges. He needed to prove something. At his retirement press conference, he said he would look for something to satisfy the competitive side of his personality. Watching the grass grow didn't cut it. Baseball did. On February 7, 1994, the White Sox invited more than 250 reporters to IIT to watch Jordan work out—field ground balls, catch fly balls, and take batting practice—with other members of the team. Rather than demonstrating an ability to play the game—the first two ground balls went right through his legs—Jordan showed the competitiveness needed to make this endeavor seem more than a whim. White Sox second baseman Joey Cora teased him about whiffing at a batting practice pitch. Jordan focused on the next pitch, hit it hard, then turned to Cora and yelled, "That's gone," as if the hit would have sailed out of the park and not just bounced high off the back of the batting cage. It was one of the few times he smiled during the day's events.

Whether Jordan had the ability to play major league baseball was never important to him. Those who observed MJ through his first three weeks of spring training in Sarasota noticed his most proficient attributes to be bunting and running. He was timed going from home to first base at 3.8 seconds, the fastest on the team. The reason he wanted to play baseball became obvious when the White Sox were going through a sliding drill early in March at Ed Smith Stadium. Shortstop Ozzie Guillen led a barrage of players challenging Jordan to slide into second and in the process upend Coach Terry Bevington, simulating the effort necessary to break up a double play. Jordan dug in and sent Bevington flying, then came up flashing the kind of look he used to show after driving past Gerald Wilkins to score.

"A couple of players challenged me to play some basketball," Jordan said one morning on his way to spring training practice. "That's not the challenge I'm here for. I have this dream that I hit a home run, circle the bases, hit home, and just keep running out of the park. I have proved the point I wanted to prove."

Michael never said that moment would have to come at Comiskey Park playing for the White Sox. In fact, when he was assigned to play in the team's minor league organization after a month of spring training, MJ claimed he was still focused on the challenge of proving he could play this game.

Nevertheless, critics continue to claim Jordan could never succeed as a baseball player. He would fail miserably, they argued, and in order to keep from facing the prospect of quitting he would instead announce his return to the Bulls.

At his daily media briefings during spring training, Jordan repeatedly came forth with two messages. His first confirmed that he would never return to the NBA.

His second: "Ten years from now I'll be hiding out, playing golf somewhere." Like his nine years in the NBA, his attempt to play baseball proved that no matter what happens, he will always be a man in search of a challenge.